A CHINESE LINEAGE VILLAGE

Sheung Shui

Sheung Shui from the air (1963)

A CHINESE
LINEAGE VILLAGE

Sheung Shui

HUGH D. R. BAKER

1968

STANFORD UNIVERSITY PRESS

STANFORD, CALIFORNIA

Stanford University Press
Stanford, California
Copyright © 1968 Hugh D. R. Baker
Library of Congress Catalogue Card No. 68–23023

Printed in Great Britain

To

SUE, ESTELLA, ALEX AND STUART

Preface

THIS book is, with minor alterations only, my thesis, entitled
A Lineage Village in the New Territories of Hong Kong, approved
in 1967 by the University of London for the Ph.D. degree.
It is the result of field-work carried out in the New Territories of Hong Kong from the autumn of 1963 to the spring
of 1965 under the auspices of the London–Cornell Project for
East and South-east Asian Studies. The Project, which is
financed jointly by the Carnegie Corporation of New York and
by the Nuffield Foundation, very generously paid my travel,
research and subsistence expenses throughout this period, and
continued its grant for some months upon my return to London.
For other grants made to me during a pre-field-work prepara-
tion year and during the time which has been spent in writing
up the material both for my thesis and for publication, I am
grateful to the Universities China Committee, the School of
Oriental and African Studies, the Department of Education and
Science, and the Ford Foundation.

When I went into the field, it was with no fixed idea of studying a lineage village, my intention being to make a general study
of a small village community; but a short while spent in following up the suggestions and contacts made by Professor Maurice
Freedman, whose own researches in the area had been unfortunately cut short through ill health a few months previously,
was sufficient to convince me of the importance of the major,
long-established lineage settlements. The village of Sheung Shui
was first on Professor Freedman's list of priorities, and, through
the introduction with which he provided me, it was a simple
matter to establish myself in the village.

The Village Headman, through whose good offices my entry

vii

into the village was made easy, found me a village house to rent, and furnished it for me himself. He remained a considerate and helpful friend throughout my stay. Arrangements were made for me to eat twice a day with a group of the school-teachers, whose excellent meals were taken in the kitchen of the main ancestral hall. Through these connections with the hall and with my neighbours, I was well launched in village society from the beginning of my stay. Language was something of a problem, my 'standard Cantonese' proving inadequate when faced with the village accent and slang. By the end of my stay I was still in difficulties when listening to some of the older villagers, but I believe that I was right to have dispensed with an interpreter in this instance, where the best results seemed to come from personal, private conversations.

My field-work methods were dictated by circumstances, but took as their basis Informality. I did not hold 'interviews' (except on one occasion towards the end of my stay), I had 'conversations'. Furthermore, I quickly found that direct questioning brought very unreliable answers, and that the only way to discover a required fact was to wait until conversation had swung round to the topic, when I could ask my question in context with some certainty of a valuable reply. This method proved tedious, but was doubtless no more inefficient than red-herring chasing under the other method. My days were spent walking round the village talking to people, and the evenings were almost invariably spent in my house, with the doors open, holding court. In the last three weeks of my stay, I broke my rule of informality to administer a questionnaire to all households of the walled hamlet of the village. A second set of questionnaires was left behind for completion by the members of the Village Council and the Village Watch, but this unfortunately did not materialise.

My work, then, was very largely of an impressionistic nature, and as such is in places less than satisfactory. A brief visit to Hong Kong in the summer of 1967 was taken up almost entirely with another project, and so I regretfully submit the manuscript to the publisher in the knowledge that it has short-comings which might have been avoided. In particular I am sorry that I could not take more advantage of some very pertinent and helpful criticism made by Professor G. William

Skinner of Stanford University when he kindly read a copy of my thesis.

The book is preceded by a long introduction. While this is not an integral part of the book itself, I feel that its inclusion is necessary both to set the scene and to avoid long explanatory footnotes and disruptive interpolations at a later stage. No attempt has been made to disguise the names of places or people, unless the transposition of Cantonese names and terms into Mandarin constitutes disguise. I use Mandarin in order to bring romanisation into line with standard practice; but for place names in the New Territories I have thought it advisable to adhere to the officially sanctioned *Gazetteer of Place Names in Hong Kong, Kowloon and the New Territories*. The Glossary gives Chinese characters for romanised terms.

It would be hard to imagine a government more consistently co-operative and courteous than was that of Hong Kong both during and after my field-work. Mr. J. P. Aserappa (District Commissioner, New Territories), Mr. J. C. C. Walden (Deputy District Commissioner), and the many officers and staff under their direction were inexhaustibly patient and helpful; and in particular I must thank for their friendship and interest Mr. D. Akers-Jones, Mr. K. M. A. Barnett, Mr. J. W. Hayes, Mr. G. C. M. Lupton, Mr. B. V. Williams and Mr. H. Williams, all of whom hold or have held the post of District Officer in the New Territories. Mr. K. W. J. Topley and Mr. Tsang For-piu should be mentioned from amongst the many other Hong Kong Government officers who were unstinting in their assistance.

I am especially grateful to Mr. Leung Chee-tung for a most happy friendship, and for his assistance to me particularly in the initial stages of my work; to Mr. Leung Kwok-wai, head-master of the Ho Kai School; to Miss M. A. E. Smith of the London Missionary Society; and to Dr. Marjorie Topley. Mr. Liu Yun-sum very generously took for me some of the photographs of Sheung Shui (the remainder are my own work).

My debt to the Headman, to the Headmaster of the village school, and to so many good friends in Sheung Shui would be too obvious to mention, were it not that I may express my gratitude to them by so doing.

My greatest debt is to my supervisors, Professors Maurice Freedman and Denis Twitchett, who have both been assiduous in their advice and assistance throughout. I hope that my own inadequacies in this work (which no amount of advice could wholly correct) will not be allowed to reflect to their discredit.

School of Oriental and African Studies,   H. D. R. B.
University of London
October, 1967

The Hong Kong dollar (which is used throughout the text) was, at the time of writing, calculated at HK$16 = £1, or HK$5.714=US$1.

Contents

FIGURES

Illustrations

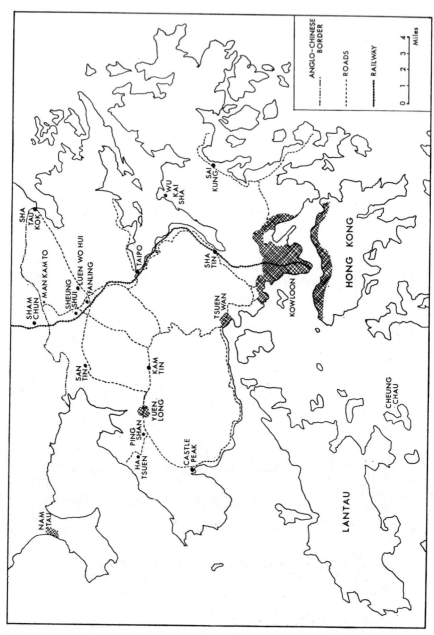

MAP I

Hong Kong and the New Territories

xiv

Introduction

I

The British Crown Colony of Hong Kong is situated on the south-eastern coast of China, and was formerly a portion of the province of Kwangtung. It lies between latitudes 22°9′ and 22°37′ N. and longitudes 113°52′ and 114°30′ E. It consists of a large peninsula and many islands of various sizes—a great number of which are uninhabited and barren—the total land area of the Colony being 398¼ square miles.[1] The terrain is extremely hilly, the rock being mainly granitic, porphyric and volcanic.[2] These hills are for the most part covered with sparse scrub and grass, and while complete barrenness is common, luxuriant growth is rare, and occurs only where there are particular circumstances of a political or religious nature militating against denudation.

Only 12·6 per cent. of the total land area of the New Territories is under cultivation, a further 0·5 per cent. being given over to pond-fish production,[3] and this 13·1 per cent. represents virtually all the cultivable land in the Colony. While pockets of arable land are to be found in small valleys and depressions throughout the area, "the only substantial areas of flat land are the plains of Yuen Long in the west and Sheung Shui/Fanling in the north which contain the bulk of the 13 per cent. of cultivable land".[4]

The climate is usually described as 'monsoon type', the winter monsoon blowing from the north or north-east from October until mid-March, while the summer monsoon blows

[1] *Hong Kong 1964*, Hong Kong Government Press, 1965, p. 241.
[2] Grant, C. J., *The Soils and Agriculture of Hong Kong*, Hong Kong Government Press, 1960, p. 2.
[3] *Hong Kong 1964*, p. 65.
[4] *NTAR 1963–64*, p. 5.

from the south or south-west; but neither of these winds is as regular or dependable as the name monsoon generally implies. The winters are dry and pleasant with temperatures well above freezing point, while the summers are extremely humid with temperatures consistently higher than 80° Fahrenheit. The bulk of the annual rainfall comes during these summer months, and typhoons are not uncommon, with winds frequently in excess of 100 m.p.h.[5] Despite the heavy summer rainfall, shortage of water is a constant problem as the denuded hills lack powers of water retention, and streams and rivers have only short courses. Consequently the winter months see the drying up of most of the streams in the area, and a summer of only light rainfall ensures a whole year of hardship. The best watered areas are the two plains mentioned earlier, it being through these that the two largest river systems flow. In 1898 a steam pinnace was able to navigate the Yuen Long River as high up as Kam Tin in the centre of the plain,[6] but this would not now be possible owing to the rising of the land on the west side of the area.[7]

The frost-free climate and prolonged heavy rainfall ensure that a double crop of rice may be grown in the Colony. Double-cropping with a winter catch-crop of vegetables has been the traditional agricultural pattern, but the last fifteen years have seen a dramatic change in this pattern, and much paddy land is now under full-time vegetable production, only the most remote areas being totally unaffected by the boom in market-gardening. There has been an accompanying change in land values, proximity to roads and quick communications taking perhaps as important a place in the reckoning as soil quality.

The area is occupied by two groups of peoples, discounting the many non-indigenous groups which have come in during the last twenty years. The larger group comprises the Cantonese

[5] For a summary of the climate in graph form see Grant, *op. cit.*, Fig. 1 (f).

[6] *Report by Mr. Stewart Lockhart on the Extension of the Colony of Hong Kong* (*Lockhart Report 1898*), 8th October 1898, in Eastern No. 66, Colonial Office, 1900, p. 38.

[7] There is good evidence that the New Territories is tilting in such a way that the east side is submergent while the west is emergent. See Barnett, K. M. A., 'Hong Kong before the Chinese', in *JHKBRAS*, Vol. 4, 1964, p. 44: also Grant, *op. cit.*, Fig. 1 (c) and p. 1.

speakers, usually called Punti. These people speak a language which "is probably the oldest established form of Chinese in the southern provinces, and has developed independently of the Northern language at least since the tenth century of our era, and in all probability since much earlier".[8] Some of the Punti lineages can trace nearly a thousand years residence in the area, while perhaps the majority were established before the start of the Ch'ing dynasty in 1644. Most have genealogical histories showing a southward migration from other provinces. The larger areas of good agricultural land are in the hands of these Punti people, while the other group, the Hakkas, occupy small areas of good land, and much higher, less fertile land.[9] They speak a language distinct from Cantonese, but which "like Cantonese, differs from standard Chinese particularly in being more archaic, but its archaism is less pronounced".[10] Some Hakkas are said to have begun to settle in the district at about the same time as the first Punti settlers, but it was not until the end of the Ming dynasty and the beginning of the Ch'ing that they came in in large numbers.[11]

When J. H. S. Lockhart toured the whole of the area on a fact-finding mission in 1898 prior to the British assumption of control, he set the population at 100,320 persons;[12] but while this estimate may have been a fairly accurate one, based as it was on personal observation of all the villages and towns included, the figure is only of use if it is first subjected to some pruning, for Lockhart included whole areas which were not in the end leased to Britain. From the breakdown of the figures which he gives it is possible to calculate that some 16,310 of his total did not come under the British lease when it was finally settled, giving an amended population figure for the New Territories in 1898 of 84,010, as in Table 1. It has been stated that 10,000 of the Lockhart figure of 100,320 were fishermen,[13] though no source was given for the statement; but, if it is

---

[8] Forrest, R. A. D., 'The Southern Dialects of Chinese', Appendix I in Purcell, V., *The Chinese in Southeast Asia*, 2nd ed., London, 1965, p. 569.

[9] *Hong Kong 1964*, pp. 244–5.

[10] Forrest, *op. cit.*, p. 570.

[11] See Barnett, K. M. A., 'The Peoples of the New Territories', in Braga, J. M. (ed.), *The Hong Kong Business Symposium*, 1957, p. 263.

[12] *Lockhart Report 1898*, p. 55.

[13] *NTAR 1963–64*, p. 6.

B

correct, then we might take the same proportion of 10 per cent. of the 84,010, or 8,400, as being fishermen.

TABLE 1

New Territories Population 1898

Division	Lockhart's figs.		Amended figs.	
	Villages	Population	Villages	Population
Shat'au	4	5,000	—	—
Sham Chun	26	14,080	15	5,100
Shat'au Kok	55	8,600	39	6,270
Un Long	59	23,020	59	23,020
Sheung U	182	20,870	182	20,870
Kau Lung	54	15,030	54	15,030
Islands	43	13,720	43	13,720
Total		100,320		84,010

A census was taken in 1901, and again in 1911, 1921 and 1931.[14] No further census was taken until 1961, but an estimate in 1954 put the New Territories population at between 200,000 and 250,000,[15] while noting that "there has been a steady inflow of settlers, particularly since 1950". In March 1955 an unofficial census of the New Territories population was taken, the results showing "a total figure in the region of 265,000 to which should be added about 50,000 fishermen operating from bases in the New Territories. Since then the population has increased . . . to an estimated 305,912 at the end of March 1957 excluding the fishermen."[16]

The definitive census of 1961 gives a total New Territories population of 456,404, made up of 409,945 landsmen and 46,459 boat dwellers.[17] The population totals from 1898 to 1961 are summed up in Table 2.

[14] See Census Reports in *Hong Kong Sessional Papers*, by Wodehouse P. P. J., in 1901 and 1911, by Lloyd, J. D. in 1921 and by Carrie, W. J. in 1931.

[15] *NTAR 1953-54*, p. 1.

[16] *NTAR 1956-57*, p. 3.

[17] Barnett, K. M. A., Census Commissioner, *Report of the Census 1961*, 3 vols., Hong Kong Government Press, 1962, Vol. II, Appendix XV, Table 1.

TABLE 2
New Territories Population 1898–1961

Year	Land population	Boat population	Total population
1898	75,770	8,400	84,010*
1901	—	—	102,254*
1911	94,246	9,855	104,101*
1921	—	—	82,947
1931	—	—	98,157
1955	265,000	50,000	315,000
1961	409,945	46,459	456,404

* Totals include New Kowloon (Kowloon City and Sham Shui Po), the population of which in 1911 was 13,624.

II

At the negotiations for the lease of the new territory to Britain in 1898, Lockhart pressed strongly for more territory than was in fact granted, arguing that Sham Chun was a market centre for a great part of the leased territory, and that inconvenience would result if a boundary were drawn between it and its market catchment.[18] There is little doubt that Lockhart was correct in his assessment of the importance of Sham Chun to the area. Geographically the Sham Chun Plain is one with the New Territories area, a range of hills isolating it from other agricultural and population centres to the east, north and west. The town lies at the heart of the plain and is surrounded by fertile rice lands.

In Sham Chun was situated the council chamber of the *Tung P'ing Kuk*, the Council of Peace for the Eastern Section,[19] which Lockhart describes as being "a general council for the whole of the *Tung Lo* or Eastern Section".[20] It consisted, we are led to assume, of the representatives of the various *Tung* ("Divisions", such as Shat'au Kok Tung and Sheung U Tung already

[18] *Lockhart Report 1898*, p. 50, for his detailed comments on the advisability of including Sham Chun. See also Eastern No. 66, Enclosure No. 2 in No. 102, pp. 118–21 for verbatim reporting of Lockhart's negotiations.

[19] *Ibid.*, p. 45. The only other reference to the Tung P'ing Kuk which I have seen is in Eastern No. 66, p. 29, Enclosure to No. 30, a letter dated August 1898 addressed to the Unofficial Representatives from "we the undersigned members of the Tung P'ing Kuk and Tat Tak Sieh. . ."

[20] *Ibid.*

mentioned above in connection with population) which went to make up the Eastern Section, and acted as a higher appeal court for either criminal or civil cases which had passed through the hands of the Village Councils and Tung Councils; a fairly elaborate semi-official judicial system which avoided recourse to official law in the person of the *Hsien* Magistrate and his assistants. Hence perhaps Krone's statement that "the Mandarin of Fuk-wing . . . though he is supposed to rule over 200 villages, confided to me, in a conversation that I had with him, that he had nothing to do but to eat, to drink, and to smoke".[21] The Tung P'ing Kuk's council chamber in Sham Chun was so sited because this town was "regarded as the centre of the Eastern Section".[22]

As far as I have been able to ascertain, Sham Chun served the whole of the plain as an intermediate market,[23] the three days in ten on which its markets were held being kept free by all standard markets of the area. Its markets fell on the 2nd, 5th, 8th; 12th, 15th, 18th; 22nd, 25th, and 28th days of the lunar month—that is, it had a 2–5–8 schedule. All the other markets operated either the 1–4–7 or the 3–6–9 schedule.

The Kowloon–Canton Railway was begun in 1905, the British section of it completed in 1910, and the Chinese in 1912; but even by 1921 the railway had apparently been unable to destroy the influence of Sham Chun. In that year an official report could state: "The opening of the Railway seems,

[21] Krone, Rev. Mr., 'A Notice of the Sanon District', *Transactions of the China Branch of the Royal Asiatic Society*, Part VI, 1859, p. 73.

[22] *Lockhart Report 1898*, p. 45. There seems no reason to disbelieve Lockhart's account of this hierarchical system, but it adds confusion to an already confused terminological situation, for it means that at least three different sets of sub-administrative group names were in use in the 19th century, to Lockhart's *Lu-tung-hsiang* being added the *Ssu-tu-li* of the 1819 edition of the *Hsin-an Hsien-chih*, and the *Ssu-tu-t'u* of the Sheung Shui *Liao-shih Tsu-p'u*. Furthermore, the 1688 edition of the *Hsien-chih* uses a fourth set, *Hsiang-tu-li*. To what extent these terms were interchangeable or described completely different aspects of sub-administrative groupings is not known. They do not exhaust the permutations of nomenclature given by Hsiao Kung-chuan (*Rural China: Imperial Control in the Nineteenth Century*, Seattle, 1960, Appendix I), nor indeed does Hsiao indicate that such variety might occur at the same time in one *Hsien*.

[23] I use the terms standard market and intermediate market as the lowest periodic market and next higher-level market respectively, following Skinner, G. W., 'Marketing and Social Structure in Rural China', *Journal of Asian Studies*, Vol. XXIV, Nos. 1–3, 1964–65, No. 1, pp. 6–7.

contrary to expectations, to have produced little change; market supplies for Hong Kong still come from the Canton Delta as before, and paddy still remains the predominant crop."[24] The villagers of the northern part of the New Territories, about whom this was written, had remained Sham Chun oriented, rather than become Hong Kong oriented and begun to produce perishable foodstuffs for city consumption. None the less, the process of change had begun, and political instability in China turned the New Territories increasingly towards Hong Kong. In 1949 the change of government in China finally brought about the virtual closing of the border, communications with Sham Chun became difficult, and marketing in the town almost impossible.

There were two main routes from the New Territories to the Sham Chun area, and thence to other parts of the Hsien and the Province. The first was by land over narrow tracks made of slabs of cut stone. The chief of these followed a line along the east side of the New Territories and joined Sham Chun with Kowloon City. Parts of it are still extant near Sheung Shui and in the hills behind Kowloon. The second route was by sea, boats from the New Territories being able to reach not only Sham Chun, whose river was navigable for some miles, but also other important towns of the Hsien, including the Hsien capital, Nam Tau.

The communications system now also underlines the fact of Sham Chun's decline in importance for the area. A start on road-building was made soon after the lease, and the ring road, which is still the major part of the New Territories road system, was completed in 1920.[25] It connects many of the main population centres with Kowloon, while spurs have been run out from it to more remote areas, and a few roads now run across through the middle of the ring. The railway from Lo Wu to Hung Hom was completed in 1910, and extended to Tsim Sha Tsui in 1916.[26] To a large extent it acts now as a commuter service for New Territories people working in the

[24] Lloyd, J. D., *op. cit.*, Introduction.
[25] Endacott, G. B., and Hinton, A., *Fragrant Harbour*, Hong Kong, 1962, p. 120.
[26] Lam Po-hon, 'Kowloon-Canton Railway', *The Government and the People*, Vol. II, 1964, p. 46.

cities. The towns and major villages are provided with telephone services, while radio receivers able to pick up signals from Hong Kong, Macao and Mainland stations are owned by the majority of households. Electricity and piped water are installed in the towns and larger villages. Many smaller villages now also have an electricity supply, but water is usually taken from wells and streams.

III

The Colony was originally an approximately three-fifths part of the 600 square miles of territory[27] of the Hsin-an Hsien of Kwangchow Prefecture, Kwangtung Province. To the north and north-west of the Hsien lies Tungkwan Hsien, while to the east and north-east it is bordered by Kweishan Hsien.[28] The South China Sea and Pearl River estuary constitute the remaining borders.

On 26th January 1841 the British first landed on the island of Hong Kong, it having been ceded by China under the terms of the Convention of Chuenpi. This Convention, drawn up during the First Opium War, was disavowed by both governments, and the hostilities, which it had temporarily halted, broke out again within the year.[29] The island continued to be occupied, however, and when the war was finally brought to an end by the Treaty of Nanking on 29th August 1842, it was ceded in perpetuity to the British Crown.[30]

Hong Kong was not at that time a place of any size or intrinsic importance, its area, plus that of several smaller islands ceded with it, totalling only 29 square miles.[31] The population in 1841, including 2,000 boat people, was probably about 5,650.[32]

During the second Anglo-Chinese war part of the Kowloon peninsula facing the island across a narrow strait was occupied by British troops, who used it as a camping ground. In March

[27] Ng, Peter Y. L., *The 1819 Edition of the Hsin-an Hsien-chih*, unpublished M.A. Thesis, University of Hong Kong, February 1961, p. 43.
[28] Kweishan Hsien falls within the Prefecture of Waichow, while Tungkwan is in Kwangchow Prefecture.
[29] Endacott, G. B., *A History of Hong Kong*, London and Hong Kong, 1958, p. 17.
[30] *Ibid.*, p. 22.
[31] *Hong Kong 1964*, p. 242.
[32] Endacott, *op. cit.*, p. 65

1860 a lease in perpetuity was obtained, the lease being cancelled by the Convention of Peking in October 1860, and the area ceded outright.[33] Including Stonecutters Island, this territory added a further 3¾ square miles to the Colony,[34] and is known as Kowloon.

By the end of the 19th century the Colony had grown considerably in size and importance. At the same time a 'battle of the concessions' was being waged among the various foreign powers as each scrambled to obtain concessions of land in China. Involved in this, and partly as a result of this (for fear lest a second foreign power should gain a foothold near the Colony and cut its communication lines with China),[35] the British negotiated for a lease of more land adjoining their Kowloon territory. The Convention of Peking of 9th June 1898 leased to Britain for a period of ninety-nine years some 365½ square miles of land, consisting of the Chinese mainland adjoining Kowloon, and many islands in the vicinity.[36] This leased area is known as the New Territories.

The Hsin-an Hsien, from which the New Territories was excised, had existed as an administrative unit only since the first year of the Ming Wan Li reign (A.D. 1573) when it was created out of the southern part of Tungkwan Hsien.[37] Briefly, between the fifth and eighth years of the Ch'ing K'ang Hsi reign (1666–69),[38] it reverted to Tungkwan, owing to the depopulation of its territory under the coastal 'scorched earth' policy,[39] but thereafter it was reinstated as a full Hsien under the Kwangchow Prefecture.

The government of the Hsien prior to the lease has been described by both Lockhart[40] and Krone[41] in some detail. At

[33] *Ibid.*, p. 110.

[34] *Hong Kong 1964*, p. 241.

[35] Endacott, G. B., *Government and People in Hong Kong*, Hong Kong, 1964, p. 127

[36] *Ibid.*, p. 126.

[37] Wang Ch'ung-hsi *et al.*, *Hsin-an Hsien-chih*, 24 chüan, 1819 (*HAHC 1819*), chüan 1, Historical table.

[38] *Ibid.*, footnote to table.

[39] Lo Hsiang-lin *et al.*, *I-pa-ssu-erh-nien i-ch'ien chih Hsiang-kang chi ch'i tui-wai chiao-t'ung*, Institute of Chinese Culture, Hong Kong, 1959, pp. 129–36.

[40] *Lockhart Report 1898*, pp. 44–5.

[41] Krone, *op. cit.*, pp. 82–5.

the head was the Hsien Magistrate (*Chih-hsien*), residing at the Hsien capital, Nam Tau, and invested with overall authority in matters civil and criminal. He had under him an Assistant Magistrate (*Hsien-ch'eng*), who lived at Tai Pang and had juris-diction over 104 villages in that area; and two lower officials with the title *Hsün-chien-ssu*, which title Krone calls 'Chief Officer of a Township' and Lockhart 'Deputy Magistrate'. One of these officials resided at Kuan Fu (Kowloon City), with control over 492 villages, including all the New Territories villages; and the other at Fuk Wing, being in charge of 185 villages. A still lower grade official, called by Krone the Director of Police (*Tien-li*), also based at Nam Tau, presided over 73 villages in that area.[42]

The above administrative officers may all be thought of as being imposed from above, an official body composed of élite outsiders, ruling the people but not *of* the people (since in general officials might not serve in their own native provinces). The indigenous government at its highest level normally linked up with the official administration in that its members were also of the élite; that is, they were literati and perhaps officials themselves too. This highest level was the Tung P'ing Kuk, the Council of the Eastern Section, mentioned above. Below it were the various Tung, six of these being included in whole or in part in the New Territories lease.[43] The Council of the Tung was composed of the leaders of the *Heung*[44] which fell within its territory. The Heung leaders were, wherever they existed, the literati and officials belonging to the villages.

The British approach to government of the New Territories when they were leased in 1898 was to "interfere [with the civilisation and way of life of the settled population] as little as possible, and to adapt as far as was feasible the existing methods

---

[42] Lockhart does not mention this last official. It is possible that, in the forty years which had elapsed since Krone wrote, the post had been abolished.

[43] Sham Chun, Sha Tau Kok, Yuen Long, Sheung U, Kau Lung and Islands.

[44] *Heung* (Mandarin *hsiang*): a unit of variable size and make-up as far as I can discover. It might consist of one large village, or, more likely, of a large village and its surrounding area of influence, including perhaps other weaker villages coming within its power sphere. Although it is the same Chinese character, it should not be confused with the very much larger unit described by Hsiao, *op. cit.*, p. 12.

of government to the new conditions".[45] This policy was in keeping with the undertaking made at the time of the lease to the people of the New Territories that "your commercial and landed interests will be safeguarded, and that your usages and good customs will not in any way be interfered with".[46] Not surprisingly, the system of government adopted parallelled the old system fairly closely. Imposed from above was an alien élite government, represented by District Officers stationed at key points in the territory. These officials (there are four of them at present) were responsible for all aspects of public order, for land administration, for civil and criminal judgements, for health and sanitation, etc., much as the former officials of the Hsin-an Hsien had been. The position of District Officer has gradually changed over the years as more and more specialised functionaries have moved into the New Territories sphere. The principal specialised responsibility still retained by them is that of supervision of land matters, but they have important general functions of "co-ordinating all Government activities in their areas".[47]

The four districts are co-ordinated by the New Territories Administration, headed by the District Commissioner, a post created in 1948.[48] The Administration is responsible direct to the Governor of the Colony, who appoints the District Commissioner,[49] and its main task is "to ensure that the interests of the people of the New Territories are taken into account in the formation and execution of Government policy".[50]

Under this 'imposed' administration was an indigenous self-governing system patterned after the original Tung Lo-tung-heung hierarchy. The whole area was divided into 48 sub-districts, each "identified as closely as possible with the geographical divisions long recognised by the Chinese inhabitants

[45] Collins, Sir Charles, *Public Administration in Hong Kong*, London and New York, 1952, pp. 135–6.

[46] 'Despatches and other papers relating to the extension of the Colony of Hong Kong', *Sessional Papers 1900* (*Extension Despatches*), No. 93, Governor to Secretary of State, 15th April 1899, Enclosure No. 5, Translation of the Chinese Proclamation issued by the Governor.

[47] *NTAR 1963–64*, p. 15.

[48] *Ibid.*, p. 7.

[49] Hsüeh S. S., *Government and Administration of Hong Kong*, Hong Kong, 1962, p. 81.

[50] *NTAR 1963–64*, p. 7.

themselves. A sub-district usually comprised a single valley with its self-contained group of villages and hamlets, or a single island."[51] A committee for each of these sub-districts was formed, the members being nominated by the villagers, and usually being "those who possess influence in their own immediate neighbourhood, whose advice is listened to, and whose lead is generally followed".[52] Above these 48 sub-districts were created 8 districts, the intention being to set up "village tribunals"[53] to try petty cases in these districts, presumably in much the same way as the Tung councils had undertaken judicial responsibilities.

This system of indirect rule was not very successful, an official report in 1912 pointing quite clearly to the reason. "Reference should also be made to the waning influence of the village elders throughout the Territories. It was the intention of Sir Henry Blake [Governor of the Colony at the time of the lease] that 'existing village organisations should continue to decide local cases'. But it soon became clear that the authority of the village elders was of no account, with the stronger authority of the magistrates so easily accessible, and the idea of local tribunals had perforce to be dropped. Under Chinese rule, the remoteness, the danger, and the expense of the central courts had left much authority to local elders, and especially to those entrusted with powers of collecting taxes."[54]

In spite of the misleading term 'elders', it would be wrong to suppose that the downfall of the system was owing to the administration's mistake in calling on the wrong class of people to serve on its tribunals; indeed it is clear from the above quotation from Lockhart's 1900 Report that no such mistake was made. The error of judgement involved was in the original supposition that a parallel system to the old one was being worked out; for the former viability of the unofficial governmental system rested on the unwillingness and inefficiency of the official one. In the case of the British administration, the official, imposed government was designed to be efficient and

[51] Endacott, *Government and People*, p. 130.

[52] Lockhart, J. H. S., 'Report on the New Territory', 7th February 1900, *Sessional Papers 1900*.

[53] Collins, *op. cit.*, p. 137.

[54] Orme, G. N., 'Report on the New Territories, 1899–1912', *Sessional Papers 1912*.

was staffed by men schooled in a tradition of devoted public service. The venality of the former officials resulted in cases being taken for preference to the less venal unofficials; but when after the lease officials of integrity were accessible, the unofficials were neglected. This confidence in and reliance upon the official system led to dissatisfaction on the part of the unofficials themselves, and they became unwilling to serve. As late as 1948 it was reported that "the idea of unselfish public service is new and strange, and office-holders show a tendency to look for the perquisites of office rather than opportunities for service".[55] Indirect rule, then, was not particularly successful at first, but the administration could and did make use of the unofficials as informants on such matters as local customs, disputed successions, *feng-shui* problems, and so on.[56] In 1926 the usefulness of this advisory service was underlined by the creation of *Tsz Yi* or 'head-boroughs', advisors appointed by the District Officer to assist him in local matters. The honour was designed to give recognition to elders with long and faithful service.[57]

In 1946 the first elections were held in some districts in implementation of a new policy of rural representation.[58] A system, based on the pre-war system of village representation, was devised whereby each village was to elect or otherwise appoint (according to custom), representatives to serve it in all its dealings with Government.[59] Each village of from 50 to 100 inhabitants in this way selected a representative, and sometimes a deputy representative as well, and large villages could have up to three representatives. These men were to serve on the various Rural Committees which were proposed. The Rural Committee usually is centred on a communications centre such as a market town, or at least the area from which its representatives are drawn is a recognised, discrete one. Some difficulty was experienced in forming these Committees, and it was not until 1960 that the last one was formed to complete the network of twenty-seven Committees covering the New Territories.[60]

[55] *NTAR 1947–48*, p. 3.
[56] Orme, *op. cit.*
[57] Endacott, *Government and People*, p. 134.
[58] *NTAR 1946–47*, p. 3.
[59] *NTAR 1963–64*, p. 17.   [60] *NTAR 1960–61*, p. 37.

Altogether there are approximately 900 Village Representatives serving on the twenty-seven Rural Committees.[61] Neither institution has well defined functions, the Rural Committee in particular being of a somewhat nebulous nature. In practice they act as bridges between the British administration and the people, a function which becomes more important as official procedures proliferate, imposing a barrier of intricacies between District Officer and people, so that the layman now often finds it worth while to deal with the District Office through his Village Representative, who has the knowledge of how to tackle the complicated procedures. Arbitration and mediation are useful functions performed by both institutions.

The Tsz Yi advisors grew into a representative organisation known as the *Heung Yee Kuk* or Rural Consultative Council, which now comprises the Chairmen and Vice-chairmen of the twenty-seven Rural Committees and a number of special Councillors. Elections to the Executive Committee of the Council are held every two years, immediately after the Rural Committee elections. All matters concerning the welfare of New Territories people are discussed by the Council, which keeps in close touch with the New Territories Administration, the latter frequently consulting the Council.[62]

It is thus possible to equate the old Hsin-an Hsien system of unofficial government with the present-day British system, Heung representatives becoming Village Representatives, Tung Councils becoming Rural Committees, and the Tung P'ing Kuk materialising as the Heung Yee Kuk. None the less, the functions of these latter-day equivalents bear little resemblance to their originals, owing largely to the substantial part in local administration which is played by the official British administration.

IV

The village of Sheung Shui lies at the heart of the Sheung Shui/Fanling Plain, the second most important and second largest of the plains of the New Territories. The Indus River flows through the northern half of the plain, entering it in two

[61] *NTAR 1963–64*, p. 17.
[62] *Ibid.*, p. 19.

main tributaries from the south-east and the north-east, and flowing out at the north-western corner to join the Sham Chun River some four miles before it reaches the sea. The river is tidal as far as a dam to the north-west of the village, passing through a narrow defile between hill ranges shortly before the dam. Abnormal rainfall creates a bottleneck at this defile, and the whole of the north-western quarter of the plain is subject to flooding in these conditions. Rice harvests may be totally ruined by these floods, heavy rainfall occurring most frequently in the summer months when the crops are growing. A recent Government scheme to lay a pipe-line from the river, connecting with the Colony's reservoir system, was under way at the time the study was made:[63] and it was hoped that by pumping flood waters through this both the Colony's perennial water shortage and the local flooding might be ameliorated.

Since 1949 the percentage of land planted to vegetables has been steadily increasing, and rice cultivation has diminished accordingly. Furthermore, some land which was formerly under two-crop paddy cultivation only is now under two-crop paddy and a catch-crop of vegetables. Ease of communications has without doubt been a major factor in the rapid development of vegetable growing in the plain, since vegetables have to be within fast and easy reach of markets in order to remain fresh. Grant, in discussing the rise in vegetable cultivation in the plain, remarks on the "favourable disposition of soil, climate, water, market and communications".[64]

The north-western quarter of the plain was previously an area well known for its sugar-cane production, as indeed were the neighbouring Hsien of Hsin-an and Tungkwan,[65] but this speciality fell into decline in the 1930s, and the heavy, buffalo-powered, stone milling equipment used in juice extraction abandoned; mill stones may still be seen lying beside the paths and used as seats in the villages. There is, however, a new speciality in its place. The well water of this quarter is peculiarly suited to the requirements of goldfish and tropical fish; and a fish-breeding industry of some size has arisen within the last

[63] *Ibid.*, pp. 24–5.
[64] Grant, *op. cit.*, p. 107.
[65] Shen P'eng-fei, *Kuang-tung nung-yeh kai-k'uang tiao-ch'a pao-kao-shu*, Canton, 1929, pp. 153 and 189; pp. 158–9 give details of the sugar producing process.

decade.[66] It has the advantage of taking up little ground space, and can be started on a small scale without great capital investment. The fish are exported.

For communications the plain is probably better off than any other part of the New Territories. The railway runs through its centre, with stations at Shek Wu Hui and Fanling. Passenger trains run from early morning until late evening at least once per hour in each direction.[67] Several roads cross the plain. The ring road runs through it from the south-east to the west; the only main road to the Mainland border enters through a pass in the north-west to join the ring road; a recently opened road runs south-west from Sheung Shui, linking the plain with the upper half of the Yuen Long Plain; and a fourth road runs north-east from Fanling to the border town of Sha Tau Kok. Along all these roads frequent buses run, and privately owned 9-seater taxis constitute a third form of public transport, supplementing buses on the main routes, with fares only fractionally more expensive.

The market towns of the plain, Shek Wu Hui and Luen Wo Hui, have not up to the present seen any large-scale industrial development, owing largely to lack of amenities such as waste disposal and sufficient water supplies. Minor factory undertakings are there in abundance, however, the oldest being a peanut-oil factory in Shek Wu Hui. Lorry transport is a thriving business, particularly in Shek Wu Hui, which as well as being well placed on the New Territories road network is also the last town on the road from Hong Kong to the Mainland, so that it has been able to a large extent to capture the international road haulage custom, such as it is.

Both towns are virtually newly built, Luen Wo Hui having come into existence only in 1951,[68] while Shek Wu Hui, described in an official report of 1948 as "the filthiest and most indisciplined market town in the New Territories",[69] has undergone planned rebuilding following complete destruction by fires in 1955 and 1956. Both towns boast cinemas, banks, clinics, doctors and dentists; and Shek Wu Hui has in addition

[66] An article headed 'Hsiang-kang je-tai-yü te se-hsiang' in the Nan-hua Wan-pao, Hong Kong, 3rd May 1964, gives some details of the industry, and calls attention to its prevalence in the Sheung Shui district.
[67] Lam Po-hon, op. cit., p. 48.
[68] NTAR 1950–51, p. 2.
[69] NTAR 1947–48, p. 4.

a fire station, a post office, a bath house, a social centre and a library. Luen Wo Hui has to cater for a more cosmopolitan custom than does Shek Wu Hui, and its amenities include bars, which are used almost exclusively by members of the British armed services stationed nearby. Both towns rely increasingly less on periodic marketing, permanent shops selling a wide variety of goods being a major feature now; but the market schedules are still observed, and most livestock transactions take place on the periodic market-days.

Politically the plain lies within the Tai Po District, and is divided into two sub-districts, represented by the Sheung Shui Rural Committee in the western half, with its offices in Shek Wu Hui, and by the Fanling Rural Committee in the eastern half, with offices in Luen Wo Hui. The original Chinese reticulation placed the plain in the Sheung U Tung.

V

The plain is not completely flat, small hillocks and larger slightly raised areas intruding on the cultivable land. The village of Sheung Shui is largely built on one of these raised areas, being some two to three feet above the level of the surrounding agricultural land. There are of course advantages in siting a village on such a spot, both with regard to protection from flooding, and to avoidance of encroachment on productive paddy-growing land.

The land around the village was originally devoted entirely to paddy growing, two crops without a winter catch-crop being the norm, but like other areas this one has not been unin-fluenced by the recent trend towards vegetable growing. From Fanling the circle of land under vegetables has grown wider, and has now reached as far to the north-west as the walled hamlet of Sheung Shui. On all other sides of this village, with the exception of a small patch of miscellaneous crops immedi-ately to the north-east, two-crop paddy is still grown, but a catch-crop of vegetables is now usual in the area, where Grant in 1959 notes no catch-cropping.[70] Grant's division of the plain into 'villages' for the purpose of his survey of cultivated land is not well enough documented for it to be possible to say

[70] Grant, *op. cit.*, p. 108.

where the boundaries of the divisions are drawn, and apparent discrepancies between his table on p. 108 and the Land Use Map (Fig. VI. o.) make it difficult to attempt to discover these boundaries. Because it is some guide, however, the figures Grant gives for acreage under certain crops in 1959 for his 'Sheung Shui Wai' village are set out in Table 3.

TABLE 3

Sheung Shui crop acreages 1959

	Crop	Acres
1	Paddy (2 crops)	208·45
2	Paddy (2 crops and catch-crop)	—
3	Vegetables	15·83
4	Orchard	2·00
5	Miscellaneous crops	23·88
	Total	250·16

Much land falling within category 1 in this table must now be in categories 2 and 3. It may also be noted that to the north and north-west of the village there is much land which is uncultivated, though it has been cultivated in the past, and remains of the bunds which divided the fields may still be seen.

The land around the village is mostly irrigated by the Indus River, which runs in a rough semicircle from the east to the north-west of the settlement. Numerous small effluents of this river run through the plain, eventually rejoining the main course. But the land is so level (as witness the bifurcating tendencies of the river) and so low-lying, that a small rise in water level brings serious danger of flooding. Such flooding occurs perhaps once every three years, when even the village itself may be flooded to a depth of several feet. Periods of drought, and especially the dry winter season, quickly reduce the flow of the river to a small trickle, and dams have been built to avoid wastage of water in these conditions. One dam is to the north-west of the village, marking the end of the tidal stretch of the river; and a second large one lies higher upstream to the east of the settlement.

The village was originally on the main stone path from Sham

Chun to Kowloon, the path entering the plain from Lo Wu through the same narrow gap by which the Indus River escapes. Other paths in pre-British times led from the village to Man Kam To, to Sha Tau Kok, and to Tsung Pak Long and thence to Kam Tin and other villages on the west side of the New Territories. A concrete road wide enough to take one vehicle, with passing space here and there, has been built into the village from the Man Kam To road, and this feeder road has been continued in a semicircle through the heart of the village and out again on to the main road, while an offshoot of it penetrates into a further part of the village. The village is now very easily accessible to motor transport. The railway station is fifteen minutes walk away.

There is one telephone in the village, an internal phone linking the Junior School with the Middle School, which is outside the settlement. Electricity is fitted in almost every house, and piped water in a few—perhaps in one in twenty.

The village consists of eight sub-villages, which I shall call 'hamlets'. Each hamlet has a separate name by which it is known within the village, these names mostly being suffixed with the word *Ts'un*; while the whole complex of eight is known as *Sheung Shui Heung* or *Fung Shui Heung*. Boundaries between hamlets are often merely narrow alleys or slightly larger paths, but they are recognised clearly by the inhabitants of each hamlet and there is no confusion. The village is planned facing approximately west-south-west, and almost every house in the entire complex faces in this direction. The reasons for this, and for a grove of trees which screens the back of the village are connected with *feng-shui*.

The walled hamlet, known as Wei Nei, was the first of the hamlets to be built. The wall has almost completely disappeared, though about 25 yards of it survive on the north side of the hamlet, from which it can be seen to have been of formidable proportions. Approximately 30 feet high above the ground level outside, it is slotted at the top, presumably for small-arms fire. Round the inside of the wall runs a ledge on which the defenders could stand without committing their bodies to the aim of the enemy. It is about two feet thick at the base, and is constructed entirely of bricks. There is still only one entrance, through the main gateway on the east side. It is a narrow gap through which

C

it is necessary to walk in single file, the approach being commanded by positions built over the gateway. Gates made of iron bars and iron chain are still in position in the doorway, and are said to be the original gates, first installed over 300 years ago. Wooden bars slotted into the masonry of the wall provided extra security, and a few bars are still in place. A similar gateway, but without iron gates, exists in the wall on the south-west side, and leads out on to a small surround of land which lies between the walls and the moat. This surround has been planted with lichee trees and a few patches of vegetables, and rice-straw is kept there for firing. All around the hamlet runs a moat, two or three feet deep, and from 30 to 50 feet wide, a drawbridge formerly allowing entrance at the main gate, but for many years the moat has been filled in at this point in order to allow easy access.

The other seven hamlets vary much in size, but all have in common the direction in which they face, and the ranks of terraces one behind another, a gap of only about six feet separating one row of houses from the next. The normal length of a terrace is six houses. The narrow alleys between the terraces

TABLE 4

Hamlet Population 1961[71]

Hamlet	Households	Male	Female	Total
Wei Nei	129	263	301	564
Pu Shang Ts'un	363	658	795	1453
Men K'ou Ts'un	135	230	294	524
*Chung Hsin Ts'un	38	67	68	135
Shang Pei Ts'un	67	120	121	241
Hsia Pei Ts'un	102	196	200	396
Ta Yüan Ts'un	212	361	465	826
†Hsing Jen Li	64	131	140	271
Total	1110	2026	2384	4410

* Also known as Ta T'ing Ts'un.
† Also known as Hsin Wei Tzu.

[71] After Census information not published in the 1961 Census Report, but made available through the kindness of certain Hong Kong Government Officers.

are often paved with granite blocks, but in some cases with concrete. The houses are small, generally about 30 feet by 12 feet, and consist of one large room half covered by a cockloft, with a kitchen-cum-washhouse forming an entrance hall.

The population of the entire village in 1961 was 4,410 divided between 1,110 households. The division of this population between the eight hamlets was as in Table 4.

Since 1961 the population has certainly increased, though I am unable to produce figures to prove this. A questionnaire administered to all households in the walled hamlet shortly before I left the village in March 1965 yielded the following figures (shown in Table 5 compared with the 1961 figures).

TABLE 5
Wei Nei Population 1961–65

	Households	Male	Female	Total
1961	129	263	301	564
1965	116	281	310	591
Increase	−13	+18	+9	+27

% increase   4·8 in four years.

The increase of 4·8 per cent. in four years in the population of the walled hamlet falls well below the estimated annual growth of the Colony's population of 4·1 per cent., which was given by the Census Department.[72] However, it is doubtful whether the New Territories population is in any way typical of the Hong Kong population in general, and, furthermore, the fact that the hamlet is walled places limitations on growth which must upset any estimates based on the Colony as a whole. The other hamlets almost certainly have higher growth rates than does Wei Nei. For convenience I propose to take 5,000 as being a close approximation to the 1965 population. This represents a growth of 13·4 per cent. in four years, a rate below the estimated Colony rate, but greater than that of Wei Nei.

The traditional pattern of life in the village was almost

[72] Mok, Benjamin N. H., *Hong Kong Census 1961: Population Projections 1961–1971*, Government Press, Hong Kong (1962?), p. 15.

entirely an agricultural one. Aside from scholarship, there was apparently little diversity of occupation, the vast majority of villagers farming for a living, and selling their high quality rice to buy cheaper grain and other goods. Today the position has changed radically. Agriculture has become of only indirect importance, and while many people derive an income from it, few of them actually work at it. In 1961 only 29·87 per cent. of the working population of the New Territories were employed in agriculture and fishing combined.[73] Opportunities for taking other employment have been increasing since first Hong Kong was established in 1842, and since the Second World War and the change of government in China in 1949 these have been augmented considerably.

TABLE 6

Occupations: Wei Nei 1965

Occupation	Numbers engaged
Abroad/at sea	15
Accountant	3
Army Civilian Employee	3
Carpenter	1
Clerk	2
Commerce	8
Construction worker	9
Farming	12
Foreman	1
Government servant	14
Medical	5
Nun	3
Police	3
Rattanware	5
Servant	3
Teaching	10
Tea-house	1
Transport	15
Workman	7
Total	120

[73] Barnett, *Report of the Census 1961*, Vol. III, p. 28, Table 242.

In the walled hamlet in 1965, out of 120 people whose occupations were given, only 12, or exactly 10 per cent., were found to be engaged in farming of some kind. The range of occupations represented in the hamlet is given in Table 6 in roughly generalised categories. 'Workman' includes all who called themselves *kung-jen* (workman, servant, someone not self-employed) or who replied *ta-kung* (to work for someone else, be a servant, etc.). 'Transport' includes both lorry owners and transport workers, one of whom is a bus conductor. 'Medical' includes doctors, nurses and other hospital personnel. 'Government servants' includes both white-collar and labouring personnel.

With the exception of those employed in agriculture, the nuns, the rattanware workers, a few of the teachers and a very few from some of the other categories—with these exceptions these occupations are carried on outside the hamlet and outside the village.

No detailed data concerning household income and expenditure were gathered, but general questions on income were included in the questionnaire. I have reservations about the accuracy of the answers given to these questions, believing that in many cases income was understated (particularly through not taking into account income, such as rents from fields, which was not received *per mensem*, and through ignoring income from part-time jobs); but the average income per household in Wei Nei according to these answers was HK$334.83 per month, while the average number of people per household was 5·1. It should be borne in mind that by local custom an extra month's money is payable at New Year on most salaries which boosts the annual income considerably.

CHAPTER ONE

Lineage History

I

THE village of Sheung Shui was founded by, is still largely occupied by, and is wholly owned and controlled by the Liao lineage. An account of the history of the foundation of the village and of the lineage may be found in the genealogies maintained by certain lineage members, while a few other sources of historical information exist in the *Hsin-an Hsien-chih*, inscriptions, and the genealogies of other lineages. In addition there is a small fund of lineage history which has been handed down orally.

There is little possibility at this stage of verifying the genealogical account of lineage history. Certainly there are points in the account which must be regarded with some suspicion. Not least of the weaknesses is the fact that there appears to have been no genealogy maintained by the lineage until the version of Liao Hung was made in the 16th year of the Ch'ing Chia Ch'ing period (1811),[1] allegedly nearly five hundred years after the foundation of the lineage. Hung's preface describes this version as a "revision of the old genealogy",[2] implying the existence of an old copy; but it must be doubted whether any copy could have survived for five hundred years, where books only forty years old are almost unreadable owing to the combined effects of the rudeness of village life, the damp destructive climate, and the ravages of bookworm.

The influence of other genealogies borrowed from lineages of the same surname is obvious,[3] and there are thus grounds for

[1] *Liao-shih tsu-p'u*, combined MS, various dates (*LSTP*). Preface to the genealogy of the Ying-lung line.

[2] *Ibid.*

[3] E.g. the inclusion in the *LSTP* of a preface from the genealogy of the lineage in Lungnan, Kiangsi.

supposing that the entire earlier part of the genealogy may have been 'borrowed' when Hung prepared his version. The absence of prefaces composed by lineage members earlier than Hung[4] almost certainly demonstrates that the 'old genealogy' must have been one from another lineage.

A change of name of the first ancestor of the lineage at the point where its genealogy links up with the earlier established Fukien branch of the surname group[5] may well be an indication of a connection deliberately made by posterity in order to acquire an ancient and lustrous heritage. Examples of the forging of spurious links with an established genealogical line are not uncommon.[6] The ancestors, whether acquired or genuine, were certainly inordinately talented: of the thirty generations from Tzu-chang to Chung-ta, fourteen in the direct line were either government officials or holders of high degrees.

Whether the connection is genuine or not, historically the course of events which is recorded in the genealogy is a reasonable one, and could well have taken place at the times given. In the last analysis, it is of the greatest importance that lineage members not only believe implicitly in their history as it is recorded in the genealogy, but are prepared to act on that belief.

II

The Liao surname is said to have originated with the descendants of Po Liao, the son of King Wen of Chou;[7] but another account places the origin back in Shang or pre-Shang times with a Liao Shu-an,[8] (or Liao[A] Shu-an), the surname being derived from the state of Liao with which he is said to have been enfeoffed.[9] The lineage genealogy follows this latter account, claiming that the surname Liao[A] was changed to Liao by Liao[A] Po-kao, who lived in the Ch'un-ch'iu period.[10]

[4] Chinese genealogy compilers religiously reproduce the prefaces and colophons from previous editions.

[5] See below, p. 27.

[6] See for example Freedman, Maurice, *Lineage Organization in South-eastern China*, London, 1958, p. 71.

[7] Chang Shu, *Hsing-shih hsün-yüan*, 1838, chüan 35.

[8] *Ibid.*

[9] *Ch'un Ch'iu Tso Chuan*, Chao 29th Year, '*Hsi yu Liao[A] Shu-an*'.

[10] *LSTP*, Lungnan Preface.

Serious attempts to trace descent begin with Tzu-chang of the Hsi Chin dynasty (A.D. 265–316), who is given the title Originator of the Lineage (*T'ai-shih-tsu*). One section of the prefaces to the genealogy gives the names of all the generations between Shu-an and Tzu-chang, making the latter to be of the 68th generation,[11] but this sequence of names is repudiated elsewhere.[12]

Tzu-chang is said to have been created General, Guard of the Left, Protector of the State (*tso-wei chen-kuo ta-chiang-chün*) by the Chin emperor Wu in A.D. 276, as a reward for military service.[13] His elder son succeeded to the title, but the line is traced through the younger son, Ts'ung-hsien, who moved to Chekiang Province from Loyang.

Ts'ung-hsien's son, Wu-kuei, was made Governor, Guard of the Left, Subduer of Wu (*cheng-Wu tso-wei ta-tsung-kuan*) by the Chin general Tu Yü; and Wu-kuei's son, Ch'in, succeeded to the title of Governor. Ch'eng-hai of the 5th generation was Prefect of Yangchow (*Yang-chou t'ai-shou*), but moved south because of the incursions of the Wu Hu barbarians.

His grandson, Yen-kuang, held office as Prefect of Chingho (*Ch'ing-ho t'ai-shou*), while his great-grandson, Yü-ling, of the 8th generation, became Prefect of Hukuang (*Hu-kuang chün-shou*). In the 11th generation Yen-ling held office as Prefect of Wuwei (*Wu-wei t'ai-shou*), and was given the title of Duke of Wuwei Prefecture (*Wu-wei chün-kung*). His son, Ch'ung-te, was Magistrate of Chienhua District (*Ch'ien-hua hsien-ling*) in the early years of the T'ang dynasty,[14] and he settled there after his term of office, founding a branch of the lineage.

Ch'ung-te's eldest son, Lan-chih, was a *chin-shih* of A.D. 668; while his grandson, Kuang-ching, of the 14th generation, who was born in A.D. 689, held office as Prefect of Hsuanchow (*Hsüan-chou tz'u-shih*), and moved to Tiaochou in A.D. 710. Ssu-shih-i-lang of the 16th generation moved to Ninghua District in Fukien.

From Ssu-shih-i-lang there are three generations for which no names are recorded. The genealogy attempts to explain the

[11] *Ibid.*, Remarks on the origins and development of the Liaos.
[12] *Ibid.*, Lungnan Preface.
[13] *Ibid.*, Liao-shih tsung-hsi. Other biographical details below are also drawn from this source, unless otherwise stated.
[14] Chienhua is a District of Kiangsi Province; later known as Ningtu.

deficiency in terms of years of unrest causing temporary abandonment of record-keeping; but rather than being a three-generation deficiency it appears that it may be a three-generation insertion—that is to say that the three nameless generations were inserted as a rationalisation of the chronology, which a compiler had found to be faulty.[15] There is mention that in other genealogies variants are to be found, and certainly in one other work the three generations are missed out entirely.[16]

The 20th generation is represented by Wen-hsing, who held the office of a Grand Secretary (*Ts'an-i ta-fu*). His son Hua was Assistant Governor of Hu-Kuang (*Hu-Kuang ts'an-cheng ta-fu*), and was buried in Tingchow Prefecture, Fukien. Min of the 23rd generation was a Sub-Prefect of Tean Prefecture (*Te-an-fu t'ung-p'an*). Chün-shou, of the 28th generation, is said to have been a contemporary and colleague of Wen T'ien-hsiang, the Sung Chief Minister, but the statement is probably an attempt to link the coincidence of his name with the "Liao Shou-weng of Meichuan" mentioned in Wen's preface to the genealogy. Meichuan is in Hupeh Province, not in Fukien.[17]

The 30th generation from Tzu-chang is represented by Chung-ta, who is said to have moved from Tingchow in the middle years of the Yuan dynasty. He settled within the jurisdiction of the Deputy Magistrate at Kuan Fu, then in Tungkwan, but later coming within Hsin-an Hsien;[18] changed his name to Chung-chieh, "because his name was the same as that of the elder son of San-shih-san-lang of the 24th generation";[19] and became the founding ancestor of the Liao lineage of Sheung Shui.

III

Although it seems likely that no genealogy was maintained in the lineage from the arrival of Chung-ta (i.e. Chung-chieh) in the Yuan dynasty until Hung's version was made in 1811, it is probable that most of the record is genealogically correct.

[15] *LSTP*, Lungnan Preface.

[16] (*Hua Shan*) *Liao-shih tsu-p'u*, MS, 1938, Hsing-tsu yüan-liu.

[17] Playfair, G. M. H., *The Cities and Towns of China*, Shanghai, 1910, p. 325.

[18] *HAHC 1819*, chüan 1, Hsien-chih yen-ke-piao.

[19] *LSTP*, Liao-shih tsung-hsi, 29th generation.

There must have been at that time sources of information, chiefly ancestral tablets and grave-stones, which could serve as accurate guides to the composition of the ancestral line.

Oral tradition has it that Chung-chieh was an itinerant tinker and blacksmith. Informants in another village which I visited also volunteered statements that certain of their ancestors were engaged in this trade. In each case the men were Hakka, and I was told that tinkering was largely a Hakka occupation in this part of China.[20]

When he moved from Fukien, Chung-chieh is mentioned as staying first at Tuen Mun (now known as Tsing Shan or Castle Peak), a sea-port of some importance up until the Ming dynasty.[21] Thus it is conceivable that he had journeyed from Fukien by sea, especially since "Fukien communicated with other parts of the country almost entirely by sea".[22] He next moved to Fuk Tin, a village north of the Sham Chun River, close to the border with the New Territories; and finally into the Double Fish Division (*Sheung U Tung*), to the area where the lineage is at present. The genealogy refers to this area as being in "the 21st Sub-sector (*t'u*) of the 2nd Sector (*tu*), under the jurisdiction of Kuan Fu",[23] but the *Hsin-an Hsien-chih* of 1688 places it in the 6th Sector.[24]

Chung-chieh married a Hou, and they had one son, Tzu-yü. Chung-chieh later returned to Fukien according to the genealogy, but the oral tradition is that he died before getting there. At any rate his body is represented in his grave by a silver plaque.[25]

Tzu-yü had three sons, who each had two sons, these two generations being of great importance for lineage segmentation.[26] Their many descendants lived scattered all round the Sheung Shui/Fanling plain in small settlements of segmentary

---

[20] Mr. James Hayes has indicated to me similar findings from his researches into the history of the area.

[21] Lo Hsiang-lin, *I-pa-ssu-erh-nien* . . ., p. 21 *et seq.*

[22] Fitzgerald, C. P., *China: a Short Cultural History*, revised ed., London, 1961, p. 4.

[23] *LSTP*, Summary of Historical Movements.

[24] Chin Wen-mou *et al.*, *Hsin-an Hsien-chih*, 13 chüan, K'ang Hsi 27 (1688). (*HAHC 1688*.) Chüan 3, 'Villages'.

[25] *LSTP*, Tsung-hsi. "Kung yung yin p'ai . . . tsang yü Chin-ch'ien-hsiang-ts'uen hou."

[26] See below, Chapter Four.

kin. One of these settlements was in Ping Kong, which is a Hou village now, and perhaps was then, though the Hou genealogy is not clear on this point.[27] It is worth noting that not only Chung-chieh, but also a member of the 3rd generation, took Hou wives, so that a fairly intimate connection between the two surnames at this point may be inferred. A series of settlements (Kak Tin, Lung Ngan Yuen and Ha Shui) were sited on the north bank of the (Indus) river, downstream from a settlement which bore the name Upstream (Sheung Shui) and which later gave its name to the village. Other settlements mentioned in the genealogy are Wang Mei Shan, Siu Hang and Ling Ha, the last being occupied jointly by two distinct lineage segments.

Nan-sha of the 7th and Chün-hui of the 8th generations from Chung-chieh were both geomancers,[28] and it is they who are credited with the unification of the lineage and with the plan and site of the village which the unified lineage came to occupy. The *feng-shui* of the site consists of a dragon traced through the surrounding hills and over the plain: on the head of the dragon is built the main ancestral hall; while Wei Nei, the original village, is built in front of the dragon's head in the stylised shape of a pearl—the dragon traditionally chasing a pearl.[29]

Although the genealogy does not mention the fact, there is an oral tradition that the site was at that time (the Wan Li reign of the Ming dynasty 1573–1619) already occupied by the Chien lineage. No reasonable explanation is forthcoming from the Liaos to account for the evacuation of the Chiens from the site to the village of Tsung Pak Long in an area of inferior land nearby, where their descendants still live. One Liao informant said, "Nan-sha asked Chien Kung[30] to move, and he agreed", but a Chien informant claimed that a Liao gained a foothold in the village by marrying the daughter of Chien Kung; and that later the Liaos grew powerful and drove the Chiens out,

[27] *Hou Shan Hsing T'ang tsu-pu*, MS, Ho Sheung Heung, no date, notes on 13th generation. The founder was of the 16th generation, *fl.* A.D. 1500?

[28] Chün-hui is said to have studied under a geomancer called Chung Hsin-i of Hang Chieh Ts'un in Tungkwan Hsien.

[29] Burkhardt, V. R., *Chinese Creeds and Customs*, 3 Vols., Hong Kong, 1953, 1955, 1958, Vol. I, p. 121.

[30] Several informants used the name Chien Kung in talking of the transfer of Sheung Shui from the Chiens to the Liaos, but there was much disagreement about who he in fact was, and what role he played.

forcing them to purchase from the Liaos new land near Tsung Pak Long.

The end of the Ming dynasty brought disturbances to the area, and in particular trouble was caused by Li Wan-jung, a defeated Ming loyalist who engaged in bandit activities from 1647 until his capture by Ch'ing forces in 1656.[31] The genealogy gives these disturbances as the reason for deciding to build a wall round the village.[32] The work was begun in October 1646 and completed the following year. The village was divided into four wards (Tou), each of which was occupied by one kinship segment. The wards were of unequal size and were known simply by the quadrant of the compass which they occupied; thus North Ward, South Ward, etc.

Pirate raiding had long been the scourge of this coast. In the Ming dynasty, in 1551, Chung-shan of the 7th generation had been captured by pirates and held to ransom, his wife taking his place and then committing suicide so that he had not to pay the ransom.[33] In the K'ang Hsi reign the problem had reached such magnitude that it was felt necessary to institute a scorched earth policy, evacuating all inhabitants within 50 li of the coast. Sheung Shui was within the affected area, and the lineage was evacuated in 1662. There is no knowledge now of where the next seven years were spent, the genealogy merely recording "homeless wandering with untold suffering";[34] but in 1669, as a result of strong action by certain provincial officials, the Hsin-an Hsien, which had been merged with Tungkwan in 1666, was re-established,[35] and the evacuees were allowed to return to their homes.

IV

The size of the lineage at this time is unknown, but it was probably not greater than 500 strong, since under present crowded conditions the walled hamlet houses 591 people. By

[31] Lo Hsiang-lin, I-pa-ssu-erh-nien . . ., p. 146, note 17.

[32] Lo, ibid., points out that many other villages in the area built walls at this time.

[33] HAHC 1819, chüan 20, 'Virtuous wives'. The pirates may have been those under Ho A-pa, who was active in the area in that year (HAHC 1688, chüan 11, 'Bandits'). Lo Hsiang-lin thinks so (I-pa-ssu-erh-nien . . ., p. 199).

[34] LSTP, Summary of Historical Movements.

[35] HAHC 1819, chüan 1, Hsien-chih yen-ke-piao.

1688, however, expansion out of the walled hamlet had already taken place, and Pu Shang Ts'un had been founded.[36]

The dates of foundation of the other hamlets are unknown. The 1819 edition of the *Hsien-chih* records the names of only the two hamlets of Sheung Shui (i.e. Wei Nei) and Pu Shang Ts'un, and this is some evidence that perhaps no other hamlet had then been founded. The Earth God of Men K'ou Ts'un (which is said to have been the third of the hamlets founded) bears the date tenth year of Hsien Feng (1860), but this is not necessarily the year in which the hamlet was founded. The Wei Nei Earth God is dated seventeenth year of Chia Ch'ing (1812), but this date cannot be connected with the foundation of the hamlet. There are no dates on any of the other hamlet Earth Gods. It would probably be safe to assume that all the hamlets other than Wei Nei and Pu Shang Ts'un were founded between 1819 and 1898.

The market of Shek Wu Hui, which was controlled by the lineage, was originally sited at and called Tin Kong Hui, by which name it is mentioned in the 1688 edition of the *Hsien-chih*.[37] By 1819 it was established in the present location,[38] though at the end of the 19th century it was moribund. It has not proved possible to locate Tin Kong Hui.

The present main ancestral hall, the Wan Shih T'ang, apparently dates from at least the *hsin-wei* year of the Ch'ien Lung reign (1751). The evidence is a board hung in the hall, bearing the name of the hall, dated, and presented by Liao Ying, a *chin-shih* of the 21st generation of the Yungting lineage in Fukien.[39] None of the memorial boards to individual members of the lineage predates this. The two smaller ancestral halls, owned and maintained by certain lineage segments, were built in the following century; the Ming Te T'ang in 1828, and the Hsien Ch'eng T'ang in 1838. (I am assuming that the dates on the title boards in each case bear close connection with the dates of foundation.)

[36] *HAHC 1688*, chüan 3, 'Villages'.
[37] *Ibid.*, chüan 3, 'Markets'.
[38] *HAHC 1819*, chüan 2, 'Markets'.
[39] According to the *LSTP*, the Yungting lineage was founded by Liao Hua of the 21st generation. Twenty-one generations from him is equivalent to the 12th generation of the Sheung Shui lineage, and this generation flourished in the first half of the 18th century.

V

By the use of the information about individuals which is in the extant genealogies, in the *Hsien-chih*, and on the ancestral tablets and memorial boards of these three ancestral halls, it is possible to trace the broad pattern of development of lineage wealth and importance. Figures given cannot be accurate for the following reasons. First, some of the genealogies are more detailed in presentation than others; second, the two subordinate halls are concerned with only two of four major segments of the lineage; third, there is a proliferation of honorific terminology used, which makes it difficult to distinguish actual attainments from wishful; and fourth, the *Hsien-chih* is only of use for the years before 1819, when it was last revised. The figures, then, serve only as a guide to the pattern, being certainly lower than the actual figures. The Wan Shih T'ang has tablets for some of the members of the two segments unblessed with halls, and furthermore some information is contained in the genealogies of these segments: perhaps to add 20 per cent. to the figures given would result in a close approximation to the actual.

The first indication of the lineage's growing wealth and importance was the invitation, in the Ming dynasty, to a man of the 7th generation to participate in the 'district banquet ceremony',[40] a distinction conferring on him the title *Chün-pin*.[41] Probably this occurred in the second half of the 16th century,[42] somewhere about the time when the new village was built.

The system of purchasing degrees began in the Ming dynasty, and was continued later by the Ch'ing.[43] The most widely purchased degree was the first or *sheng-yüan* degree, which in the latter part of the 19th century was attained by examination by only two-thirds of its holders.[44] Because there is no distinction

[40] In the Ch'ing dynasty this was held twice each year, on the fifteenth day of the first month of Spring, and on the first day of the first month of Winter. (*HAHC 1688*, chüan 7, 'Ceremonies'.) There is no information available for the Ming.

[41] For some details see Chang Chung-li, *The Chinese Gentry*, Washington, 1955, p. 16.

[42] See generation times, below, p. 42.

[43] Ho Ping-ti, *The Ladder of Success in Imperial China*, New York, 1962, pp. 30, 33–4.

[44] Chang Chung-li, *op. cit.*, pp. 138–40.

in the terminology used on the tablets and in the genealogy between degrees gained by purchase and those gained by examination at the level of this first degree, it has not proved possible to differentiate them here. No fewer than seven different terms for first-degree holders are used, but I shall refer to them all as Licentiates.[45] Nine members of the 9th generation were Licentiates. In the 10th generation there were three of these degree holders, one of whom was also a district banquet guest; while in the 11th there were two Licentiates, two men with the 8th rank honorary title *Hsiu-chih-lang*,[46] and one with the title *Shou-kuan* for longevity.

The most flourishing period in the history of the lineage commenced with the 18th century, when its rising power and wealth were demonstrated in the building of the great, three-halled Wan Shih T'ang, and in the increasing number of holders of degrees.

Chiu-wo of the 11th generation was born in 1666 and was admitted to the Hsien college in 1688. In 1715 he graduated as a Licentiate of the Supplementary List, and was given salaried status (*lin-pu tseng-sheng*). He donated a large piece of ancestral trust land for the endowment of the Hsien school (the *Wen Kang Shu Yüan*) in 1724,[47] and finally in 1732 purchased the degree of Senior Licentiate (*tseng-li kung-sheng*). He also purchased the title *Hsiu-chih-lang*. Two men from the 12th and one from the 13th generations were Senior Licentiates, while ten from the 12th, thirteen from the 13th and eight from the 14th generations held first degrees.

Three men from the 13th generation and one man from the 14th were district banquet guests. One man from the 14th was selected as a student of particular merit (*Yu-hsing hsüeh-sheng*), and was given the honorary title *Wen-lin-lang* (7th rank). A 13th generation man purchased the 8th rank title *Hsiu-chih-lang* and later was raised to *Wen-lin-lang*; while in the next generation a purchaser of the 9th rank title *Teng-shih-lang* was raised to *Cheng-shih-lang* (rank 7b). One from the 12th and two from the

---

[45] I use the terminology of Mayers, W. F., *The Chinese Government*, London, 1897, pp. 76–9.

[46] *Ibid.*, p. 70; as also for other titles below.

[47] *HAHC 1819*, chüan 23, Chi-hsü. 'On building the Wen Kang Shu Yüan.'

13th were *Teng-shih-lang,* and the rank 9b title *Teng-shih-tso-lang* was given to a 14th generation man. In the 12th generation one man was honoured for longevity, his tablet bearing the title *Kuan-tai shou-kuan.*[48]

The 19th century saw the continuation of lineage prosperity. The first half of the century in particular was a flourishing period, the smaller ancestral halls both being built then, the first ancestor's grave being elaborately rebuilt in 1816 (the less impressive grave of the second ancestor having been rebuilt in 1793), the genealogy being written, and honours and examination successes of unprecedented height being won.

Liao Hung of the 14th generation was born in the latter half of the 18th century. In 1819 he was a Salaried Licentiate, and with this qualification was one of the six Assistant Editors of the *Hsin-an Hsien-chih* produced in that year.[49] In 1820 he became a Senior Licentiate. He purchased the title *Hsiu-chih-lang,* and was honoured also with the 7th rank *Wen-lin-lang.* The first "revision of the old genealogy" was undertaken by him in 1811. In his preface he has written: "Although there have been notable people in each generation, no one has yet made a revision of the old genealogy."[50] A highly successful man by village standards, his own success was not all that he would have wanted recorded for posterity. In 1786 his second son was born, and this man, Yu-chih, in the space of a short life of only twenty-one years completely eclipsed his father's academic record. An infant prodigy—he talked fluently at two *sui,* extemporised witty poetry (one piece of which is extant) at seven, and wrote essays at eleven—he came second in the Prefectural Examinations in 1803,[51] fifth in the Hsien College entrance examinations in 1804, and in 1807 passed 61st on the list of *chü-jen,* a scholastic achievement not excelled by any other member of the lineage. Said to have been selected as a Hsien magistrate, Yu-chih died the same year, poisoned, according to village tradition, by a jealous maternal uncle.[52]

[48] See Ho, *op. cit.,* p. 21.
[49] *HAHC 1819,* chüan shou, 'Hsing-shih'.
[50] *LSTP,* Ying-lung Preface.
[51] There is a mistaken character on the back of his tablet, where this account is found, but 1803 seems to be the correct date.
[52] A Teng from Lung Yeuk Tau. Sheung Shui people ascribe the deterioration of this Teng lineage to retribution for the poisoning.

The elder brother of Yu-chih, Yu-jung, was a Senior Licentiate (*sui-kung-sheng*) of 1839. He held the purchased title *Hsiu-chih-lang*, and was given the title *Ju-lin-lang* (rank 6b), and 6th rank military title. He held office as a Sub-director of Studies (*Hsün-tao*), and was a Chief Guest at the district banquet. Traces of his local works remain in an iron temple-brazier, dated 1833 and presented by him when still a Licentiate; in the title-board of the Hsien Ch'eng T'ang, written by him in 1838; and in the stone altar, still used, raised by him in 1839 on a nearby hill-top for the purpose of praying for rain. A renowned doctor, a water-damaged contemporary portrait of him is still preserved in the village.

In the 16th generation a second man, Ju-i, passed the *chü-jen* degree. He was born in 1807 and came first on the list of Licentiates at the age of 20 *sui*. After repeated failures, he finally gained his *chü-jen* degree at the age of 42 *sui* in 1849, being placed 36th on the list. He purchased the title *Wen-lin-lang*, and opened a school in the Eastern Sector of the Hsien. Unfortunately he was at one stage imprisoned as a result of (unspecified) tax troubles in which the lineage was involved,[53] and this apparently caused the suspension of his honours. Public restoration of his fair name by a local official was accorded him, but no acknowledgement of his reinstatement was forthcoming from the Board (*Li Pu?*), and he did not take the Metropolitan Examinations. He died in 1863.

One man from the 17th and one from the 19th generations purchased Senior Licentiate degrees. Of holders of first degrees there were one in the 14th generation, four in the 15th, eleven in the 16th, three in the 17th, and two in the 18th.

In the 14th generation one man was a *Teng-shih-lang*, purchasing the title *Ju-lin-lang*. A 15th generation man purchased both *Cheng-shih-lang* and *Ju-lin-lang* titles, and held minor office in a Prefectural government. In the 16th generation there was a purchaser of a 6th rank military title. Seventh rank military titles were held by one man from the 15th and two from the 16th; while a 15th generation man bore the title *Wu-te ch'i-yü-*

---

[53] *LSTP*. The gentry of Hsin-an refused to pay taxes in 1852 (see Wakeman, Frederic, Jr., *Strangers at the Gate*, California, 1966, p. 135), and it is possible that Ju-i's imprisonment was connected with this more general movement.

D

lang, and held office as a Battalion 2nd Captain (*Ying-shou-fu*).
One man each from the 14th, 15th and 17th generations held
the title *Teng-shih-lang*, and a 15th generation man received the
Teng-shih-tso-lang title.

Two men, one from the 14th and one from the 15th generation, were district banquet guests.

VI

At the close of the 19th century occurred the leasing of the
New Territories to the British Crown. The lineage was opposed
to the leasing, and joined with other lineages of the area in
organising resistance to the new administration.[54] The inevitable
collapse of the resistance was fortunately not made an excuse
for vengeance by the British, and there were few reparations
exacted from the villages. The chain-mail gates of the Teng
walled village of Kat Hing Wai were blown down and removed
by British forces,[55] to be returned from exile in Ireland in
1925;[56] but a similar fate does not appear to have befallen the
gates of Sheung Shui Wei Nei, unless it was this village which
the errant Captain Simmonds attacked on his mistaken march
to the Fanling area.[57] None the less, the village was considered
to be sufficiently a danger to public order to require the building
of a police station there immediately.

Receptivity of the villagers to Western ideas was no more
ready than to Western rule. The London Missionary Society,
working through the Hong Kong and New Territory Evangelization Society, engaged in a protracted battle to gain a foothold
in the village. In 1909 the first convert in the village was made,
but this "evoked strong opposition which took the form of
persecution and entailed suffering for the truth's sake". Events
in the village at the time "recall, in a marked manner, features
of early apostolic life".[58] "The villagers generally are strongly
opposed to Christianity now well represented in their midst,

[54] See below, Chapter Seven, p. 196.
[55] *Extension Despatches*, Lockhart to Governor, 18th April 1899.
[56] See stone tablet in wall of Kat Hing Wai. Also Sung Hok-p'ang,
'Legends and Stories of the New Territories', *Hong Kong Naturalist*, Hong
Kong, 1935–36, pt. III, 'Kam Tin', 1936.
[57] *Extension Despatches*, Lockhart to Governor, 19th April 1899.
[58] Hong Kong and New Territory Evangelization Society, *Minute Books
1904–1932*, Report, 1909.

and they have been successful in driving out one family, whose house has been closed up *by the officials* [my emphasis—this must surely refer to 'village officials'] and we believe sold."[59] Even the apparent success of the Society in finding premises for a chapel in the village was destined to turn into failure. The building was provided by a villager in return for a money-loan which he undertook to repay after seven years. A girls' school was run by him in the building during the week. At the end of the seven years he renounced his Christian professions and took a concubine, and since he was a man of some wealth and influence there was a "retrograde movement" in the village.[60] I was told that the man was a Sun Yat-sen supporter, who used the building in question as a hostel and secret meeting place for revolutionaries, so that his school and chapel activities were perhaps a deliberate blind. There is no mention of mission work in the village after 1919. A London Missionary Society nurse, Miss Mary A. E. Smith, ran a maternity home on the outskirts of the village from 1954 until 1964, but she did not proselytise. A Mormon mission nearby has tended to concentrate its attentions on the market town in the six or seven years of its existence.

In 1925 Shek Wu Hui revived as a market next to the village. The revival was due to the joint initiative of a lineage member and a non-lineage man.[61] The market is built very largely on lineage land, and apart from the benefits of private trading carried on by lineage members there is a large income from market dues. The market has been prosperous since 1925, with temporary setbacks caused by the Japanese occupation, and by the two fires of 1955 and 1956. In 1898 it had a population of 120,[62] which had decreased to 43 in 1911.[63] In 1955 it was estimated at 5,000,[64] in 1961 it was 14,286,[65] and an estimate for 1964 gives 35,000.[66]

[59] *Ibid.*, Report, 1912.
[60] *Ibid.*, Minutes, 22nd October 1918, and Report, 1918.
[61] *Shih Hu Hsü Ch'ung-chien Hsin-shih Lo-ch'eng: Ta-hui T'e-k'an*, Hong Kong, 1964. Chairman's speech.
[62] *Lockhart Report, 1898.*
[63] Wodehouse, *Report on Census, 1911.*
[64] *Gazetteer of Place Names in Hong Kong, Kowloon and the New Territories*, Hong Kong Government Press, 1960, p. 206.
[65] *NTAR 1961–62*, p. 3.
[66] *NTAR 1964–65*, p. 6.

A small group of Hakkas of the Liao surname appeared in the area in 1929 from Waichow in Kwangtung. Despite the lineage's complete identification with the Punti element, recognition of the newcomers as kin was given on the production of a genealogy showing a common ancestor in Liao Min of the 23rd generation from Tzu-chang.[67]

In 1932 the first major concession to Western values came with the founding of a school in the Wan Shih T'ang. Replacing the numerous small tutorial institutions which had traditionally catered for the educational needs of the village, the new school taught a Western-type syllabus, and was the foundation of the thriving present-day school.

The Japanese invaded the Colony from China on 8th December 1941, and the village, being close to the border, was soon engulfed. The final surrender of British forces took place on 25th December, the occupation lasting until August 1945.[68] Conditions in the village were rigorous, food and fuel were extremely scarce, and severe disciplinary methods were adopted by the Japanese, some of whom were quartered in the police station. Over thirty people are said to have died of starvation during this period, and foods such as are usually given to pigs, and congee made with unhusked rice, were eaten. The economic hardship of the period necessitated the abbreviation of many important ceremonies and the excision of some lesser rites.

In the late 1940s the unrest in China caused many people to seek refuge in Hong Kong. The rise in population of the Colony from 1948 onwards was not without effect on the village, and the change in composition of the village population and in the local economy has been of great importance.

The Korean war of 1950–53 led to the embargo on trade with China,[69] and this in turn brought opportunities for smuggling on a large and lucrative scale. By all accounts many local people, both of the lineage and not, were engaged in this activity, and some of the richest men of the area are said to owe their present fortune to the period when the severity of the sanctions against China was accompanied by the highest prices for embargoed goods.

[67] (*Hua Shan*) *Liao-shih tsu-p'u*, genealogical table.
[68] Endacott, *History of Hong Kong*, p. 300.
[69] *Hong Kong Annual Report, 1956*, Hong Kong Government Press, 1957, p. 10.

In population the village is one of the largest of the New Territories, and has been so since the first available population estimates. Table 7 shows the growth in population size for years for which there are figures.

TABLE 7
Village Population Growth

Year	Population	Source
1647	500	My estimate.
1898	1800	Lockhart Report 1898.
1911	1441	Wodehouse, Report on Census 1911.
1921	1400	Lloyd, Census Report of 1921.
1955	3600	Gazetteer of Place Names, p. 206.
1961	4410	Unpublished 1961 Census information.
1965	5000	My estimate.

The 1898 figure makes Sheung Shui the third largest village in the area after San Tin and Kam Tin. In 1911 it was the second largest, but Kam Tin was not considered as one village in that count. In 1921, again with the exclusion of Kam Tin, it was the third largest village, after San Tin and Yuen Long. Present-day conditions of population movement have made it unhelpful to place the village in a comparison of size with other settlements, particularly with the blurring of village boundaries and with the rise of the market towns.

VII

The Liaos were Hakka, as lineage tradition maintains,[70] and their pattern of movement southwards through the centuries follows closely the common Hakka migratory pattern worked out by Lo Hsiang-lin.[71] The original home of the Liaos in Loyang places them firmly in the area of origin of the Hakkas, while the moves south in the 3rd and 4th centuries accord with Lo's first wave of migration (even to its being expressly stated

[70] And as Lo Hsiang-lin believes. See his *K'o-chia Shih-liao Hui-p'ien*, Hong Kong, 1965, p. 357.

[71] Lo Hsiang-lin, *K'o-chia Yen-chiu Tao-lun*, Taipeh, 1942, map and commentary facing p. 98.

in one case that the Wu Hu were the cause). The moves to Kiangsi and Fukien in the 7th and 8th centuries follow Lo's lines of migration but not his chronology. The final move from Fukien to Hsin-an agrees with Lo's third wave both as to time and direction, though there is no evidence in this case that, as Lo suggests,[72] resistance to the Mongols in support of the Sung was the cause.[73]

From the first ancestor, Chung-chieh, it was seven generations before a lineage member achieved recognition in the outside world, a 7th generation man being a guest at the district banquet; and yet two more generations before the first degree-holders of the lineage. There are probably several reasons to account for this. First, it must be expected that a man moving from his native district to settle down permanently elsewhere (unless he is doing it as the result of a posting as an official or some similar reason) will be landless, poor, and therefore possibly illiterate. Second, in pioneering new settlements it is unlikely that either he or his immediate descendants will have leisure or money to indulge in studies, particularly such onerous studies as were demanded by the Chinese examination system. Third, there must of necessity be an interval of time during which he and his descendants make the adjustment from Hakka speech and customs to Punti: not to mention the interval of residence necessary to qualify as a local inhabitant for official purposes.[74] It would, then, be highly unlikely that a lineage could produce scholars until several generations had passed in which wealth and population could be built up.

By the same token it is reasonable that no genealogy is kept up by a new lineage, for genealogies tend to be works of some literary pretension. A bare record of names of the dead may well be all that is preserved, and even then perhaps only on ancestral tablets. If this hypothesis is correct, it follows that there is in many cases a built-in weakness in the chain of record of descent, which very readily lends itself to juggling in the

[72] *K'o-chia Shih-liao Hui-p'ien*, p. 7.

[73] Unless the connection with Wen T'ien-hsiang, mentioned above, may be adduced.

[74] Chang Chung-li, *op. cit.*, p. 80, note 32: "It usually took a long time before an immigrant could be considered as a native of a locality and participate in examinations . . . in Yung-ning thirty years were required before an immigrant could be registered as a native."

hands of the lineage member who eventually undertakes to produce a genealogy. Where ancestry is lost beyond a certain point, the temptation to find an illustrious line on which to weld the lineage must be great, though there is no reason to suppose that the welding is not carried out in good faith in most instances. The Liao genealogy was not made until the 14th generation, and a change of name of the first ancestor is recorded: both factors could be evidence of just such a case of 'ancestral juggling'.

As Hakkas in a predominantly Punti district, pressures must have been great to change orientation, and it seems likely that the Liaos would have become Punti-oriented before the evacuation of 1662 took place. On their return to the village in 1669 the position would be even more one forcing them into a coincidence of interests with Punti elements. Many of the people who had been evacuated did not return,[75] and large tracts of land were left vacant, these being settled eventually by Hakka immigrants.[76] Those people who *had* returned to their old holdings would have had opportunity to lay claim to larger areas of good land than they had possessed before. Furthermore they would constitute an élite of long-established, well-landed, and thus comparatively wealthy lineages. A group of such lineages founded the *Chau Wong Yee Yuen*.[77] The Liaos were members of this group, their membership indicating an identification with the Puntis rather than with the later Hakka arrivals. In 1819 the village was sufficiently Punti not to be listed under the Hakka section of the *Hsien-chih*.[78] Thus, the evacuation and return may well have helped the lineage to consolidate its position as a major power and land-owner in the area.

From the little personal detail which is available for early generations an attempt has been made to work out a table of dates of birth of each generation up to the present day. Table 8 gives the probable dates of birth of two separate lines of descent,

[75] *HAHC 1688*, chüan 6, 'Population figures'.
[76] See Lo Wan, 'Communal Strife in Mid-nineteenth-Century Kwangtung', *Papers on China (Vol. 19)*, Harvard University East Asian Research Center, December 1965, pp. 92–3. Also Barnett, 'The Peoples of the New Territories', p. 262.
[77] See below, p. 194.
[78] *HAHC 1819*, chüan 2, 'Villages'. The 1688 edition does not distinguish Hakka from Punti villages.

both of which are taken from genealogies of the lineage. The computation leans heavily on one date—the date of birth of the 3rd generation ancestor of Line 'A'. It has been assumed that this date is correct, mainly because it is the only date of birth for an ancestor earlier than the 9th generation contained in any of the genealogies, and therefore has some weight, since no attempt has been made to invent dates for the other early ancestors. In addition, it is a date which fits very plausibly into

TABLE 8

Probable dates of birth by generation

Generation	Line 'A'	Line 'B'
1	1308	1308
2	1341	1344
3	1374	1379
4	1408	1415
5	1441	1450
6	1474	1486
7	1508	1522
8	1541	1557
9	1574	1593
10	1608	1628
11	1641	1664
12	1674	1700
13	1708	1735
14	1741	1771
15	1774	1806
16	1808	1842
17	1841	1878
18	1874	1913
19	1908	1949
20	1941	—

a physically possible sequence of generation spans. The average length per generation between this date and the date of birth of the sixteenth generation ancestor of Line 'A' has been worked out and used to trace back to find a probable date of birth for the founding ancestor. This last date has then been used as the base for calculating the generation spans of other lines. This method of calculation must of course be highly suspect, but none the less it does produce a series of dates which bear a strong relation to historical facts. Each of the four genealogies in my possession was studied by this method. Three of them result in such a closely similar series of figures that it is only necessary here to take one of them (Line 'A') to represent them all. The fourth is represented by Line 'B'.[79] Obviously there were individual exceptions to these dates, but in general the two lines probably cover the dates between which the majority of each generation was born.

While this table is of use in that it gives a general picture of the historical span of each generation, it does not demonstrate any change in generation span over the centuries, since it deals in *average* spans only. In fact, by utilising other dates given in the genealogies, it is possible to show a marked shortening in generation span in the later years of the lineage's history. In Line 'A', for example, the average length per generation between the 1st and the 10th ancestors is 35·1 years, while from the 10th to the 16th it is 30·5 years. In Line 'B', between the 1st and the 9th it is 36·5 years, but between the 9th and the 18th only 34·9 years. Taking into account the increase in wealth in the lineage over the centuries, these differing averages tend to lend strong support to the theory of later marriage in poorer families. As Freedman has said, "Poverty postponed marriage".[80]

With Table 8 as a reference, the figures already produced for scholars of the lineage may be reappraised to discover a recognisable historical pattern of development. Figure 1 plots the numbers of scholars and honoured men (known usually by the term *kung-ming*) against the generations in which they were born. Chang Chung-li estimates the average age of attaining the first degree by examination as about 25,[81] but for purchased degrees and titles the likelihood, it seems to me, is that the average age would be higher, owing to the probable inability of a younger man to find the necessary money. I have therefore considered that 30 would be the average age of attaining degrees and titles, whether by purchase or examination, and

[79] In fact the 2nd generation ancestor is the same man for both lines, so that Line 'B', 2nd generation, must necessarily be wrong; but it was not considered important to change the base of calculation from the first ancestor since both dates are only hypothetical.

[80] *Op. cit.*, p. 28.

[81] *Op. cit.*, p. 95.

have added this number to the dates of birth arrived at in Table 8, thus giving a rough indication of the times during which each generation flourished.

The member of the 7th generation who was a district banquet guest was a particularly wealthy man, and the founder of the fortunes of his line, according to the genealogy. It is not until the 9th generation that there is a burgeoning of successful men,

FIGURE 1
Honours per generation

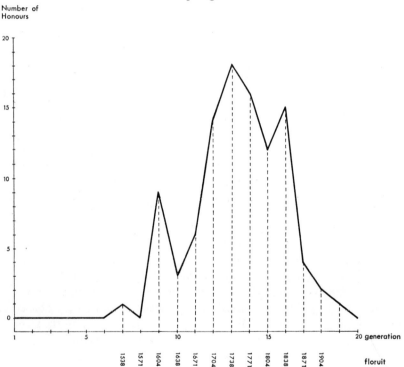

the period coinciding with, or being slightly later than, the founding of the village. The same wealth and strength of numbers which made possible the founding, no doubt contributed to the rise of lineage fortunes at this time. The time at which the 10th generation might have been expected to attain honours is also the time of the disorders and confusion of the change of dynasty from Ming to Ch'ing, and it is significant that the number of successful men is very low in this generation. Similarly the 11th generation's opportunities for success must have been reduced with the evacuation of the lineage from 1662 to 1669, though there are signs of the beginning of a recovery of lineage fortunes. The long years of the K'ang Hsi, Yung Cheng and Ch'ien Lung reigns, when "the Chinese Empire attained its maximum material prosperity",[82] followed by the Chia Ch'ing and Tao Kuang reigns, marked the zenith of lineage prosperity. The disturbances in Kwangtung in the 19th century, occasioned by the Opium Wars, the Taiping Rebellion, and the Hakka/Punti struggles, no doubt account for the steady fall in numbers of successful men after the 16th generation. The one member of the 19th generation, who was a Senior Licentiate by purchase, is one of the exceptions to this general pattern of generation birth.

A great deal of lineage history hinges on the genealogy prepared by Liao Hung in 1811, but his recording of lineage affairs did not stop with this work. His influence on the 1819 edition of the *Hsien-chih*, of which, as has already been noted, he was an Assistant Editor, seems to have been very strong. A comparison of the 1688 and the 1819 editions emphasises this. The map of the Hsien marks the Double Fish Division in 1819, but not in 1688. The only geographical feature near Sheung Shui mentioned in 1688 is the mountain formation called *Shuang Yü Ling*, which is described as being near Ho Sheung Heung.[83] In 1819 the description changes to place it near both Sheung Shui and Ho Sheung Heung.[84] In addition, mention is made of Tai Leng Shan, "behind Sheung Shui village: when the year is dry, the local people pray for rain here with certainty of success";[85] of the pass through which runs the Sheung Shui–Sham Chun road; of three dams near the village, constructed for irrigation purposes;[86] of four bridges near the village;[87] and of many individuals of the lineage who are considered worthy

[82] Fitzgerald, *op. cit.*, p. 547.

[83] *HAHC 1688*, chüan 3, 'Mountains'.

[84] *HAHC 1819*, chüan 4, 'Mountains'.

[85] *Ibid.* The present-day stone altar on this same hill was raised by Hung's elder son in 1839.

[86] *Ibid.*, chüan 4, 'Waters'.

[87] *Ibid.*, chüan 7, 'Bridges and fords'.

of fame on grounds of long-preserved virtue, old age, and so on. While most of these items concern constructions and persons which came into existence after the 1688 edition, it is true that some of them are natural phenomena which the 1688 edition chose to ignore. A large space, moreover, is devoted in 1819 to the story of the wife of the 7th generation man who was captured by pirates in 1551.[88] This event happened long before 1688, but does not appear in the *Hsien-chih* for that year. It must therefore be an insertion by Hung, and his source for it must have been oral tradition, since there was no genealogy before his time, so that the accuracy of this tale is in some doubt. The fact that the 1819 edition refers to the above matters when the 1688 edition does not is, it seems to me, a reflection not of their importance, but of the desires and ambitions of Hung to enlarge the reputation of the village and the lineage. That the reputation of the lineage was being enlarged anyway is demonstrated by the very fact of one of its members being in the position to manipulate *Hsien-chih* material.

[88] *Ibid.*, chüan 20, 'Virtuous wives'.

CHAPTER TWO

The Lineage: A Kinship and Ritual Group

I

THE questionnaire administered in the walled hamlet in 1965 reveals that of the 116 households 78 were lineage households, and that 399 of the 591 inhabitants were lineage members. Thus 67·5 per cent. of the inhabitants of the hamlet were lineage members. Applying this percentage to the total village population of 5,000[1] we reach the figure of 3,375 persons for the size of the lineage in 1965. This figure accords well with the "3,000 or so" estimated by the village leader most knowledgeable in such matters, and with the figure of 3,000 which is the 'official' lineage size.[2]

The lineage comprises all the living agnatic male descendants of Chung-chieh, their wives, concubines and unmarried daughters. Since the lineage was founded no segments or individuals are known to have hived off from it in such a way as to form a new lineage elsewhere; nor, indeed, is there record of more than a very few individuals being lost to the lineage. A notable exception to this is the case of Ying-wu of the 4th generation, who is said to have accompanied Chung-chieh on his journey back to Fukien;[3] while of at least one man it is recorded that "when young he went overseas, but it is not known where he ended up".[4]

Membership of the lineage is conferred on women by their marriage or concubinage to a male of the lineage, and on children by their birth into a lineage family. Up until the beginning of the 20th century it was necessary for the membership in

[1] See Introduction, p. 21.
[2] 'Official' in that it is the figure used in District Office land records for the membership of the lineage trust.
[3] *LSTP*, Liao-shih tsung-hsi, 4th generation.
[4] *Ibid.*, 16th generation.

the lineage of a newly-born son to be recognised and confirmed by lineage leaders in the presence of the elders of the lineage (*fu-lao*). On the first new year after the birth of a son, his father was obliged to hoist in the ancestral hall an ornate lantern in his name. In addition it was required of the father to give a feast in the hall to the elders, in return for which a certificate of lineage membership (*chu-shu*) would be issued by them, being signed by the Lineage Headman and his deputy, and by the head of the major segment into which the son had been born. This recognition of membership entitled the son to receive his share of lineage and segment benefits, and furnished him with irrefutable proof of this right, while at the same time binding him to observe concomitant obligations towards these groups. It also confirmed in the son his right to inherit land and property. The ceremony, known as *K'ai-teng*, was also obligatory for males being adopted. Poor members of the lineage were allowed to dispense with the provision of a feast. To a certain extent, then, it was true that the more a man stood to gain by lineage membership the higher the cost of ratifying that membership.

This fairly rigid system of registration of lineage males on the one hand provided an opportunity for the lineage to scrutinise the legitimacy of claim to inheritance of all aspirants to lineage membership, and on the other gave proof of right to inheritance in all relevant segments to all who were so registered, no doubt lessening considerably the chances of inheritance disputes among lineage members.

Sung-nan of the 18th generation was born in 1871 and became a Licentiate and an influential man in the lineage. He is said to have been the first man *not* to register the birth of his sons in this way. His reasons for refusing to hold the ceremony are unknown, but the custom quickly began to lapse following his example. The elders were perturbed by the demise of a ceremony which not only helped to maintain the stock of the Liaos untainted by unsanctioned adoptions, but also served to emphasise their own importance and vestigial power; and steps were taken to encourage the revival of the custom by offering to provide pigs from lineage funds to assist with the cost of the feasts. The incentive apparently was effective for a time, but the thin end of Sung-nan's reforming wedge was secure and the incentives were beginning to lose their force when the Japanese occupation set a period to all extravagancies. After the occupation the custom did not in general revive, although a few lanterns and feasts are in evidence still each year on behalf of adopted sons or sons born to concubines.[5] Some people content themselves merely with worshipping the ancestors in the hall at New Year.

In particular it is when a son is adopted that the ceremony is still usually held. One of the functions of the feast and the signing of the certificate was the opportunity which these gave for questioning the validity of an adoption, rules for which were laid down in the genealogy: "Male children may not be given in adoption to families of another surname, nor may males of a different surname be taken in adoption.[6] Anyone lacking an heir should adopt a son of one of his own brothers. If there should not be one to adopt, then he must choose a suitable male of the next generation and nearest collateral branch of the lineage. . . . If even in the whole lineage no heir can be found, the line should be marked 'ended'."[7] The elders could check easily on the claims of anyone presented to them for ratification of adoption. After the Japanese occupation, however, these rigid rules were ignored to such an extent that it became possible to adopt any male provided he were of the Liao surname. Now so little attention is paid to this that it is generally held that any male is eligible for adoption provided that he is presented to the elders as of the Liao surname; the inference being that a well-told lie about surname is a non-reprehensible falsehood. I was told that one adoption had been disallowed of recent years because it was openly known that the adoptee was of another surname.

No ceremony is held for daughters, because they are only temporarily members of the lineage, surname exogamy ensuring that they will be married out to become members of other

[5] In other lineage villages of the New Territories the ceremony is still considered essential for all males born or adopted into the lineage during the previous year. One reliable informant whose sister is married into the Teng village of Tai Po Tau said that in that village fines are levied by the ancestral hall on parents who neglect the custom. Failure to make good the omission the following year incurs even heavier fining.

[6] A very common proscription, some of the reasons advanced for which are given in Liu Wang Hui-chen, *The Traditional Chinese Clan Rules*, New York, 1959, p. 74.

[7] *LSTP*, Rules for revising the genealogy, Rule 4.

lineages. In any case as women they are precluded from inheriting within and stand to gain nothing from the lineage, so that they need no claim to lineage membership. "Daughters have no concern with descent and need not be entered in the genealogy. . . ."[8] An unmarried woman who passed the age by which she might have been expected to have married must have had a hard life in the village (if indeed she could have stayed in the village). Informants claimed that a spinster of that age is a phenomenon unknown to Sheung Shui.

Protracted marriage ceremonies make unnecessary further claim to membership on the part of wives. Concubines, however, are frequently taken with no ceremony at all, and tend to achieve full recognition only through bearing sons, who themselves only achieve recognition in many cases through the *K'ai-teng* ceremony. "Where a concubine has no son, there is no need to enter her in the genealogy."[9] Whether a concubine's son needs to be registered in this way or not at the present time depends on circumstances which are not clearly defined. It seems to be that a concubine taken openly or with the consent of the wife is in a strong position and her son would not need to be registered. No *K'ai-teng* ceremonies were undertaken on account of the two sons of the Village Headman by his concubine, the circumstances of his taking her being well known, and his own eminence such that most people in the village could bear witness to the facts. On the other hand, if a man had a son by a concubine whom he kept in the city, or perhaps abroad, it would almost certainly be necessary for him to hold such a ceremony to achieve recognition of his son's claim to membership.

Members are lost to the lineage by daughters marrying out; by expulsion—"If any male becomes an entertainer, or a lictor, or is adopted into another surname group, or becomes a priest, or commits a serious offence against lineage rules, his name should be expunged from the genealogy"[10]—though no instances of this are known to me; by divorce, but this is almost unknown; and by death.

While men, women and children are all members of the

---

[8] *Ibid.*, Rule 7.
[9] *Ibid.*, Rule 8.
[10] *Ibid.*, Rule 6.

The Wan Shih T'ang.

The Village Council Hall.

Offerings at the grave of Ju-chang, focal ancestor of the Second Branch.

The Lineage Headman offers wine at Ju-chang's grave.

lineage, as may be seen from the size of the 'official' lineage and from the lineage's assumption of control over all three categories, it is not true that all are equal members. The rights of individuals vary according to age, but the greatest difference is that between the sexes. Unmarried girls are only temporarily members of the lineage and wives are only members through their husbands: and neither of these categories normally has the right to participate in lineage ceremonies, or to have a share in such economic benefits as may from time to time be forthcoming from the lineage, or to assist in the administration of lineage affairs. Females are thus in fact something less than full members of the lineage, and most informants in the village tended not to include them in their talk on lineage matters. In my first attempts at establishing lineage size I was misled by the exclusion of women from informants' estimates into thinking the group smaller than it in fact was. Thus, in the eyes of many informants the lineage comprises only *ting*, *ting* being defined as all males from birth onwards (and not as adult members only, a more common definition).[11]

Amongst the *ting* there is an inequality of rights based on age, the major difference being marked by the coming of age 61 *sui*, after which a man becomes an 'elder', provided that he fulfills certain conditions. Previously it was usual for a man to give a feast to mark his sixty-first birthday anniversary, inviting to it all the existing elders and other village dignitaries. If the man were poor, however, the feast could be waived. Essential to becoming an elder was the attendance in that year at the Autumn grave ceremonies held on the ninth and tenth days of the ninth lunar month, the aspirant elder being required to come forward alone to worship at the graves at the end of the main ceremony. Failure to perform this essential worship meant foregoing the privileges to which an elder was entitled. The process of becoming an elder was and is known as *Shang-shou*.

C. K. Yang, talking of lineages in Nanching, a village of P'an-yü Hsien, perhaps 100 miles away from Sheung Shui, says: "The council of elders, who served without compensation, consisted of males over sixty-five years of age. When a man

[11] Ho Ping-ti, *Studies on the Population of China 1368–1953*, Harvard, 1959, pp. 24–5.

E

reached his sixty-fifth birthday, he gave a big feast to the entire clan in order to qualify for council membership. . . . The requirement of giving a feast for the clan had the actual significance of making wealth as well as age a qualification for council membership. In fact, there were several poverty-stricken old men in the village whose age was well above sixty-five, but who had never sat on the council of elders."[12] In Sheung Shui, the poor were not similarly handicapped, but on the other hand the position of elder was not as responsible as in Nanching. I found no traces of the existence of a council of elders as such in Sheung Shui.

What then were the privileges of an elder? They seem to have consisted largely of the right to participate in feasts held as part of lineage ceremonies. Such feasts always included meat, and, where meat was a rare item in the village diet, this privilege must have been of some account. In addition an elder was entitled in person to worship the first ancestor. This privilege may not necessarily have meant increased supernatural benefits for the elder, for the first ancestor is worshipped for the benefit of the entire lineage and not for individuals, but it would have increased his standing in the eyes of the rest of the lineage, since he became one of the individuals through whom contact between ancestors and living was maintained. The older a man became the greater were the respect shown to him and the amount of food given to him on ritual occasions. Thus portions of pork in addition to what could be eaten at the feast were given to elders at the following rates—to those 81 *sui* and over, 4 *liang* ('ounces') each, and to those 91 *sui* and over, a pig's head and a whole wooden tub of pork. (We have already seen that, in the wider sphere, long-lived men were sometimes granted honorary titles.)[13]

Respect and feasting were the rewards of elderhood, but no overt political control was exercised by these men. The elders in Nanching did have some degree of political power through the council which they composed—"The clan was directed by the council of elders and the business manager. In principle, the council of elders was the centre of authority that made all

[12] Yang C. K., *A Chinese Village in Early Communist Transition*, M.I.T., 1959, pp. 93–4.
[13] Ho, *Ladder of Success*, p. 21.

important decisions concerning the affairs of the clan . . ."[14]— and, at the same time, the required qualifications for entry into elder status were higher. Thus the system worked to exclude from responsible position the financially inept and the poor. In Sheung Shui there was no council of elders, and only a simple non-excluding entry qualification.

One essential difference between the Liao lineage and those lineages of which Yang is talking is size. Of the five lineages in Nanching the largest was less than 600 strong. In a small lineage the likelihood of there being a literati-pecuniosi group of any size would seem to be remote, hence the gerontocratic tendency. The large Liao lineage produced and supported many scholars, depressing the value of elderhood. Mrs. Liu's material consists of the genealogies of large and wealthy lineages (presumably so, since the genealogies were printed), and it is remarkable that no mention of a council of elders is to be found in her work;[15] negative evidence of a correlation between small lineage size and responsible elderhood. In Kulp's Phenix Village the lineage was something less than 650 strong. Control by elders had been the norm, but modern economic conditions had changed this, and in 1925 Kulp could write: "Control is shifting from the hands of conventional leadership to natural leadership", and "At present the ages of the two principal leaders of Phenix Village are thirtynine and forty-five years".[16] It is implied that elders had traditionally served on a 'Council of Leaders', the operation of which Kulp does not detail; but, even before the advent of modern change, Phenix Village had not relied solely on its elders, for it had been exceptional in producing successful scholars.

Now the requirements of elderhood in Sheung Shui are age alone. Few bother to go through any part of the *Shang-shou* ceremony; mere attainment of the age of 61 *sui* is sufficient to qualify for participation in lineage feasts. In 1964 one man of very conservative ideas worshipped alone at the Autumn grave ceremonies to mark his coming of elder-age, but no one had

[14] Yang, *op. cit.*, p. 93.

[15] Liu Wang Hui-chen, *op. cit.*, Chap. IV, 'Clan Organization'.

[16] Kulp, D. H., II, *Country Life in South China*, New York, 1925, pp. 106–10.

done so the previous year. In 1964 also a wealthy man held a coming of elder-age feast for over 400 guests, but did not worship alone at the grave ceremonies—perhaps because, through his activities as a political leader, he had already been worshipping at the ceremony for many years. Again, the decline in importance of even these simple ceremonies may be correlated both with the decline in respect for old age which has been one result of Western influence and education, and with the rise in living standards, which has made meat an everyday food, and destroyed its drawing-power as a luxury, so that feasts are not as interesting to the elder as they once were.

II

Only by tracing ancestry back to Chung-chieh (or rather to his son) can all members of the lineage find common kinship, and, since kinship is the foundation and essence of lineage unity, the ancestors may be said to be an important element of lineage organisation. The strong accent on ancestor worship and memorialism indicates how heavily the living lineage leans on its dead forebears.

Chung-chieh having had only one son, both the first two generations of the lineage are worshipped and commemorated as the trunk of the tree of lineage descent, but Chung-chieh himself is counted the first ancestor, and it is in his name that most lineage ceremonies are conducted. The main ancestral hall may be said to be built primarily to honour his memory, but his is by no means the only tablet contained in the hall, nor in point of fact is it the oldest.

Ancestral tablets have been allowed entry to the hall on three different grounds, and, in general, each of the three altars of the hall is devoted to tablets of one of the three types only.

The central altar of the three is considered the most important. It is at this altar that the major parts of the ancestral hall ceremonies take place. Thirty tablets are arranged in three rows, nineteen of them being enclosed in eleven small, gated cabinets (*tu*) forming the top two rows. The tablets themselves are placed according to precedence of generation and age, the rule of precedence for this hall being the same as that for the

other two halls of the village, namely that the higher the row
the more important, that the tablets in the centre of a row are
more important than those at the ends, and that, where two
tablets are equidistant from the centre of the row, the one on
the observer's right hand side as he faces the altar has precedence.
Thus the centre position of the topmost shelf is the one of
greatest honour.

FIGURE 2
Tablet Precedence

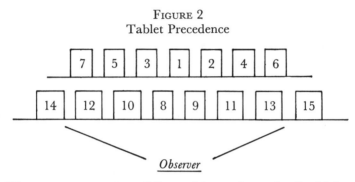

Observer

The top row consists of five cabinets, in each of which are
two tablets; the middle row has six cabinets, three of which
contain two tablets each, and three only one tablet; the
bottom row comprises eleven single tablets without cabinets.
Where there are two tablets per cabinet they are man and wife.
The tablets of the top five cabinets and of the fourth cabinet
from the left in the middle row all represent ancestors senior
to Chung-chieh: they are (each of course with his wife):

A. Kuang-ching:	14th	generation from Tzu-chang.
B. Wen-hsing:	20th	generation from Tzu-chang.
C. Hua:	21st	generation from Tzu-chang.
D. Ch'ang:	22nd	generation from Tzu-chang.
E. Min:	23rd	generation from Tzu-chang.
F. San-shih-san-lang:	24th	generation from Tzu-chang.

On the tablets they are referred to as First Ancestor, Second
Ancestor, etc., down to Sixth in the above order, and are called
by the one or two villagers who are aware of their existence by
the name *T'iao-tsu*. It is not at all clear why these particular
six ancestors should be worshipped and why certain others

should not. It *is* clear that in some way the knowledge of the import of the six cabinets has become divorced from other genealogical knowledge in the lineage. First, the six are numbered in consecutive generations, but according to the genealogy there was an interval of six generations between Kuang-ching and Wen-hsing.[17] (It is true, however, that some other genealogies of the Liao surname do give the six in consecutive order.)[18] Second, the tablet for the wife of Wen-hsing leaves blank the place for her surname, yet the genealogy does have her surname. Third, all but one of the genealogies of the lineage trace the line down through San-shih-i-lang, the third son of Min, not through San-shih-san-lang, his fifth son; and the one genealogy which does trace descent through San-shih-san-lang has been clumsily altered to do so—it was last copied by one of the few men who know something of the cabinets. Fourth, there is an inexplicable gap of six generations between the last of the six ancestors and Chung-chieh. Informants said that the six were there because they were famous scholars, but not all of them were successful men according to the genealogy. It does not seem possible now to account for the presence of these particular tablets, but they seem to have come to represent for the lineage all the ancestors senior to Chung-chieh, and in this guise they are not without effect on lineage ceremony, as will be seen below.

The other two cabinets containing pairs of tablets are for Chung-chieh and his wife and his only son Tzu-yü and his wives; while the remaining three cabinets contain the tablets of Tzu-yü's three sons. The bottom row consists of six tablets of the 4th generation, four tablets of the 5th, and one of the 15th. This last tablet is that of the man who held office as a Battalion Second Captain.

The tablets on this main altar, with one notable exception, owe their position of importance to seniority of birth, and it may be pointed out that the most senior of these honoured few are further favoured by the inclusion of tablets for their wives. The point at which wives are not represented is that point at which the lineage divides internally for the first time, and thus

[17] *LSTP*, Liao-shih tsung-hsi.

[18] See for example Liao Shao-hsien *et al.* (eds.), *Liao-shih tsung-ch'in tsung-hui tzu-chih hui-so k'ai-mu chuan-k'an*, Hong Kong, 1960, 'P'u-tieh' (Hsin-an K'uei-yung-tung Liao-shih kua-tieh t'u).

the importance of Chung-chieh and his son for lineage unity is emphasised in pictorial form. (The significance of the single tablets of this altar will be discussed in a later chapter.) The one tablet which does not owe its position to seniority of birth—that of the 15th generation man—remains something of an enigma, and its presence on this altar can only be ascribed to historical reasons not transmitted.

The second most important altar—following the above order of precedence—lies on the right. Tablets on this altar commemorate ancestors of particularly high academic success. The two tablets which have positions here (again in wooden cabinets) are those of the two *chü-jen* degree holders of the lineage. On the higher shelf is the tablet of Yu-chih of the 15th generation; Ju-i having been of the 16th generation his tablet is on the lower shelf.

The altar on the left of the main altar houses 156 tablets in eight rows. It is traditional in the village that, when the ancestral hall is restored, those who subscribe money for the work are entitled to have their tablets set up in the hall, and it is on this left-hand altar that such tablets are placed. Analysis of the distribution of tablets on the altar seems to show that this system of introducing tablets into the hall has pertained since first the lineage was unified, and indicates at the same time that there was an ancestral hall in existence many years before the existing one was built. On the altar in due order of precedence are tablets representing members from the 6th generation down to and including the 18th generation. The numbers of tablets per generation in chronological order are:

7, 7, 8, 15, 11, 9, 15, 7, 12, 18, 31, 12, 4.

At any time at which the hall was rebuilt or restored there would be members of several generations alive and able to subscribe, and consequently tablets of more than one generation would be placed on the altar. The majority of subscribers, however, would be likely to come from that generation which was largely in flourishing adulthood at the time, so that each rebuilding should produce a peak number of tablets for one generation.[19] The tablet numbers have been plotted in the same

[19] I am assuming that I was correctly informed that it was not possible to purchase places for the tablets of ancestors or others.

FIGURE 3
Honours and hall restoration

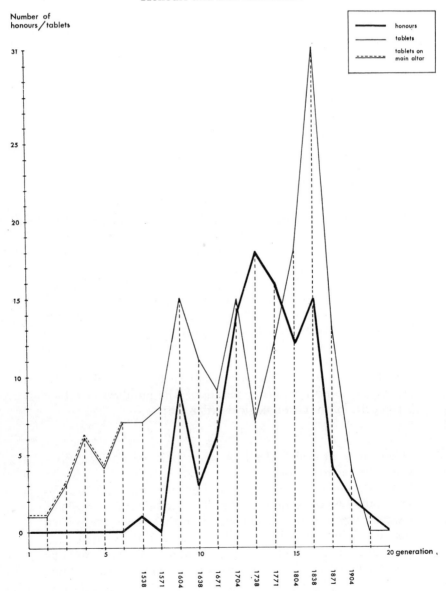

way as were honours numbers in Figure 1, and the two graphs are shown together in Figure 3.

It may be seen that there are three peaks on the tablet graph, occurring in the 9th, 12th and 16th generations, and indicating work on the hall on three occasions, which we may roughly date as the beginning of the 17th century, the beginning of the 18th century, and the middle period of the 19th century. The first building (rebuilding?) coincides with the rough date which we have for the unification of the lineage and the founding of the village (1573–1619).[20] Since the village was built to the plan of the geomancers Nan-sha and Chün-hui, it is reasonable to suppose that a hall would have been built at the same time. Roughly one hundred years later the hall was rebuilt, a century, during which the evacuation had taken place, probably having been sufficient to ruin the first building. It was approximately 150 years under more normal conditions before the hall required rebuilding again.

The coincidence of the tablet graph peaks with the honours graph peaks should not pass unnoticed. Of the three peaks on the tablet graph two of them (in the 9th and 16th generations) occur in exactly the same generations as peaks on the honours graph, while the third peak (in the 12th generation) is co-incident with a number of honours unprecedented at that time, though afterwards to be exceeded. The coincidence of the two graphs is not remarkable. Honours were obtained through wealth in most cases, either directly by purchase or indirectly by a man's having the leisure, which only wealth could provide, to study for examinations. The expensive rebuilding of the ancestral hall would also be likely to take place at a time when the lineage was comparatively wealthy. Hu Hsien-chin reaches a similar conclusion with regard to the growth of common property.[21]

One section of the tablet graph makes rather less sense than the above—the tablets of the 6th and 7th generations could hardly have relevance to the peak of the 9th generation, since it is unlikely that there would be a large spread of generations alive at that early stage in lineage history.

[20] *LSTP*, Historical Movements.
[21] Hu Hsien-chin, *The Common Descent Group in China and its Functions*, New York, 1948, p. 78.

The relative importance of the three altars is demonstrated in lineage ceremonies. In the Spring Rites, held each year in the hall, the major part of the ceremony takes place before the main altar. A short ceremony follows before the altar which houses the *chü-jen* tablets, the participants here being both fewer and of lower ritual standing. The third altar is not worshipped, though tea and incense are set out before it.

The Wan Shih T'ang was last restored in 1932, when it was made more suitable for the opening of a Western-style school. No tablets were added to the left-hand altar, but another commemorative device was resorted to. On the internal walls separating the main altar from the two side altars were hung framed photographs of those twenty-six people who had contributed largely to the restoration, each photograph being inscribed with the name of the contributor, the words "Helper in building the school" (*Ch'uang-hsiao tsan-chu-jen*) and "Commemorative photograph taken in January 1932". One of the photographs was that of the same man who had begun the practice of not holding *K'ai-teng* ceremonies, and it was possibly his idea to remove the commemoration from the religious sphere, even though it would have been possible to make room for more tablets on the altar.[22] One result of this device was that it was possible to include the photographs of two women married into the lineage and two men not of the lineage, all of whom had had a share in the rebuilding. The photographs, which are still there, are not worshipped or tended.

Aside from the altar tablets and the photographs, there is yet another vehicle for memorialism in the 'honours boards' (*kung-ming-p'ai*) which are hung round the walls. There are fourteen of these in the hall, each one normally dedicated to one man of particular merit only, the standard form being an honorific title written large in the middle of the board, on the right of which are inscribed the qualifications and name of the man who is dedicating the board, the dedicatee's name and achievements being written on the left. Each of the two *chü-jen* has a board, as has Liao Hung, the man who compiled the genealogy. One board is dedicated jointly to Yu-chih and Yu-

[22] In one of the halls of the Wen lineage of the nearby village of San Tin I have seen banks of especially narrow tablets obviously made so in order to squeeze more on to the altar.

yung and bears the honorific title "Graduate Brothers". Other boards concern scholars of the Liao surname who apparently were not members of the lineage, and two boards have become so badly defaced that I could not read the inscriptions. The most recently hung board bears the title "Bachelor of Arts" (*Wen-hsüeh-shih*), and is dedicated by the Lineage Headman to a lineage man who graduated with an Upper-second Class Honours Degree at Hong Kong University in 1961. These boards represent individual honours in which the whole lineage can take pride and find example: they are not, however, worshipped in any way.

Although it is not uncommon for there to be a genealogy for a whole lineage kept in the ancestral hall,[23] in Sheung Shui there is no such genealogy. I discovered four separate genealogies for different segments of the lineage, but not only is none of these wide enough in scope to do duty as a lineage record, none of them is wide enough even to represent in anything other than very sketchy terms the segment of which it is the record. Liao Hung made his version for his own segment, though he had hopes that it would serve as the basis for a lineage genealogy.[24] One man now living expressed to me his intention of compiling a lineage genealogy, but it may have been little more than a pious hope.

III

The ancestral tablets and the hall which houses them may be said to be the physical representations of kinship with the dead, and hence evidence of lineage unity. Ancestor worship is the spiritual representation of this kinship tie, a ritual vehicle of communication between the living and the dead, and is a strong sanction behind lineage unity.

Freedman, surveying the literature on ancestor worship, sets out a neat system whereby an ancestor is worshipped in the home for approximately five generations, after which time his tablet is destroyed, either to make way for his promotion to an

[23] I have seen the genealogy kept in one of the halls of the Teng village of Kam Tin, for example. See also Taga Akigorō, *Sōfu no Kenkyū*, Tokyo, 1960, p. 40.

[24] *LSTP*, Ying-lung preface.

ancestral hall or to mark the near extinction of his memory.[25] In Sheung Shui there is no 'promotion' of tablets to the ancestral hall, the only way of securing a place there being to be alive (and sufficiently wealthy) at the time the hall is restored. Concomitantly ancestors are worshipped for a much longer period in the home, many homes having paper 'tablets'[26] representing "all the ancestors of the Liao surname", while others have paper 'tablets'[26] recording the names of individual ancestors of ten generations or more (wooden tablets have disappeared from the home).[27]

A much closer approximation to Freedman's model is shown in grave worship and tending. Individual families go to the graves of their recently dead to worship during the Ch'ing Ming festival in the spring, or in some cases during the autumn Ch'ung Yang festival. By and large the graves (or unburied urns) worshipped are those of ancestors known personally to the living, thus only a few generations may be worshipped in this way. The most distant ancestor's grave known by me to be worshipped was that of a great-grandfather of the youngest agnatic descendant present (though he was great-great-grandfather to a non-agnatic descendant who also worshipped). Beyond this limit in generation depth graves are not worshipped by individual families, *but* grave-worshipped ancestors may be 'promoted' to communal grave-worship and thus saved from extinction of memory, in much the same way as are the tablet-worshipped ancestors of Freedman's account. 'Promotion' of this nature rests entirely on the forming of a trust in the name of the ancestor, the land held in trust being required to produce an income sufficient to cover the costs of grave-worship and subsequent feasting. These trusts are known as *t'ang* or *tsu*, and will be described in more detail in a later chapter. It is significant here that just such a trust did exist in the name of the father of the great-grandfather above, who marked the limit of individual worship.

[25] *Op. cit.*, pp. 82 ff.
[26] The 'tablet' is in each case a large sheet of red paper, pasted on to the altar.
[27] Informants showed some dread of wooden tablets, several people enquiring quite seriously after my health when I had been handling such tablets in the halls. Until recently—ten or twenty years ago perhaps—there were wooden tablets in some homes, but "the children were frightened of them", I was told, and paper tablets have now completely superseded them.

Because of the absence of promotion to the hall, the tablets placed in the hall when it was first built are, by and large, the only ones of which it is possible to say "Once an ancestor had been placed in the shrine belonging to a hall he had ceased to be an object of personal devotion and had become part of the ritual centre of a lineage segment".[28] The tablets of the main altar have merged their separate identities to become a conglomerate body forming the 'ritual centre' of the lineage, but those on the left-hand altar are much less merged into one indiscriminate whole. These latter tablets were placed there through the actions of the individuals themselves when alive, and it is arguable that they are there for the selfish satisfactions of those individuals, so that there is no onus on the lineage as a whole to worship them once dead. I was told that the tablets are in fact worshipped still as individuals by direct descendants, who affix small gold-paper 'ears' to the particular tablets which are the objects of their veneration. These tablets play little part in lineage ceremonies, and, as mentioned above, it is the main altar and the *chü-jen* altar which are more truly central to lineage worship.

Furthermore, these tablets were placed on the altar when the restoration was complete, as early even as in the lifetime of the subscriber:[29] and if, as Freedman claims, "no other tablet could stand for the same person",[30] then the whole basis of the home ancestral cult would be swept away, for a link between generations would be lost to the descendants of the subscriber. Here it must be mentioned that there is a difference in wording between tablets in the home and tablets in the halls. Home tablets are invariably worded *shen-wei*, while hall tablets use the term *shen-chu*. But these two forms of wording do not seem to imply two different forms of tablet; that is to say, it is apparently not the case that one form is the true tablet and the other the copy, as is reported in other studies.[31] If such were the case, then, supposing *wei* to be the 'true' form, the tablet of the first ancestor, which is found only in the halls and not in any homes, should use the *wei* form and not *chu*, which is in fact used; and, supposing *chu* to be the true form, it would not be possible for

[28] Freedman, *op. cit.*, p. 84. Or, of course, of a complete lineage.
[29] The way in which this is done will be described in a later chapter.
[30] *Op. cit.*, p. 82.   [31] *Ibid.*, pp. 82–3.

there to be identical tablets for one man found in both a segment hall and the main hall both using the *chu* form, which duplication is in fact quite common. The two forms seem merely to be recognised as appropriate to the situation of the tablet, without regard to duplication or promotion. There seems to be no bar to setting up more than one tablet to the name of an ancestor.

It may be added here that the practice of 'dotting' the soul into the tablet is virtually unknown at the present day, though some of the tablets in one of the segment halls have certainly undergone the process. An informant learned in lineage lore was quite dumbfounded when I pointed this out to him, and professed complete ignorance as to the meaning or even the existence of 'dotting'.

Formerly all the tablets were exposed to the full view of the hall, so that not only were the ancestors thought to be apprised of all activities which took place there, but those who used the hall were constantly reminded of the existence of the ancestors and of the bonds which held the living together as a unity. When the hall was modified in 1932 to house the school, the two side altars and the spaces in front of them were enclosed by low wooden walls to make classrooms. Being temporary, these walls are perhaps not considered to obstruct the view of the tablets, but it is significant of the greater importance of the main altar that no enclosure was made around it. The main altar, indeed, can be enclosed behind the hinged and decorated doors of the screen, but I did not see these doors closed at any time during my stay in the village.

The major ceremony held each year in the Wan Shih T'ang is the *Ch'un-chi* (Spring Rites), which takes place on the second day of the second lunar calendar month. Like other lineage ceremonies, it is conducted partly in a speech foreign to the village, which is said by the villagers to be "Ch'ing dynasty officials' language", but which bears little resemblance to Mandarin. The ceremony lasts approximately three-quarters of an hour, and is split into two main parts. The first part is performed with the gates of the tablet cabinets on the top shelf of the main altar open, while the gates of the middle row of cabinets are opened for the second part. The two halves of the ceremony are quite clearly meant to point the importance not only of the lineage itself but of the yet more ancient line which the assortment of pre-Chung-chieh tablets is taken to represent. (It seems to have escaped lineage attention that one of this latter group is housed on the middle shelf.) A short ceremony of perhaps two or three minutes at the *chü-jen* altar concludes the proceedings.

Traditionally eligible to take part in and witness the ceremony were the elders and the *kung-ming*. Other people were shut out of the hall for the ceremony—"beat thrice on the drum, play music loud and soft, fire the crackers, seal the door . . ."[32]—and up until the Japanese occupation children who had wandered into the hall before the ceremony were turned out *instanter*. Now women and children tend to come in at will to watch, and no objections were raised to the presence of an anthropologist with tape-recorder, camera and flash equipment. Those who take part in the ceremony too have changed. The elders still predominate, and village leaders from outside the elderhood have replaced the *kung-ming*, but a considerable contingent of representatives (usually including some women) from the Liao Surname Association in Kowloon now has the privilege of worshipping the ancestors as guests. Pre-war some five hours were required for the ceremony, compared with the mere three-quarters of an hour now taken.

An essential part of this ceremony, and of most ceremonies which take place in the village, is the banquet which is held in the hall later the same day. Formerly attended by the *kung-ming* and elders only, the participants now are the elders, the village leaders (that is, members of the Village Council), members of the lineage who are middle school graduates (or higher), and the guests from the Surname Association. That middle school graduates qualify to partake is not, I think, widely publicised—indeed not one of this category was present at the banquet which I attended in 1965—and it is possible that if it became popularly known the increasing numbers of eligible graduates would render necessary the closure of this category.[33] The foods eaten at the meal are determined by

[32] The opening instructions of the 'Ch'un-chi Wan Shih T'ang Li-wen' in Liao Jui-ch'üan (*Shang Shui Liao-shih Chia-li*) *T'ie-shih*, MS, 1946.

[33] On the other hand, many of these graduates would have neither time for nor interest in such ceremonies.

tradition, most of them having previously figured amongst the offerings to the ancestors.

At New Year the *K'ai-teng* ceremony is held in the Wan Shih T'ang, and once again dichotomy of purpose of the ceremony is manifest. Notice of the introduction of a new member to the lineage is given to the ancestors by hanging the lanterns in front of the main altar, and to the living by giving a feast.

On the eighteenth of the tenth lunar month is celebrated the anniversary of the birth of Chung-chieh. The ceremony lasts a little over five minutes, and is addressed to the tablet of Chung-chieh, the gates of only his cabinet being opened. Few elders take the trouble to be present, probably merely a dozen men, including non-elder officiants, in contrast to the fifty or sixty or more who attend the Spring Rites. None the less, many more than the dozen are present at the feast which follows later in the day, though the fare is not as elaborate as at the Spring Rites' feast. An informant, lamenting the degeneration of lineage ceremonial since the Japanese occupation, said that before the war the ceremony lasted for hours; that all the elders would have attended it on pain of the displeasure of the Lineage Headman and other leaders; and that it was most unusual for one who had missed the ceremony to dare to attend the feast. The feast too, of course, is held in the Wan Shih T'ang.

These three ceremonies constitute all the regular ceremonies of ancestor worship carried on in the hall, though it must be noted that a caretaker is employed to offer incense and tea to the ancestors every day of the year as one of his duties. The hall, however, does not serve merely as the home of lineage ancestral rites; it is also a building for the accommodation of communal activities, a physical expression of the unity of the lineage, and even, as we shall see below, in some sense a concrete manifestation of the first ancestor himself. Nor are all ancestral rites carried on in the hall. Ceremonies of at least equal importance, the Autumn Rites (*Ch'iu-chi*), take place at the lineage graves.

In the New Territories there is a strong belief in geomancy (*feng-shui*), and in particular in *feng-shui* of the *Yin-chai* type, concerned with grave-making.[34] Attention paid to graves is

---

[34] For much detail see Freedman, Maurice, *Chinese Lineage and Society: Fukien and Kwangtung*, London, 1966, Chap. 5.

A typical terrace of houses, the front row in Pu Shang Ts'un.

Between newer buildings in Chung Hsin Ts'un stand the dilapidated remains of a *hsi-min*'s mud-brick house.

The *chü-jen* altar in the Wan Shih T'ang.

doubly great because of this, descendants wanting to ensure not only the peace and contentment of the ancestor buried in the grave, but also the good fortune accruing to themselves through the effects of *feng-shui* acting (apparently) on the grave itself. While in many respects Sheung Shui may be said to be laggardly as regards *feng-shui* beliefs, there is no doubt that the Liaos consider the Autumn Rites to be extremely important, and that in the case of the Second Ancestor's grave *feng-shui* considerations add appreciably to this importance.

Chung-chieh having had only one son the lineage has in effect a double first ancestor, since all members are descended from both of them equally. The consequent double duty of worship on the part of the lineage may be ignored in the ancestral hall, where the two tablets stand side by side, but is called for in grave-worshipping rites, since the two ancestors are buried in separate graves some miles apart. Two ceremonies are necessary, being held on consecutive days; Chung-chieh's grave is worshipped on the ninth day of the ninth lunar month, Tzu-yü's on the tenth day.

Chung-chieh's grave lies just over two miles from the village as the crow flies, perhaps three miles by the route usually taken. Its massive brick-built structure actually consists of three separate tombs: the centre tomb contains the silver plaque representing Chung-chieh, and the bones of his wife; the right-hand tomb contains the remains of a 7th generation ancestor and his wife; and in the left-hand tomb are those of an 8th generation man and wife. These two side tombs were perhaps added when the grave was rebuilt in 1816 by members of the 14th and 15th generations. A little later the same year the earth god protecting the grave was rebuilt. The site of the grave is apparently satisfactory from the point of view of *feng-shui*, though a geomancer whose opinion I asked could only *enthuse* over the grave of the Second Ancestor.

This latter (much smaller) grave is again at about three miles walking distance from the village, though in another direction. It was last rebuilt in 1793, and its earth god six years later, at which time an inscribed stone bearing the prophecies of the officiating geomancer was let into the side of the grave wall. The site is called the "Fierce tiger descending the hill", the tiger in this case being considered beneficial to the *feng-shui* of

F

the grave provided that he is ritually fed each year—thus a large, round boulder below the grave is always smeared with a mixture of lime, pig's blood and chicken feathers before the ceremony of worship of Tzu-yü begins. Much of the 19th century academic success of the lineage is attributed to the good *feng-shui* of this grave, one of the principal features of which is a nearby hill-top similar in shape to a writing-brush stand. The present-day emphasis on the *feng-shui* of this grave can doubtless be put down in part to fears of ill-effects arising from the use of the surrounding hills as a public cemetery,[35] the threat to lineage prosperity being sufficient to keep alive moribund geomantic interest.

Traditionally the graves were worshipped by the same members of the lineage who were eligible to worship at the Spring Rites: namely the elders and the *kung-ming*, who processed to the graves accompanied by flag bearers, fire-cracker throwers, and men bearing the many offerings to be used in the worship. The long ceremony concluded with the worship by the recently come-of-age elders, following which a feast (*ch'ih shan-t'ou*) was held near the graves.

Recently (approximately the last ten years) a new element has been introduced into the ceremonies. In a deliberate attempt to encourage a sense of lineage unity in the young, all the Liao school-children have been made to take part in the procession. Between the normal worship and the coming of elder-age worship (if any) senior pupils go through a miniature ceremony, making offerings of flowers and fruit, and reading an address to the ancestor modelled on the lines of the address read in the main ceremony. The rest of the children watch, and join in singing songs accompanied by members of the school band. Lineage funds are not intended for feeding children, and a new method of financing the feast has had to be devised in order that all present may participate.[36] Some of the representatives of the Surname Association who take part are women, and they also have a share in the feast, contrary to custom.

[35] See *NTAR 1947–48*, p. 3, for the year in which work on this cemetery apparently commenced.

[36] In 1964–65 there were over 600 children surnamed Liao enrolled in the junior and middle schools of the village. It is probable that a small number of these were not of the lineage, but came from the nearby Hakka village of the same surname.

In 1964 it was proposed to restore the First Ancestor's grave, which had become quite dilapidated since the last rebuilding in 1816. A geomancer was consulted, and he pronounced the year unsuitable for the work. The ceremony was held as usual. Shortly after I left the field I was told that the work had been started, and the grave was completed in time for the 1965 *Ch'ung Yang* ceremonies. The mimeographed order of procession which I was sent, and which I translate below, gives some idea of the departures from tradition on an occasion when (as was the declared intention of some of the organisers) everything was to have been "as in the old days".

Order of procession: *Ch'ung Yang* visit to the grave of the First Ancestor.

(Maintaining of communications has been entrusted by the school to the Boy Scouts.)

1 One cloth banner [reading] "The Liao lineage of Sheung Shui visits its grave".
2 One pennant.
3 One pair of silk lanterns reading "The Liao lineage visits its grave".
4 One pair of wooden sign-boards.
5 One pair of flautists.
6 One two-man gong.
7 Two roast pigs. } To be put in roast-pig trays and carried
8 One lamb.   } on three cloth-covered banquet tables.
9 Motor-car for the especial use of the lineage elders (intended for the use of the Lineage Headman and Second-in-the-Lineage only, but the Branch Headmen may also ride in it).
10 The three Village Headmen on foot.
11 The elders and gentry [*sic : shen-ch'i*] on foot.
12 University graduates on foot.
13 Middle school graduates walking in pairs.
14 Village Councillors and representatives of the Surname Association walking in pairs.
15 One school cloth-banner [reading] "The students of Fung Kai School visit their grave".
16 The Headmaster and Chairman of the Board of Governors walking together (and four junior school pupils carrying fresh flowers).

17　One school flag.

18　The school brass band.

19　The Brownies.

20　The Wolf Cubs.

21　The girl junior school students (attended by the Girl Guides and a contingent of teachers).

22　The boy junior school students (attended by the Boy Scouts and a contingent of teachers).

23　The girl middle school students.

24　The boy middle school students.

25　The corps of drums.

26　The teachers.

27　Any villagers may freely join in at the end of the procession.

28　Any villagers in cars should follow behind the procession.

29　Any villagers on bicycles should either go on ahead or keep right to the rear.

30　Helpers and equipment should either go on ahead or keep to the rear.

CHAPTER THREE

The Lineage: A Community

I

THE Chinese lineage is founded in both kinship and ritual, which are complementary and largely interdependent, but in the case of a lineage village it is also a community, so that community functions are mainly inseparable from those of kinship and ritual. It may safely be said that until the late 1940s the Liao lineage was community as well as kinship group and ritual group. The history of change over the last twenty years has been in many ways the history of the separation of community interests from lineage interests, and the growing importance of the former in contrast with the rapid decline of the latter.

The uses to which the ancestral hall is put typify the close interrelationship of kinship-ritual and community. We have seen the importance of the hall in certain lineage ceremonies: it is also used for non-ritual purposes. Each year on the day of the Winter Solstice (*tung-chih*) a public meeting is held in the hall at which anyone from the lineage, male or female, may be present and speak. There is no agenda, any matter may be brought up for discussion, and it seems mainly to function as a forum for those with criticisms of the village leaders, who are usually present in force. In 1964 there were twenty-seven people at the meeting, all of whom were men, all of them of the lineage, and most of them of the leadership. The only matter brought up for discussion was the recent completion of a concrete road through the heart of the village, the road being considered by many to be dangerous to playing children, so that it had not been opened to traffic. In spite of the fact that most of the leaders, including the most influential of them, were eager to open the road, albeit under a severe speed restriction, opposition was such that four

71

months later, when I left the village, the road was still closed. This annual meeting is a comparatively recent innovation, no official channel for public discussion existing until after the Japanese occupation.

In addition to the annual meeting, special meetings are occasionally called by village leaders when important matters of general interest arise. In August 1964 such a meeting was called to discuss plans for building a new Village Council Hall, the old one being in a dilapidated and soon to be condemned condition. Twenty-five men were present, many of whom were of the leadership. The meeting was asked to endorse a plan for the siting of the new hall in a section of the moat of the walled hamlet, the moat to be filled in at this point; and public approval for the renovation of the first ancestor's grave was also sought. This meeting demonstrates the way in which community (the Village Council Hall) and kinship-ritual (Chung-chieh's grave) may both come under the roof of the Wan Shih T'ang; while it is indicative of the changed basis of power of the leadership that it felt constrained to call for public endorsement of its policies in this way, and thus to place the responsibility of authorising the considerable expenditure involved on to the community at large.

The hall may be used for private purposes too, and, indeed, I attended a birthday anniversary feast there for an old woman married into the lineage. However, the use of the hall by the school night and day has put a stop to its free availability, so that less and less is it used for such private purposes, and its function as a casual meeting place for conversation has been wholly undermined. It is in its use as a school that the hall performs a community function of the highest importance.

II

Until 1932 education in the village was carried on under tutors who set up schools by invitation in halls or private houses. Most of the tutors seem to have been members of the lineage. Fees, and therefore income, were low, dividing the tutors into two types; the poor, who relied on this occupation for a living, and the rich, who must have done it in some measure as a voluntary service. Such schools (*ssu-shu*) existed in the Wan

Shih T'ang, and in at least four other halls in the village,[1] while the school mentioned above in connection with the Hong Kong and New Territory Evangelization Society was also still running at this time. From the scanty information which I have on the subject it appears that schools in segment halls catered exclusively for segment members, but all pupils were fee-paying, whether studying in the Wan Shih T'ang or in segment halls. The schools were open seven days a week from the beginning of the second month to the end of the eleventh. I came across no evidence that there was in any sense a hierarchy of schools; that is to say, the school held in the Wan Shih T'ang does not appear to have been for the use either of more intelligent or of older children than those who used the segment hall schools. Tutorial schools having no curricula, the necessity of using the halls for ceremonies, feasts or meetings could not cause undue interference with schooling, and this community function of the halls could flourish without impinging on the kinship-ritual function, which had priority of importance.

The lineage did not help with education other than by allowing the use of the Wan Shih T'ang rent free. One informant spoke of the former setting aside of certain lineage land, the income from which (known as *hsüeh-ku*) was used to assist in the maintenance of 'scholars and literati'; but I received no confirmation of this fact, most people stressing that the lineage had never maintained a policy of educational assistance. Money would, however, be spent by the lineage on ceremonies of welcome to scholars returning successful from examinations, the ceremonial doors of the Wan Shih T'ang being opened especially, and a feast given.[2]

Fees in the tutorial schools were low enough that very few males of the lineage were prevented from becoming literate. After 1899 a government-aided school, also run on tutorial lines, was held in a temple in Shek Wu Hui, and the purely nominal fees charged at this school brought education within the financial reach of virtually all. Girls in general were not educated.

---

[1] The Ming Te, the Hsien Ch'eng, the Yün Sheng and the T'u Nan T'ang.

[2] This last occurred in 1961, when the graduate of Hong Kong University already mentioned was feted by the lineage.

The refurbishing of the ancestral hall in 1932 marked a change both of syllabus and educational method. The new-style school taught classes rather than individuals. It also began to concentrate exclusively on a syllabus biased to the demands of the westernised Hong Kong educational system.

The people who were instrumental in forming this new-style school, and whose photographs hang now in the hall, do not all seem at first glance to be of the stamp which might have been expected to perform this reforming action. One of the richer type of tutor played a major role in the change-over, for instance. He was a Licentiate, a product of the traditional Chinese educational system, and taught in the Yün Sheng T'ang. But he seems to have been in many ways a remarkable man. He it was who first neglected to perform the *K'ai-teng* ceremony. Personally rich, and respected and powerful in the lineage, much of the land of which he managed, he was evidently aware of the necessity to run with the tide of westernisation. Others of the reformers were already committed to Western concepts, not least of whom were the Sun Yat-sen supporter whose encounters with the Evangelization Society have been mentioned above; his concubine, a Western-trained doctor and practising mid-wife; a clerk in the Hong Kong Government Service; and an active and capable man who combined his trade as a herbal pharmacist with providing banking facilities for lineage members who had gone overseas, and who was eventually decorated by the Crown for his services to the village and to the New Territories as a whole.

The hall was not greatly changed by the reforms. Both sides of the middle *chien* of the three were converted into rows of classrooms by the erection of wooden partitions, the side altars were similarly enclosed to make two more classrooms, and the front *chien* was converted into teachers' rooms. Teachers, not necessarily of the lineage, were even allowed to sleep in the hall. While I was in the village the two teachers who slept in the hall were neither of them lineage members.

As demand for education grew, probably particularly as numbers were swelled by the widening popularity of educating girls, so the hall became more cramped. After the Japanese occupation an L-shaped extension to the hall was built, providing several more large classrooms with access to the hall through its side door. This in turn became inadequate, and in the late 1950s and early 1960s a large modern school was built on the outskirts of the village. Into this building moved the Middle School and a small part of the Junior School, the greater portion of which remained in the Wan Shih T'ang. A kindergarten was started in the Hsien Ch'eng T'ang. The Junior and Middle Schools are known as the Fung Kai Public School and are operated as a Government-subsidised School.

Grant schools are eligible for up to 50 per cent. subsidy from Government on new buildings, equipment and so on. The rest of the money must be found by the directors of the schools. A subscription list (dated 18th November 1960) for the building of the new school reveals that by no means all the subscribers were lineage members. In fact only 171 of the 441 subscribers were of the lineage, though they donated HK $59,752.15 of the total $113,496.95 collected. The large number of non-lineage benefactors demonstrates the widespreading connections of the lineage, but it is also a result of the school policy of throwing open its doors to all comers.

In 1964–65 the enrolment of the Junior and Middle Schools was as in Table 9.

TABLE 9
Enrolment in Fung Kai Public School 1964–65

| | Number of classes | Students | | |
		Liao	Others	Total
Junior School	23	508	498	1006
Middle School	11	104	344	448
Total	34	612	842	1454

Since the school is under the management of the lineage, which works through a board of directors, its prowess reflects on the name of the lineage, so that much 'face' accrues to the lineage both from the magnanimity of the school in catering for outsiders and from its ability to attract students from a much wider area than the village and its immediate environs.

The school was incorporated as a limited liability company without share capital in 1961. The eleven members of the board of directors were all lineage members.[3] The board now has expanded in size a little,[4] but all the directors are still Liaos, while the body of up to 100 Members of the School (provided for in the Articles of Association)[5] from which the board is elected is also composed purely of lineage members. The school has always been headmastered by a Liao, the present incumbent being a graduate of a well-respected University in Shanghai, a man of wide educational experience, the son of one of the men who founded the school in 1932. The teaching staff comprises only very few members of the lineage.

Admission to the school is open to all; however, it is recognised that lineage children have a certain priority of entrance. There is little difficulty in securing admission to the Junior School for these children, but the New Territories is singularly ill-equipped with secondary schools, and there is very keen competition to enter the Fung Kai Middle School. It is here that the lineage students have a particular advantage, though it should be pointed out that a high standard is required of them, and that duller members cannot gain entrance from brighter non-lineage students. The difference in proportion between Liaos and others in the two schools is well pointed in Table 9 above. The fees in grant-aided schools are standardised by Government, so that there is no discrimination between lineage and non-lineage students. Treatment of students is also equitable, though there still remain vestiges of a system of class time-allocation which is slightly unfair to non-lineage Junior School students.

Unlike the Middle and Junior Schools, the Kindergarten is not subsidised. Its profits are ploughed back into the general Fung Kai educational purse, so that in part it supports the activities of the parent school. Its headmistress is not in any way related to the lineage, but she is considered to be under the overall authority of the Fung Kai headmaster. Not being government-subsidised there is no restriction on fee-charging,

[3] Hastings and Company, Solicitors etc., *Memorandum and Articles of Association of Fung Kai Public School*, Hong Kong, 1961, p. 14.

[4] To fifteen.

[5] Hastings and Company, *op. cit.*, p. 12.

and here discrimination is made between lineage and non-lineage children, the fees being $12 and $15 per month respectively. The reason given for the extra charge to outsiders is that the hall must be rented, but no rent was actually paid for the use of the Hsien Ch'eng T'ang. Of the 306 children enrolled in eight classes in 1964–65 121 were Liaos.

The effect of the founding of the school in 1932 and of the increasing scope of its activities since the war may be seen in the data on education elicited by my questionnaire of 1965. Of the 92 lineage males aged seven and above about whom detailed information was given only three had received no education at all, all three being past school age in 1932. Education in Hong Kong was sadly affected by the Japanese occupation, indeed only 4,000 children were found to be attending school in the whole colony when war ended,[6] and a drop in the number of years of school-attendance is noticeable for those who grew up in the village at this time. From the war until the present there has been a steady rise in number of years attended, so that from an average of less than $4\frac{1}{2}$ years attendance for those born between 1926 and 1935, the average figure for those born between 1946 and 1950 is just over 9 years attendance. The effect on the daughters of the lineage cannot be calculated, but it may be said with certainty that very few received any education prior to 1932, while no daughter of school age born after 1945 has gone without education. Girls born between 1946 and 1950 have attended school for an average of $8\frac{1}{4}$ years, very little less than lineage males of the same age. The end of the war probably marks the point at which education of lineage girls becomes general. Of the 86 lineage wives who were over 25 years of age in 1965, 14 had been educated for an average of just over $3\frac{1}{2}$ years, the remaining 72 had received no education at all. It is likely that daughters of the lineage have been more fortunate than girls from most other areas of the New Territories, where educational facilities have been much slower to develop.

The increase in school size and in depth of education offered has come about through the initiative of lineage members who

[6] Donohue, The Hon. Peter, Director of Education, 'Education Department' in *The Government and the People*, Hong Kong Government Press, 1962, p. 10.

have been given their head by the lineage.[7] From a small number of students studying for a limited number of years, the system has expanded to the point where all lineage children receive education, the length of that education growing rapidly year by year. Fung Kai School introduced a 5th year Middle School course in 1964–65, and plans to work up to full university entrance courses. Students have the choice of taking classes conducted in Chinese or in English, the latter classes providing an obvious stepping-stone to jobs in government, international commerce, etc. The lineage already has some six or seven university graduates among its members.

Thus the lineage has done much to make easy the process of education for its members. As before 1932, however, it makes no attempt to give financial assistance towards the education at any level of *individual* members. There is a movement among a few influential leaders to set up a revolving scholarship fund to provide loans for university students, but no definite steps in this direction have yet been taken. The next stage in the expansion of the school is the setting up by the lineage of a private secondary school. When this is flourishing, as it seems probable that it will,[8] it is possible that the fund may be set up and supported by it.

III

Pirates have not been the only lawless forces to cause disruption of village life. Bandit hordes, other lineages, and casual thieves all have constituted a menace to lineage life and property over the centuries. It has already been noted that the original hamlet was walled and moated in response to the threat of the marauding army of the Ming loyalist-cum-bandit Li Wan-jung;[9] a proportion of the Chinese force which opposed the British assumption of power in the New Territories in 1899 was said to have been composed of "remnants of the followers of Chung Sui-yeung and Sun Yat-sen, who tried to create a rebellion in

[7] It is the proud boast of the Liaos that they have always had a strong tradition of education, and they point to the many successful men of past generations and to a poetry club, the *Ch'ing-nien Shih-she*, the members of which met annually to compete for bardic honours.

[8] Indeed, I understand from a correspondent that it has now opened, bringing the total enrolment of the two schools to nearly 2,000.

[9] *LSTP*, Historical Movements.

the Kwangtung province";[10] a lineage man in his fifties told me how before the war he had been tied up in the ancestral hall while bandits ransacked it;[11] and there is ample evidence that bandits were active in the area as late as 1947.[12]

Before the British administration of the New Territories there was little direct control exercised by the Central Government below the level of the cities in which the Deputy Magistrates resided, so that villages were thrown on their own resources for protection from wrong-doers. While the British administrators were thicker on the ground, with police stations established at key points, it is apparent that until after the Japanese occupation the effectiveness of the administration was not great enough to safeguard the villages. Under British rule no less than under Chinese it was necessary for villages to create some form of protection for their inhabitants, livestock, crops and property.

There are reports of crop-protection groups being set up by villages throughout China,[13] while mention may be found of organised night-guards of various kinds operating within villages.[14] In Sheung Shui the Village Watch, known as the *tzu-wei-tui* or *hsün-ting*, guarded not only crops, but livestock, inhabitants and property as well. I did not establish how long a history the Watch had, the usual answer being "there has always been one".[15] In the past the Watchmen seem to have been picked for their strength and pugnacity, the model having been a man who lived about 200 years ago and who is known to lineage posterity by his nickname 'Ploughboy'. He is said to have been capable of leaping seven rows of sweet potatoes at once, to have seen in the dark as well as in the light, and to have had great cunning. At the age of 22 he embarked on a life of crime, robbing other villages; and such was his prowess

---

[10] *Extension Despatches*, Colonial Secretary to Governor, 15th April 1899.

[11] I cannot vouch for the authenticity of his story, but that he volunteered it without any question or leading from me gives some significance (if not veracity) to it.

[12] See for example Collins, *op. cit.*, Dedication, "To the memory of Sydney Charles Collins . . . who, on 1st January 1947, was killed by bandits near Taipo in the New Territories . . ."

[13] See for example Smith, A. H., *Village Life in China*, New York, 1899, pp. 163–4; Yang, M. C., *A Chinese Village*, London, 1948, pp. 148–9; and Gamble, S. D., *North China Villages*, California, 1963, Chapter 5.

[14] Gamble, *op. cit.*, pp. 109–12.

[15] Cf. Gamble's findings on the night watch, *ibid.*, p. 109.

at this that he was made a member of the Watch, and became eminently successful at his job. The legend woven around this figure includes details of his robbing the District Magistrate for a wager, and of his eventual end in exile after his eyes had been 'neutralised' by a doctor.

Today, when with greater mobility the Hong Kong police force is no doubt capable of patrolling the village adequately,[16] the Watch continues to function as the main protecting body for the village. There is little duplication of effort. The villagers are happy to have relative immunity from police patrolling, much of the traditional distaste for and distrust of such control remaining. It is a fact that the villagers believe that the majority of policemen (and government officers high and low) are corruptible and corrupt. The existence of the Watch obviates the necessity for police patrolling. In any event the general belief is that the Watch can do a better job than the police, for the latter are organised in such a way that patrols pace the same beat at the same time each day, clocking in at well-established check-points, while the Watch is free and expected to vary both time and route from day to day.

The Watch is responsible to the political leaders of the village, of old to the *kung-ming*, now to the Village Council. There are sixteen Watchmen, all from the lineage. Each year on the 12th December[17] the sixteen positions are tendered for, tendering (*k'ai-t'ou*) being the usual way of settling lineage matters in which there is an element of financial competition. Tenders are placed in sealed envelopes and handed in to the Village Council. The sixteen highest tenders are accepted, the highest of all being made Head Watchman. The total amount paid in 1963 was HK $3,206, the money going into the general village finances. The Watchmen recoup themselves and take an income by levying a charge on property protected. A householder pays $2 or $3 per year, while crops are protected at a charge varying with the type of crop and size of field. Animals, such as water buffalo and pigs, are also charged for.

[16] To the annoyance of the villagers the police regularly manage to raid the tea-houses for gamblers.

[17] It is strange that the Western Calendar should be used in this instance, the Lunar Calendar being the most common arbiter of recurrent events in the village; at the same time it is typical of date selection that the 'double date' (i.e. 12th of 12th month) should be fixed on.

The Watchmen patrol at night only, usually in small groups: but they do not necessarily patrol every night, nor are all sixteen necessarily on duty every night. Their major responsibility is to prevent and apprehend thieves, but fire-watching and flood-warning also come within their charge. They operate from a centrally situated building outside which stands a small, antiquated, trolleyed hand-pump, with 'Wan Shih T'ang' and the maker's name cast in the metal, while inside is a large altar to an unspecified god who protects them.[18]

Their vigilance is supposed to be assured by a stipulation that they partly reimburse any victim of theft, but it seems that this aspect of their responsibility is now lacking. Indeed, a charge of $3 is levied by the Watch before they will even investigate any theft reported to them. In February 1965 my next-door-neighbour's entire stock of nine chickens was stolen overnight from the hen-house outside my door. He did not report the matter to the Watch, claiming that it would be sending good money after bad, since he would have to pay $3, knowing that the Watch would be unable to find the culprit and that he would receive no compensation for his loss.

Formerly (until the turn of this century?) the Watch patrolled with gongs in traditional manner,[19] but now they go about silently. The effectiveness of these men as detectives or captors is much in question, and it is probably mainly their ability to take wrongdoers by surprise in the course of silent and unpredictable patrols which acts as a deterrent to crime. Certainly they can take common-sense precautions against crime: barking dogs invariably attract a patrol, ripe crops are watched more closely, and it is said that thirty years ago a known thief (a drug addict) was stalemated by the Watchmen's putting a seal on his door each evening and checking the seal periodically during the night to make sure that he had not slipped out. There is in fact very little crime in the village, which argues that in some measure the Watch as an institution is not unsuccessful.

It is difficult to know quite how the Watch would act in the event that they apprehended a criminal—no arrests were made while I was in the village as far as I know. Before 1899 there is little doubt that the captive would have been hauled straight-

---

[18] The god is represented merely by a large character, *shen*.
[19] For a short account see Gamble, *op. cit.*, p. 109.

way in front of the *kung-ming*, who would have dealt with him summarily. One of the commonest forms of punishment was by beating, the guilty party's head being tied into a sack so that he could not see who were administering the blows. (It was not unknown for death to result from such beatings.) After 1899 there was little difference in treatment of criminals, but it is probably true that serious cases would have been submitted to the fairly approachable British administrators for trial and judgement. I was told that now the Watch would still be prepared to beat criminals caught by them, and that such men would be dealt with entirely within the village and without recourse to the police. I am sceptical of this claim—one informant told me that there had been no beatings since the Japanese occupation, though pre-war he had seen some—but had no means of verifying it at the time since, as mentioned, no criminals were caught. Certainly it is difficult to believe that men of the responsible cast of mind of the present village leaders would sanction such flagrant disregard for the Colony's law, but it might well be that *members of the lineage* caught in crime would be punished by the Village Council and would submit to such a punishment rather than undergo the shame for individual and lineage of a police prosecution. Mediation in disputes is still carried on by the political leaders, with much success in the cases I saw or heard about. That there is a tradition of self-sufficiency in law and order in villages of the area may be seen in the sporadic reports of village trials and punishments which are heard—even death being called for in some cases.[20]

In general it may be said that the duties and responsibilities of the Watch have diminished appreciably during this century, and that they are likely to decrease further. The Watch used to have full responsibility for the protection of the village from all dangers. It was expected to keep a watch for marauding bandits and other such groups, to warn the village and to constitute the first line of defence against them. It was expected to spot fires and to take the lead in extinguishing them; to watch for flooding and warn the village of imminent danger from it. It was expected to warn off thieves from village and crops, and to

[20] See Baker, Hugh D. R., 'The Five Great Clans of the New Territories', *JHKBRAS*, Vol. VI, 1966, p. 45, note 85.

catch those who were not timid of the gongs, to see that they were judged and to officiate in the punishments. Now there are no bandits to attack the village (and if there were, the responsibility for protection would lie with the police and other government forces); there is a fully equipped modern fire station less than a mile away in Shek Wu Hui; there is a large police force and efficient legal system to deal with any arrested persons (and to frown on villages which want to take the law into their own hands). As the 'vegetable revolution' engulfs the surrounding fields, so the people farming the fields begin to sleep in huts next to their plots, so that protection for the crops is not needed.

But it may be inferred that the Village Watch still performs one function of great importance to lineage unity. It acts in effect as a medium of village taxation, making each householder tacitly responsible to the village leadership by virtue of paying the protection fees. Accepting the necessity for protection the householder acknowledges his dependence on the Watch, which is the agent of the Village Council. If he accepts the protection of the village, he must abide by the village (i.e. the lineage) regulations. If he abides by the regulations, he may not sell his house or land within the village precinct to outsiders. In this way the lineage can still maintain its control of land ownership and of behaviour of those living in the village, for, while the actual protection of the Watch may be only partially effective, the known withdrawal of that protection can be a powerful stimulant to lawless action against the unprotected. In the last few weeks of my stay in the village there was much talk of mob action against an alleged bad character in the village, village leaders hinting darkly that unless he removed they would be unable to restrain the natural desire on the part of the villagers to attack and demolish his house. The authority of the lineage is thus acknowledged and bolstered by this indirect taxation.

IV

Another community function for which the lineage was responsible was public works—the building and maintenance of bridges, dams, paths, public buildings, and in this context the graves of the first and second ancestors too.

G

It is not possible to say what percentage of public works in the past was financed by the lineage and what by individuals. Since there were no public meetings, the decision to spend lineage money on, say, a new bridge must have been made by the leaders; and, where a historical relic bears the name of an individual of the lineage, there is no way of knowing whether he had himself paid for the work, or whether he as prime mover in the work had been the spender of lineage money. Indeed, it may well have been that the boundary between lineage funds and the private funds of the lineage leaders was in some respects a blurred and uncertain one; a point which Freedman has brought out.[21]

To the north of the village lies a modern road bridge over the Indus River, now usually known as Red Bridge (*Hung-ch'iao*). It is built very close to the site of an older bridge, the *Tung-hsing-ch'iao*, which is mentioned in the *Hsin-an hsien-chih* with the date 1748.[22] During the building, an inscribed stone, the earth god protecting the *Tung-hsing-ch'iao*, was excavated. The stone bears the name of the bridge, the words "For convenience of crossing the great river" and "The god of the earth of this bridge", and, underneath the date, the names of three Liaos who set up the stone. There is no way now of knowing by virtue of what position these three names appear on the stone. The three men may have been the three senior elders of the day, three leaders of the lineage, or perhaps three rich men who had built the bridge. They may have subscribed the money themselves or be merely representing the lineage.

The same confusion applies to other relics, but the question of the authorship of any essential public works of the past need not concern us too deeply—the lineage as a body must ultimately have been responsible for such public works, whether or not an individual had stepped in to pay for them, and while the glory of achievement might belong either to an individual or to the whole lineage, the individual and the lineage were so closely identified that either could share in the achievements of the other.

Since the Japanese occupation the position as regards public works has become at once more complicated and more rational.

21 Freedman, *Lineage Organisation*, p. 130.
22 *HAHC 1819*, chüan 7, 'Fords and Bridges'.

The rationalisation has been the emergence of two clear areas of responsibility, kinship-ritual and community: the complication lies in the advent of and expansion in Government aid, either partial or full, in local public works. In the year 1946–47 this aid amounted to HK $26,968.17 for the whole of the New Territories,[23] but twice this amount was expected to be spent by Government on one project in this village alone in 1963–64,[24] and aid to the New Territories now runs at over $2 million *per annum* in all.[25] In practice, Government aid seems to be given only to those public works which fall within the community area of responsibility.

Projects carried out in recent years include the building of a road through the village, of several wells, and of two sets of public toilets (a third was about to be started when I left the village); and the rebuilding of two dams and of the first ancestor's grave. The last of these works did not qualify for Government aid, and was wholly paid for out of lineage funds; but even of those projects aided by Government most are granted only a proportion of the cost, so that the village has to make up the full amount. That the Liaos are as well aware as Government of the difference between the kinship-ritual and community spheres (despite the fact that lineage funds and village funds are one and the same) may be demonstrated.

In 1957, after a series of dams had been destroyed by floods several times, a new dam was built at Shek Pei Tau, downstream from Red Bridge,[26] the village supplying the labour for the work. An inscribed stone, dated 16th May 1957 and raised beside the dam, gives details of the history of the dam and of its latest rebuilding. It bears the names and offices of three Liaos— the three Village Representatives, the political leaders of the village.

By contrast, when, in 1965, the first ancestor's grave was restored, the additional wording inscribed on the tablet gave the date of restoration in both Western and Lunar calendars, and bore the names again of three Liaos, but this time of the three most important leaders in the kinship-ritual sphere

[23] *NTAR 1946–47*, pp. 6 and 18.
[24] *Report of the Public Works Subcommittee of Finance Committee 1963–64*, Hong Kong Government Press, 1964(?), p. 17.
[25] *NTAR 1964–65*, p. 11.
[26] See *NTAR 1956–57*, pp. 24–5 for details of the work.

(though they are not in any way identified as such).[27] The original tablet also gave no clue to the position of the men who had raised it—what can still be deciphered appears to be merely a list of some sixteen names.

The two sets of names on the tablets—political leaders on the community project and kinship-ritual leaders on the kinship-ritual project—point the awareness on the part of the Liaos of some difference between the two spheres, even though the money which paid for the works came in each case from the same source.

V

As a kinship-ritual group the lineage practised and was bolstered by ancestor worship: as a community it gave its support to other religious practices and beliefs.

The entire village and its fields were considered to be under the protection of the God of Earth and Grain (*Hsiang she-chi chih shen*), the altar to whom was placed on the outskirts of the village near the walled hamlet. He was worshipped regularly by many women on the first and fifteenth days of the lunar month, and by women from every household once a year on the solar period *Ching-che*, when fertility (of fields and women) and good health were stressed in the rites. Principally, in his capacity as controller of insects, the god was a farmers' deity, but today, when the percentage of those connected with farming has fallen drastically, he is still worshipped as of old. His importance to the community is demonstrated by an incident which occurred in 1964. Late in October of that year a particularly violent typhoon brought massive rainfall to the colony, and the village, though raised from the level of the surrounding fields, was flooded to a depth of as much as three feet in places. The altar of the god was completely demolished. By early December the tablet had already been reset in a brand-new altar, and on the 9th December a ceremony of rededication, called *k'ai-kuang*, was held. The rebuilding and ceremony were paid for from lineage funds at a cost of $550.

[27] In fact the wording gives the names and the generation numbers of the three men followed by "and all grandsons" i.e. all living descendants of Chung-chieh.

Something of an anomaly is a second altar located in the fields on the opposite side of the village. The tablet of this altar is dated 1864 and worded "The place of the true spirit of *Fu Te*, the earth god protecting the village". The dilapidated condition of this altar and the paucity of offerings made to the god point to virtual abandonment of it. One of the men who knew of its existence told me that the two altars at different ends of the village ensured protection from evils "such as tigers" which might come to the village from outside. It is my own assumption that this second altar was raised by the community at large, but the possibility must not be ruled out that the hamlet nearest to it was responsible for its erection.

A ceremony of exorcism of ghosts is a common periodic feature in New Territories villages. The ceremony, called *ta-chiao*, is held in many villages once in ten years, in some more frequently, but in Sheung Shui only once in sixty years, always falling in the *ping-hsü* year of the sixty-year cycle. Part of the cost of the *ta-chiao*, which is heavy,[28] is met by the lineage, the rest being raised by private donations and by means of a *per capita* tax levied on all *ting* in the village.[29] The ceremony lasts for several days and is mainly under the direction of Taoist priests (*Na-mo-lao*).

Half a mile to the north-west of the village a low concrete platform stands in the middle of the fields. It is six-sided and hollow-centred, the remains of a pagoda. It is said to have been built "300 or 400 years ago" by the lineage in an effort to counteract the effect on the *feng-shui* of the village of the rock formation called Eagle Head Hill, which faces the village from a distance of about a mile and a half. It was thought that the open mouth of the eagle was swallowing some of the good fortune of the Liaos, so that male children and examination successes in particular were being denied the lineage, and a geomancer suggested that between the village and the eagle a *feng-shui* pagoda should be built to represent a bird table, thus protecting the Liaos from the bird's appetite. Unfortunately the

[28] In 1964 a *ta-chiao* was held in the Teng lineage village of Ha Tsuen. The lineage and its segments alone were said to have contributed HK\$160,000 to the ceremony, though this did not cover the cost completely.

[29] I was unable to discover the cost of the last ceremony, held in 1946, the records having been lost.

pagoda was not built on the correct site,[30] and other villages to the west benefited instead, gaining unprecedented successes in examinations. The lineage tore down the pagoda to the level at which it still stands, but did not rebuild elsewhere.[31]

In the walled hamlet are two temples which are the property of the lineage. The T'ien Hou Temple supports three nuns, a superior and two votaries. The nuns call themselves Buddhists, though they eat meat and fish,[32] wear leather sandals, gamble at Mahjong, and smoke cigarettes, while earning money at piece-work when not required for religious duties. Few people I asked knew that the nuns were Buddhists, but said they were "of the Chinese religion"—a term which seems to cover almost any religious observance other than Christianity. The same nuns also maintain the second (adjoining) temple, which is dedicated to the god Hung Sheng. The idols of this latter temple are very much dilapidated, and the temple itself is tumbledown. Very few people worship there, though the nuns keep a few sticks of incense smouldering at the altar.[33] Not only does the lineage own these temples, it also makes to the nuns a monthly grant of $6 towards their maintenance.

On an auspicious date after New Year there is a ceremony of prayers for blessings on the whole village. The ceremony (tso-fu) is conducted by a Taoist priest, whose fees are (presumably) paid by the lineage, with the Lineage Headman as supplicant. The God of Earth and Grain is worshipped, as also are two tree gods.

While the above religious practices are all concerned with the lineage as a community rather than as a kinship-ritual group, it is true that there is not in fact a completely clear division into community and kinship-ritual spheres. As a kin-ship-ritual group the lineage is tied to ancestor worship; as a community it can and does support Buddhist, Taoist, Geo-mantic and virtually any other religious practices: but the two

[30] There is a tale to account for this, involving a goose-herd's inadvertent moving of the stone which marked the spot on which to build.

[31] To this day the virtually complete depopulation of Shang Pei Ts'un is blamed on the eagle's spoiling of the *feng-shui*.

[32] "It's better for their health to eat meat", I was told by one group of women amongst whom were several who regularly make offerings at the temple.

[33] It is in this temple that the brazier donated by Yu-jung in 1833 is housed.

spheres are at times mutually reinforcing, so that there are earth gods attached both to the first ancestor's grave and to the Wan Shih T'ang, so that both a Taoist priest and the Lineage Headman perform the *tso-fu* ceremony, and so that the *k'ai-kuang* ceremony of rededication of the Earth and Grain God altar also was conducted jointly by the Lineage Headman and a Taoist priest. Blurring the picture still further is the fact that the financial source for all expenditure is the same—the Wan Shih T'ang.

VI

The uses of the Wan Shih T'ang as the venue for lineage ancestral rites and for community activities have been described above, but the name Wan Shih T'ang does not signify only the concrete hall. Embodied in the term also are at least four abstract conceptions.

First, the T'ang is an 'ancestral trust' endowed with land and property, the managers of the trust having disposal of the income from the endowment in the interests of the lineage, but the primary claim on the income lying with the ritual cere-monies of worship of the first and second ancestors.

Second, the Wan Shih T'ang was, and to a certain extent still is, the collective name of the lineage leadership, so that matters of village or lineage policy are said to be "decided by the Wan Shih T'ang", and in a conversation about the Village Watch I was told, "Yes, the Wan Shih T'ang can still punish people." I was also told that "the Wan Shih T'ang" would step in to prevent any house or land within the precincts of the village being sold to a non-lineage buyer.

Third, the name is frequently used to denote the lineage itself. Every member of the lineage, man woman and child, is a member of the Wan Shih T'ang,[34] so that the two terms are exactly synonymous and are so used. In honour of the "Inaugural Celebration of the Rebuilding of Shek Wu Hui" in 1964 both the Liaos and the Hous from the chain of villages nearby erected ornamental arches over the main road of the market

[34] The 'official' figure for the membership of the Wan Shih T'ang, given above, makes it clear that all are considered to be members (though not all are full members with rights of inheritance).

town. The wording of the Hou arch read "The Hou clan of Sheung Shui District . . .", while the Liao arch read "The Liao Wan Shih T'ang of Sheung Shui Village. . . ."[35] By extension the term also means Sheung Shui Village; that is to say the Wan Shih T'ang is the lineage as a community as well as as a kinship group. I suspect that the name is becoming less frequently applied to the community now that so many outsiders live in it; none the less an informant described the duty of the God of Earth and Grain as being "to protect the Wan Shih T'ang".

Fourth, the Wan Shih T'ang is frequently called *A-kung* ('the ancestor'). "Who paid for the rebuilding of the Earth and Grain God altar?" . . . "*A-kung* did." The ancestor is of course Chung-chieh, so that the Wan Shih T'ang is the representation of the first ancestor.

From the foregoing the importance of the Wan Shih T'ang as a unifying factor is plain. It symbolises the essential continuity of the patrilineal descent group down through history. "The first principle of filial piety is that you dare not harm your body, limbs, hair or skin, which you receive from your parents."[36] The lineage is a part of the first ancestor and they are so closely identified that either may be meant by the name Wan Shih T'ang. The physical T'ang (hall) itself is not only a unifying agent in performing its functions as a meeting place for community and kinship group, it also, by virtue of its housing the ancestral tablet in which Chung-chieh's soul (or part of it) resides, is the representation in concrete form of the first ancestor. Chung-chieh alive was the trunk of the lineage tree of descent; dead, the living branches of that tree may eventually have fallen away from each other without the introduction of the indestructible prop, the enduring hall and its inalienable endowment.

VII

As a hall the Wan Shih T'ang is a symbol of the unity of the lineage in all its aspects: as a trust the Wan Shih T'ang maintains that unity by its virtual monopoly of all lineage funds.

[35] *Shih Hu Hsü Ch'ung-chien Hsin-shih Lo-ch'eng*, photographs on front cover.
[36] *Hsiao-ching*, Book One, 'K'ai-tsung-ming-i'.

It is to be regretted that I was not able to obtain any kind of statement of the income and expenditure of the T'ang. The financial records, along with other important documents, were destroyed at the town home of the then Village Headman by one of the two fires which gutted Shek Wu Hui in the 1950s, and I was not permitted to see the more recent records. Nor are annual public statements issued by the T'ang, though some segment trusts do publish their accounts. However, I have attempted to estimate the income of the T'ang, by comparing it with that of another T'ang of the lineage, which, though with greater land-holdings, has, unlike the Wan Shih T'ang, no additional source of income. Assuming the two then to have roughly similar incomes from land, the Wan Shih T'ang should receive approximately $35,000 *per annum*.[37] I have been helped by being able to discover the amount of land held by the trust, land being the principal source of its revenue.

The first detailed land records compiled by the British administration were made in 1905 and amended in 1906 and 1907, in which form they are now preserved on microfilm. By courtesy of the New Territories Administration I have been able to consult these records. The land of the New Territories is divided into Demarcation Districts, and the records are entered under the different districts. It seemed practical to confine my researches to those districts which lie nearest to the village, so that it is possible that a very few lots of land owned by the Liaos have escaped my notice. However, having noted down every lot of land which came to my attention, whether near or far from the village, I am confident that the number of lots passed over can be measured in at most tens and not in hundreds, so that the figures given below are as close to accurate as is necessary for the emergence of a general pattern. In addition to the 1906 records, I was permitted to see the up-to-date records on land-holdings which are kept in the District Offices. It is unfortunate that the virtual lack of indexing and the diffuse nature of these records made the task of searching in them an extremely time-consuming one. This, coupled with the difficulty

[37] In a recent letter a member of the Village Council has told me that the approximate annual income of the T'ang is $26,000, but I do not know either how accurate this is, or whether he has taken all sources of income into account.

of not knowing what to look for before the 1906 records had
been consulted (they are in London), has meant the eventual
only partial coverage of these up-to-date records, though some
work done for me by a correspondent since my return from the
field has ameliorated the situation somewhat.

In 1906 the Liaos owned some 4,144 lots of agricultural land
(of varying size and quality) totalling 973·33 acres, and 726
house lots. Of these, 1,943 land lots (47 per cent. of total) and
50 house lots (7 per cent. of total) were communally owned;
that is, were owned by trusts of one kind or another. The Wan
Shih T'ang was one of the largest trusts, but not in fact the
largest of all. In addition to the hall and its large site it owned
100 lots of land to a total of 23·88 acres, as in Table 10.

TABLE 10
Wan Shih T'ang land: 1906

Class of land	Number of lots	Area (acres)	Crown Rent
1	32	9·19	27.57
2	5	0·53	1.06
3	63	14·16	14.16
Hall	1	—	1.00
Total	101	23·88	$43.79

One-third of the third-class lots were lying waste at that time.
The land was rented out for farming, leases being arranged
annually and the rents calculated and payable in unhusked rice.
Tenants could be lineage members or outsiders, and the latter
are said to have predominated; but I suspect the determining
factor to have been the area in which the land in question was
situated, land near the village being more likely to be rented to
lineage members than more distant lots. A Crown Rent per
acre of $1 for third-class, $2 for second-class and $3 for first-
class land was collected by the District Office from land owners.
The above land, however, did not constitute the full holding of
the T'ang. A further fifteen lots of land were owned jointly by
the T'ang and other persons or trusts. The up-to-date records
of the Wan Shih T'ang show that the sixty years since 1906
have been stable ones for the T'ang. I know that one page of

these records was overlooked by mischance and this probably explains the fact that there is no reference to twelve lots which were owned by the T'ang in 1906. Counterbalancing this loss, there are eight new acquisitions, and the complete taking over by the T'ang of eight of the fifteen previously only partly owned lots; so that in all, there has been an increase in the holdings. There has probably been a considerable increase also in the income from this land. Crown rent has not changed since 1906, so that it is now of purely nominal proportions to the value of the land: rents from the fields on the other hand have certainly risen, and sharply so where vegetables are being grown, while land in and near Shek Wu Hui has become of great value. Leases on the fields have tended to get longer, particularly where vegetable farming has made expensive soil improvement, so that farmers have demanded long leases to protect their investment in fertilisers, etc.; and a lease may be for as long even as ten years, with four or five years common.

The above are all openly in the name of the Wan Shih T'ang, but there are other holdings of the lineage which are not in that name. In some cases the managers of the Wan Shih T'ang extend their control to T'ang which continue to operate under an original name—thus the two temples of the walled hamlet are registered officially as the T'ien Hou Temple T'ang and the Hung Sheng Temple T'ang, but are in fact as much lineage controlled (and by the same personnel) as is the Wan Shih T'ang. Similarly placed are the skirt of land within the moat but without the walls, which is known as the Ho Hsing T'ang, and the Tse Mien T'ang, which is an alternative name of the Wan Shih T'ang.[38] In other cases the village is the owner of land and property, the Village Council being administrators. This village property seems all to have been acquired since the war. It includes an orchard, two fish ponds, two sports fields and an irrigation pump, but no agricultural land. Only the fish ponds at present yield an income, and one of those could find no tenant for 1965.

We have passed from the Wan Shih T'ang to the village, but it should be remembered that the income of both goes into a common fund; furthermore, land is not the only source of income for this fund. The tenders of the Village Watch are paid

[38] The title board of the Wan Shih T'ang bears both names.

in to the Village Council, as we have seen. Another source is the periodic market of Shek Wu Hui. It was a lineage market originally, and the lineage still draws from it a percentage of the income from the public weighing scales. Of the total income, which in 1965 was said to be about $70,000 per year, the share of the lineage is one-third,[39] the money being particularly intended for the Village Welfare Fund, which pays for public works, education, etc.

On occasion, other methods of raising money are employed. Early in 1964 the Village Council arranged to rent an area of lineage land some way away from the village to a businessman for the purpose of setting up a temporary amusement park. He was to guarantee $200 a day for forty-five days, and to have the option of continuing the lease at the same rental for a further forty-five days. The park, complete with opera, gambling and food stalls, was opened with great ceremony by the District Officer and other notables, but it was cursed with bad weather and the operator apparently attempted to default on the rent. The lineage did not in the end gain very much by the idea.

Another expedient for fund-raising is the loan. Recently when the lineage wanted to build on some land in Shek Wu Hui it raised a loan (*kung-chai*), issuing printed shares at $10 each. A fixed amount was repayable each year by the Wan Shih T'ang, the shares to be repaid being drawn publicly from a drum, until after so many years the loan is paid off. The shares are negotiable, but carry no interest, so that the loan is in no sense a profit-making investment for those who subscribe. There was still money outstanding on the loan when I left the village.

The lineage also on occasion solicits donations from or levies taxes on individual members. A large number of members subscribed to the building of the school, and again to the cost of building the new road through the village. For the sixty-yearly *ta-chiao* ceremony a tax on *ting* is imposed, and it is expected that a tax of $10 per *ting* will be charged to help pay for the proposed new Village Council Hall.

VIII

The major recurring expenditure of the lineage is on ritual

[39] See below, p. 191.

and the feasting which accompanies it. The Wan Shih T'ang does not itself undertake the work of preparing the offerings and feasts, but draws up a list of its requirements for each ceremony and puts the work out to tender. (Only lineage members submit tenders.) For the celebration of the anniversary of the first ancestor's birthday, for example, it is laid down that there should be:

a raw pig[40]
a roast pig
a whole sheep (euphemism for a chicken?)
a pig's head and spleen
a large dish of 'longevity cakes'
a tray of sweetmeats
five kinds of fruit
a dried fish (eel?)
a salted fish;

these in addition to rice, wine, tea, incense, candles, fire-crackers and paper-money for the ceremony, and vegetables, rice, wine, bean-curd, etc. for the feast afterwards. This ceremony is only a comparatively small one, the scope and number of offerings and the size and variety of the feast increasing with the importance of the occasion. The successful tender (that is, of course, the lowest figure tendered) for the more elaborate Spring Rites was $679 in 1965.

The most costly ceremonies of all are the two days of *Ch'ung-yang* at the graves of Chung-chieh and his son Tzu-yü: for these combined in 1964 a tender of $5,680 was accepted. In 1965 the cost was no doubt still higher as a result of the emphasis placed on the first of these ceremonies by the restoration of the grave. Yet the cost to the Wan Shih T'ang does not represent the total cost of the ceremonies. The inclusion of the school-children and the necessity to feed them have created problems of finance which were resolved by dividing the cost of the ceremonies between the T'ang and the school. The T'ang pays for its traditional responsibilities; the school, chiefly by subscription from the School Members, meets the cost of the extra food. In all, the cost of the two days is approximately $8,000 *per annum.*

40 Liao Jui-ch'üan, *op. cit.*, 'Order of service for birthday of Chung-chieh'.

Other regular expenses are the maintenance of the T'ang caretaker[41] and the Lineage Headman, each of whom is allocated land from the lineage holdings, the income from which land is for his use. In the case of the caretaker the income is expected to provide him also with the cost of the incense and tea which it is his responsibility to offer night and morning to the ancestors. The Lineage Headman must be provided with a long silk robe and traditional cloth shoes for ceremonial occasions, and, since he is unlikely to be a particularly rich man,[42] the income from his lineage land is no doubt intended partly to cover the cost of these. The subsidy to the nuns of the T'ien Hou Temple is also a regular charge on lineage funds, as is the annual *tso-fu* ceremony (the T'ang caretaker buying the necessary offerings with T'ang money additional to his normal income). Small salaries are paid to the scribe and business manager of the Village Council, and to the caretaker who looks after the Council Hall.

The lineage must also keep on hand reserves of cash to meet non-recurrent needs such as public works. Bank accounts are maintained, and I know that when one of these accounts was frozen by the colony-wide bank troubles of early 1965[43] there was $5,300 in it. The reserves must be large since some projects are extremely costly— $3,500 was given by the T'ang towards the building of the new school—and since some, such as the rebuilding of the altar of the Earth and Grain God, demand expenditure of quite large sums at short notice.

Public works account for the major part of non-recurrent expenditure, but there are other abnormal calls on lineage funds. In 1964 a banquet, partly subsidised by the T'ang, was given in honour of Miss M. A. E. Smith of the London Missionary Society when she left the area after ten years as a midwife in the small maternity hospital she had founded on the outskirts of the village. In 1965 I was similarly feted; and a large and expensive banquet was given to honour two local

---

[41] *Tz'u-t'ang-kung*. His duties do not clash with those of the school caretaker who also has responsibilities in the Wan Shih T'ang.

[42] Freedman, *Lineage and Society*, p. 44, "Ritual headships, based on seniority in generation, naturally tend to fall to men in less prosperous units . . ." The present incumbent is of the 17th generation and belongs to no segment below one of the 9th generation.

[43] See *Hong Kong 1965*, Hong Kong Government Press, 1966, pp. 5–8.

men (not of the lineage) who had been created Justices of the Peace. The ornamental arch (*p'ai-lou*) erected by the lineage for the rebuilding celebrations in Shek Wu Hui cost the Wan Shih T'ang $3,300.[44] Local events of importance, such as a *ta-chiao* ceremony in a nearby village or the election of a local man to the chairmanship of the Heung Yee Kuk, demand the formal congratulations of the lineage in the shape of a large ornamental hoarding (*hua-p'ai*),[45] which costs several hundred dollars, often as much as $700–800.

The permanent income of the lineage from its land and other sources is large, and is more than sufficient to pay for normal running costs of lineage and village. Large items of non-recurrent expenditure, however, tend to be met from *ad hoc* funds only partly contributed by the T'ang.

IX

Until after the Japanese occupation there was no organisation of community separate from kinship-ritual, the Wan Shih T'ang was the lineage in all its aspects. The creation of a Village Council distinct from the T'ang has thrown into relief the essential dichotomy of the lineage village, for it is an organisation which, on the face of it at least, has connection with the kinship-ritual sphere only in that all its members are drawn from the lineage. It is an organisation of which the very name— *Village* Council—indicates its concern with community matters.

Yet the Village Council may not so easily be dissociated from the Wan Shih T'ang—of itself it has virtually no income, the T'ang being the repository of the trust land which is the major source of income of the lineage. If, then, the Council has assumed the community role of the Wan Shih T'ang, it is none the less tied by financial need to the T'ang. But, tied to the T'ang, it is not merely the T'ang's shadow, for it has made the T'ang subservient to it: the ivy grows stronger than the tree. The T'ang is the trustee, the bank accounts are in its name, but it is the Village Council which now has control of the finances and which spends the money. The income of the Wan Shih T'ang

[44] *Hua-ch'iao jih-pao*, 11th March 1964.
[45] An average *hua-p'ai* is probably about 10 ft. high by 6 ft. wide, but some are very much bigger than this.

from land was primarily intended for ritual purposes, and the T'ang is a kinship-ritual group before a community group.[46] Control of this income has now passed to the Council, resulting in a shift of emphasis from the kinship-ritual to the kinship-community sphere. The implications of this change of control, which is at once a symptom and an instrument of social change, are important and will be discussed further in due course.

[46] Where lesser trusts have only a small income it is spent entirely on ritual.

CHAPTER FOUR

Segmentation

I

THE lineage is united in the Wan Shih T'ang, which is both a concrete and an abstract symbol of the ties of interest which bind the lineage. At levels lower than the full lineage similar symbols of unity are found marking off segments of kin. The functions of the various segments are not all alike, but the majority have as their primary aim the ritual worship and remembrance of a particular ancestor of a later generation than Chung-chieh or his son. Invariably these kinship-ritual segments find expression in ancestral trusts of similar nature to the lineage T'ang. The trusts are of two closely related types: first, the *t'ang* type, in some of which a hall is built, usually to house the tablet of the ancestor who is the *raison d'être* and focal point of the segment's unity, the hall and its trust normally being given a name other than that of the ancestor—thus the Ming Te T'ang, whose focal ancestor bears the name Huai-yin; and second, the *tsu* type, which is a trust not usually endowed with a hall, the name of the trust being the avoidance-name of the focal ancestor suffixed by the word *tsu*.

Kinship-ritual segments do not exist without trusts; that is to say, although the genealogical basis for segmentation is present wherever a man has more than one son, no segment is recognised unless an endowment of property in the form of a T'ang or Tsu is set aside for the worship of one of those sons (or of course each of the sons may form the focus of a trust). Theoretically, then, there is no reason why a new segment should not be formed around every ancestor who has a brother, but in practice this is not done. Segments are only formed by the setting aside of property, and where there is no property to set aside there can be no segment; nor is the availability of property an indication that it will necessarily be put into trust to form a segment. Where an ancestor has no segment focused on him, his grave falls into decay after a few generations, and his name fades away into the realm of 'all the ancestors' worshipped indiscriminately by his descendants.[1]

There is no discernible system which determines which ancestor should be made the focus of a segment. A man who has amassed wealth does not necessarily become the focus of a segment even if some of his wealth is put into trust. The formation of Tsu is always (so far as I know) on a posthumous basis, and frequently on a basis more retrospective than immediately posthumous; that is, a trust created in, say, the 10th generation may be focused on an ancestor of any generation prior to that. A T'ang, on the other hand, may, I suspect, be formed by a man during his lifetime—the fact that his own name is not necessary to its formation avoiding any charge of self-glorification—but almost certainly the majority of T'ang would be formed in the same posthumous fashion as Tsu. With this lack of system for the formation of trusts, a wholly haphazard occurrence of segments is to be observed. In some cases a series of trusts has been established around consecutive generations of ancestors in the same direct line of descent, in others seven or more generations have elapsed without new segments being formed. In some cases there is symmetrical segmentation where each one of a family of brothers has become the focus of a trust, and in others asymmetrical segmentation has resulted from only one or only some of the brothers being so focused upon.[2] In a few cases a trust is formed in the name of a man who has died childless, the income being used to ensure worship of one who otherwise would be neglected by later generations.

An individual may be a member of many different Tsu and T'ang according to the incidence of wealth in his own direct ancestry. I lack full information on this point, as some data which were to be forwarded to me from the village have not materialised, but probably the case of my next door neighbour is typical of an averagely wealthy ancestry. He is of the 18th generation and is a member of seven different Tsu and T'ang:

[1] See Chapter Two, p. 62.
[2] The situation is exactly as postulated by Freedman, *Lineage Organization*, p. 49.

they are focused on ancestors of the 1st,[3] 3rd, 4th, 6th, 7th, 9th and 11th generations. No one is a member of less than two trusts, of which the Wan Shih T'ang is one.

As far as I have been able to discover, there were in 1906, exclusive of the Wan Shih T'ang, at least 157 kinship-ritual segment trusts in existence, owning between them 41 house lots and 479·76 acres of land.

II

Chung-chieh had only one son, Tzu-yü, but three grandsons, Ju-kuei, Ju-chang and Ju-pi. Segmentation occurs in this 3rd generation, though in a form which is a little difficult to classify as either symmetrical or asymmetrical. The Ju-chang Tsu owned 9·87 acres of land in 1906, and the Ju-pi Tsu 2·73 acres; but I found no proof of the existence of a Ju-kuei Tsu. However, the descendants of Ju-kuei did own a small amount of land jointly with the Ju-pi Tsu, the joint venture itself being organised as a Tsu, the Kuei Pi Tsu. From this fact I infer the existence of a Ju-kuei Tsu to handle one half of the income of the joint Tsu. Indeed it is plain that the Ju-kuei Tsu did exist in 1906, as it does now, but I cannot explain its non-appearance in the 1906 records except by suggesting that it may have held land in mortgage or perhaps have held land a long way away from the Sheung Shui area.[4] As well as its small holding of land the Kuei Pi Tsu was in possession as mortgagee of a large amount of other land, so that it must have had an appreciable income, sufficient at least to ensure the continuance of ancestral rites for each of the participating Tsu. On this basis segmentation may, I think, justifiably be classified as symmetrical. Certainly the descendants of the three men are considered by the Liaos to constitute fully equal segments. In fact the three segments are known as the three *fang* (Branches); the Senior Branch, Second and Third Branch focusing on the first, second and third born respectively.

---

[3] The Wan Shih T'ang, of course.
[4] I have attempted to take mortgaged land into account where I consider it to alter the situation substantially.

FIGURE 4
The Three Branches

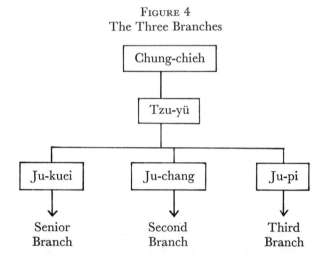

These Branches are the major ritual segments of the lineage, their importance being marked by the inclusion on the middle shelf of the main altar of the Wan Shih T'ang of a tablet to each of the three brothers. At lineage ceremonies those who worship after the Lineage Headman are the Deputy Headman of the Branch from which the Lineage Headman comes and the Headmen of the other two Branches. No rigid order of precedence in worship is adhered to after these, thus accentuating the ritual importance of the Branches. The three names on the tablet of Chung-chieh's newly restored grave are those of the three Branch Headmen.

Each of the three Branches worships at the grave of its focal ancestor on the same day—the eleventh day of the ninth lunar month—the order of grave worship thus clearly reflecting the generation order:

1st generation— 9th of 9th month
2nd generation—10th of 9th month
3rd generation—11th of 9th month

Again, the 3rd generation marks the end of strict order of precedence; later generations are worshipped on fixed dates, but not in any apparent order. Thus, in one direct line of descent recorded in the genealogy there are the following dates:

```
 4th generation—18th of 9th month
 5th generation—16th of 9th month
 6th generation—19th of 9th month
 7th generation—16th of 9th month
 8th generation—23rd of 9th month
 9th generation— 3rd of 9th month
10th generation— 4th of 9th month
11th generation— 3rd of 9th month
12th generation—13th of 9th month
13th generation—26th of 9th month
14th generation—15th of 9th month
```

The three Branches are not of equal size, nor of equal wealth. The Second Branch is nearly twice as large in numbers as the other two Branches together, as may be seen below, and the feasts which follow the grave worship of the Branches demonstrate that symmetrical segmentation does not imply equality of wealth between such segments. The Ju-kuci Tsu is comparatively wealthy, and all male members of the Branch are eligible to take part in the feast; the Ju-chang Tsu permits only its male members over 61 *sui* to participate; while the Ju-pi Tsu is at present so impoverished that their feasting has, I understand, been discontinued altogether. On the 1960 list of subscribers to the building of the school, each of the three Tsu is in evidence. The Ju-kuei Tsu donated $3,500, the Ju-chang $3,500 and the Ju-pi $700.

None of the Branches maintains an ancestral hall, but the Senior Branch does own a temple, the T'ien Hou Temple to the north of Red Bridge. This temple probably dates from at least the early part of the 17th century, for it was in this area that the Senior Branch was living before the amalgamation of the lineage.[5] There is no record of date of foundation of the temple, the earliest relic in it being a large bronze bell presented by a Licentiate of the lineage[6] in 1721; nor is there much to show that the Senior Branch is responsible for the temple other than two pairs of couplet-boards hung beside the main altar. One pair is dated 1939, and was presented by six Tsu of the Senior Branch in conjunction with the then Branch Headman and, I suspect, his deputy (the two of them presumably

---

[5] *LSTP*, Historical Movements, "The Senior Branch . . . lived upstream on the north bank of the river in a village called Sheung Shui . . .".

[6] Actually of the Second Branch.

representing the Ju-kuei Tsu) and all living descendants of the Branch. The other pair does not identify the donors, but works into the couplet the other name by which the Senior Branch is known (*Pei Tou*), a device also adopted in the first mentioned couplet. The temple was last restored in 1960. It is dedicated to T'ien Hou, normally considered to be a seafarers' goddess,[7] but contains four other gods as well. Ten nuns eke out a living in the temple from the donations of the worshippers, their fees for helping at funerals and other ceremonies, piece-work, and the income from a small piece of land with which the temple is endowed (0·29 acres of second-class land), a Senior Branch man always being manager of the trust of course. Anyone is free to worship in the temple, many of the ornaments having been presented by people other than lineage members.[8] This openness of access, and the lack of ancestral tablets in the temple, make it seem likely that the Branch has merely continued to support what is still its property by virtue of having been at one time the temple of its village.

The Third Branch similarly owned a temple, the Ta Wang Temple, which, again, was situated at one of the places where the Branch had resided before the amalgamation of the lineage, not far from the T'ien Hou Temple.[9] In its impecunious state, however, the Branch has been unable to maintain the temple, and it has rotted away. In 1906 there was an endowment cf 1·75 acres of land apart from the temple itself, but this must either now be worthless or perhaps mortgaged or sold.

III

The focal ancestor of the Second Branch had two sons, and the elder of these became the focus of a hall-owning segment, the Hsien Ch'eng T'ang. The hall is large (two *chien*), the rear *chien* containing banks of tablets arranged in the same manner as in the Wan Shih T'ang. It was built in 1838, or around that time, for the title board, by the hand of Yu-jung, bears that date.

[7] See for example Burkhardt, *op. cit.*, Vol. I, p. 13.
[8] The creation of the Restricted Area in recent years has affected the temple seriously, for it is just within the area and so inaccessible to those without passes.
[9] *LSTP*, Historical Movements, "The Third Branch . . . lived downstream on the north bank of the river . . .".

The middle altar houses 139 tablets, all 'dotted' in red, on seven shelves, the higher shelves being the place of the senior tablets, as in the case of the Wan Shih T'ang. On the topmost shelf are 18 tablets. The central tablet is a large composite one for the first three generations—that is, for Chung-chieh, Tzu-yü, Ju-chang and their wives. Flanking it are two tablets, one each for the T'ang's focal ancestor and his wife.[10] This arrangement carefully picks out the T'ang ancestor from the rest and thus emphasises his importance for the segment.

FIGURE 5
Hsien Ch'eng T'ang tablets

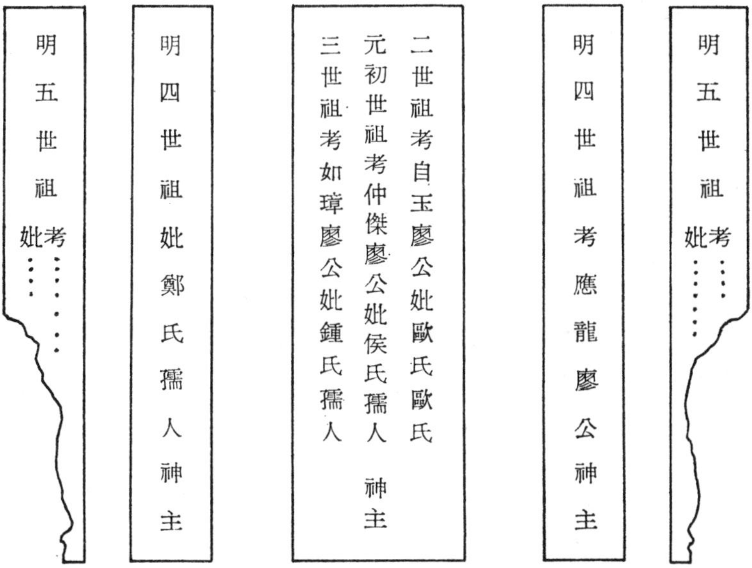

N.B. Two wives of the same surname in 2nd generation.

The rest of the tablets, which each represent a man and his wife or wives and concubines (except where he was unmarried),

[10] This is one of the very few instances in the halls of the village where a wife has a separate tablet, and the only one where the tablet is not immediately next to the husband's.

are arranged in order on either side of these, and then down on to the other shelves. There are two 5th generation tablets, two 6th generation, five 7th, three 8th, four 9th, ten 10th, eight 11th, nineteen 12th, twenty-eight 13th, twenty-seven 14th, fifteen 15th, eleven 16th and two 17th. These tablets were probably all placed on the altar when the hall was built in 1838. The reasons for the choice of these particular ancestors are not entirely clear: it seems possible that there is an element of primogeniture in the selection but, while I can substantiate this up to the 8th generation, I cannot vouch for the truth of the hypothesis beyond that, owing to the lack of genealogical information. Some of the tablets no doubt owe their selection to merit, 29 of the ancestors represented bearing honours of one kind or another. Each tablet is slotted at the back, a removable slat of wood disclosing brief biographical details of the ancestor.[11] Several of the tablets are duplicated in the Wan Shih T'ang. There is no automatic promotion of tablets on to this altar, and I was assured that there is no way now for more tablets to be added to it.

The right-hand altar, as in the Wan Shih T'ang, contains tablets of men of the segment with high honours. There are three tablets, all 'dotted', all on one shelf. The middle tablet is that of the *chü-jen* of 1807. On the right is his brother Yu-jung, and on the left the tablet of the Battalion 2nd Captain, another of whose tablets (the exception to the rule of seniority) is found on the main altar of the Wan Shih T'ang. Yu-jung's tablet must have been introduced after the founding of the hall, for he was alive at that time, and wrote the title board.

The left-hand altar also emulates the Wan Shih T'ang in that it is devoted to the tablets of those who have given money for the building and restoration of the hall. Under this system of reward the tablets are placed in the hall as soon as it is built or restored. At this time the donors will still be alive, and, to avoid the inauspicious effects of a tablet dedicated before death, each tablet is covered with a red (i.e. auspicious colour) wooden jacket on which is written the generation number and name of the donor, with the words "long life". As the donors

[11] It is considered sacrilegious to remove this slat, and, while I did in fact do so in a few cases, I did not in general collect data from this valuable source.

FIGURE 6
Hsien Ch'eng T'ang tablets and hall restoration

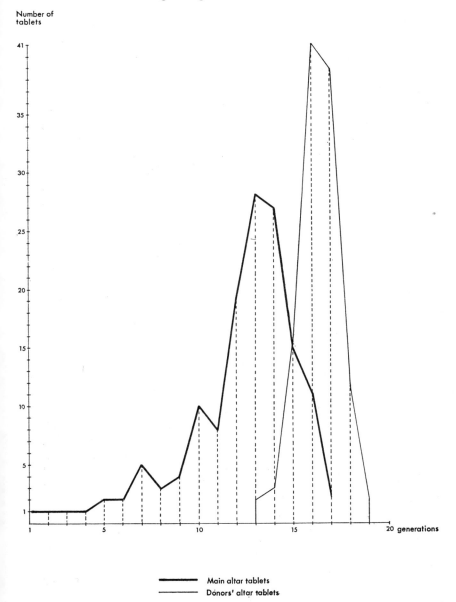

Number of tablets

Main altar tablets
Donors' altar tablets

die, so the covers are removed one by one, disclosing the ready-carved green tablets underneath. One jacket remains of the 115 donors with tablets on this altar.[12] The tablets comprise two of the 13th generation, three of the 14th, sixteen of the 15th, forty-one of the 16th, thirty-nine of the 17th, twelve of the 18th and two of the 19th.

In Figure 6 the incidence of tablets per generation has been plotted as a graph in conjunction with those tablets on the central altar of the hall. The graphs do not indicate the historical picture as clearly as do those for the Wan Shih T'ang, and yet it is beyond doubt that they represent the same processes. The explanation lies, I believe, in the peculiarly disparate nature of the segment, in which some lines have been consistently very wealthy and others consistently very poor. My neighbour, whose segment membership has been given above, belongs to no Tsu or T'ang closer than seven generations from him: in the richer half, however, those generations are liberally endowed with Tsu and T'ang, including some of the wealthiest of the lineage. In such circumstances it is to be expected that the richer lines will reproduce faster than the poorer, and a wide spread of living generations at any one moment results. The blurring of historical pattern of the graphs must be owing to this cause,[13] and one peak in the 16th and 17th generations must disguise two separate events—the building and the later restoration of the hall, which may be dated approximately as 1838 and 1923.[14] The tablets of this left-hand altar are neither slotted nor 'dotted', showing the segment's lack of interest in these ancestors as ritual objects.

In the hall are five honours-boards. Two are identical, dedicated to four successful scholars of the segment—Liao Hung, his two sons, and Chiu-wo of the 11th generation. Two honour a Liao (not of the lineage) who was a *chin-shih* and held office as a Second-class Assistant Secretary of the Board of War in the latter half of the 19th century.[15] The fifth board,

[12] Unfortunately this man lives in the city and I did not meet him.

[13] But in the case of the tablets of the Wan Shih T'ang the disparateness of this segment is doubtless lost in the general pattern formed by the lineage as a whole.

[14] Couplet-boards to mark the restoration were presented by the Ming Te T'ang in this year.

[15] There is a board dedicated to this man in the Wan Shih T'ang also.

identical to the one in the Wan Shih T'ang, is dedicated to the B.A. of 1961, though he is not a member of this segment.

The hall is used for birth, wedding and funeral feasts and, most important of all, for the Spring Rites, which are held here the day after those in the Wan Shih T'ang; that is, on the third day of the second lunar month. The Kindergarten is held in this Hsien Ch'eng T'ang, and it has interfered to some extent with the other functions of the hall, as we shall see below.

The Hsien Ch'eng T'ang is actually registered as a Tsu—in the name of the focal ancestor, of course—though it is commonly known by its T'ang name. In 1906 the Tsu owned 3·92 acres of land in addition to the hall. Its holdings now are probably about the same; not a particularly large endowment for such a large segment. It is said to be this poverty of endowment, and therefore of income, which prevents the Tsu from worshipping at the focal ancestor's grave—contenting itself with the Spring Rites worship. For this ceremony tenders are invited from segment members, in the same way that the Wan Shih T'ang seeks tenders from its members. In 1964 the successful (i.e. lowest) tender was $416; in 1965 it was slightly less at $406. Males of 51 *sui* and over are entitled to attend the feast. A donation of $3,500 was made in the name of the Hsien Ch'eng T'ang towards the building of the new school, but a note on the subscription list records the fact that the Tsu itself gave none of this money, the actual donors being three of its sub-segment Tsu. The very modest Tsu contribution of $500 went to swell the $3,500 donation in the name of yet another T'ang, the Tung Ch'ing T'ang.

IV

Segmentation at this 4th generation level is only nominally symmetrical, the younger brother forming the focus of a segment whose trust is so poor that it owns only 0·02 acres of land. Indeed, I could find no trace at all of this trust in the 1906 records, and no grave ceremonies are performed. The income from the land, if there is an income, is perhaps added to that of the Ju-chang Tsu. It is not in fact until the 7th generation that this line is segmented practically. The focal ancestor is said to have amassed a large fortune, and his descendants used this to build a hall,[16] but since the word for ancestor (*A-kung*) can, as we have seen, mean a trust endowed in his name, it is possible that the fortune was the making of his descendants rather than the ancestor himself. Informants said that the original intention was to create a trust and hall around their 4th generation ancestor, but that the opposition of the descendants of the other brothers of the 7th generation caused the segment to be focused on the 7th generation instead, thus excluding the dissenters. It is claimed that only about ten descendants of the excluded brothers are alive today, so that the trust does in fact very nearly include all the members it might have had if it had been focused on the 4th generation. The trust is wealthy and is registered under the name of the Hall, the Ming Te T'ang.

The hall was built in or before 1828 (which date is carried on the title board) and restored once early this century and again in 1964. It is of about the same size as the Hsien Ch'eng T'ang, but has an altar only in the centre of the rear *chien*. On the altar are seventy tablets on seven shelves. The top shelf supports six tablets, those of the focal ancestor and his wife and of his two sons and their wives, the tablets being placed in three husband-wife pairs. There is a tablet for each of the ten men of the 9th generation, three tablets for the 10th generation, seven for the 11th, eight for the 12th, thirteen for the 13th, eighteen for the 14th and five for the 15th. All tablets are slotted, though of the few which I managed to look at several were blank inside; no tablet is 'dotted'; and after the 8th generation wives are not represented at all. Some of the tablets are duplicated in the Wan Shih T'ang. Reverting to the dates of birth per generation as worked out in Table 8, it is clear that all ancestors represented on this altar could have lived and died by 1828. From the 7th generation to the 9th all ancestors are represented; but from the 10th generation on, merit seems to be the basis for selection, those ancestors who are not credited with a degree of some sort being designated *ch'u-shih* ('retired scholars'), and while this might be no more than an empty honorary title, it is true that a few of the tablets of the Wan Shih T'ang bear the same words, indicating a difference of some kind between *ch'u-shih* and most of the other

16 *LSTP*, Biographical Details, 7th generation.

ancestors in that hall, who are not distinguished by any such title. It will be noticed that in this case no attempt is made to link the focal ancestor with the lineage first ancestor, though the Hsien Ch'eng T'ang has adopted the device of a composite tablet for the generations before its focal ancestor.

Unlike the Hsien Ch'eng T'ang and the Wan Shih T'ang, there is in this hall no altar to individuals who have contributed to restoration work. It seems to me probable that this is owing to the superior wealth of the segment, which does not need to call for individual donations to meet the costs of such work. It must be remembered that the Hsien Ch'eng T'ang is not particularly wealthy, and that the Wan Shih T'ang income, though high, has to meet much greater commitments than those of the Ming Te T'ang. Thus no tablet has been added to this altar since 1828, and again I was assured that there is now no way of placing a new tablet in the hall.

The hall is rather bare, containing only two honours-boards, one dedicated to Ju-i, the *chü-jen* of 1849, and the other yet again to the Hong Kong B.A. of 1961. Neither of these men is of the segment, nor indeed of the Branch. Three sets of couplet boards were presented to the T'ang when it was restored earlier this century. One was given by the Hsien Ch'eng T'ang, one by the Kuei Pi Tsu, and the third by a group of individuals and firms (none of them Liaos) from Shek Wu Hui. These last were probably lessees of Ming Te T'ang land. The hall is the only one of the village which is always open and accessible, for no school is held in it, and consequently it is much used by old men who sit there to gossip.

In 1906 the T'ang owned 63 lots of land to a total of 18·84 acres, these in addition to the hall itself and a small 'reading-room' (*shu-yüan*) in the walled hamlet. The records of 1966 show that 12 of the 63 land lots are no longer owned by the T'ang, but 9 new lots are owned, including one house lot in Shek Wu Hui which is probably very remunerative. The T'ang has therefore remained fairly stable over the years. Marks of its wealth are its rather more extravagant than average feast following the Spring Rites (held on the solar period *Ch'un-fen*); its fine set of embroidered altar cloths and sacrificial vessels (the Hsien Ch'eng T'ang has none of this equipment); its gift of $3,500 towards the new school buildings; and its annual grant of $20 and one uniform to each child of the segment at school. Its finances are in a sufficiently healthy state that it could afford to charge Miss Smith a nominal annual rent of only $400 per year for the large area of land on which she built her maternity home; and the same rent is still being charged now that the buildings are used for other community purposes.[17]

But as well as this wealthy T'ang there is also a wealthy Tsu focused on the same 7th generation ancestor. The Tsu in 1906 owned 49 lots of land totalling 13·49 acres. The membership of the Tsu and the T'ang are of course identical, and both trusts were administered by the same manager in 1906 (I have no details of the present state of the Tsu). Quite why there should be this duplication is not clear to me, but it is not a unique phenomenon in the lineage, and possibly at one time it reflected a desire to avoid undue notice on the part of government officials, bandits, charitable organisations and so on. Unaware of the existence of the Tsu whilst in the village, I can only surmise that its income is used for the Autumn Rites at the grave of the focal ancestor, thus sharing the ritual duties with the Ming Te T'ang.

V

The Wan Shih T'ang, the Hsien Ch'eng T'ang and the Ming Te T'ang are the only ancestral halls (that is, halls with tablets) which still function as such. In 1906 six 'ancestral temples' were said to be in existence, but of the other three only one remains standing, and that is mostly derelict and used as a residence by three families, two of which are not Liaos. I did not go into it, but suspect that there are no tablets and that possibly there never were. Eleven other halls, labelled as 'reading-rooms' by Government (whether or not they all fulfilled this function is a moot point) were in existence in 1906. They contained no ancestral tablets. Their fate has been mixed. The largest of them, the Yün Sheng T'ang, has been mostly let to outsiders at about $300 per month, and has

---

[17] For Scout meetings, St. John Ambulance Brigade training sessions, etc. The lessee is the Village Headman.

become a small plastic goods factory—the portion not rented out is retained as a hall and kitchen for feasts by the T'ang. Another has been converted (illegally) into a biscuit factory. The rest, with the single exception of the Ming Te T'ang reading-room in the walled hamlet, have disappeared. In building halls of this nature the segments do show some signs of having a community function, especially where schools were held in them.

While the Ming Te T'ang and the Hsien Ch'eng T'ang are segments of major importance, there are many other trusts which have large holdings of land and which mark off wealthier segments from poorer. Exclusive of the Wan Shih T'ang, the average holding of land per ritual segment in 1906 was 3·02 acres. Forty-three trusts held more than this average acreage: six of the Senior Branch, six of the Third Branch and twenty-seven of the Second Branch (four of the trusts I lack evidence to identify with a Branch). The distribution of wealthy segments between Branches is thus far from equal, but within Branches there is also a marked tendency for the wealthy segments to belong to one line of descent only. Figure 7 demonstrates the bunched distribution of the majority, 31 of these 43 wealthy segments.[18]

Wealthy segments may be expected to create wealthy trusts, but there is a two-way process involved, so that wealthy trusts contribute back to the wealth of the segment. Thus some trusts make grants to the school-children of their segments in the same way that the Ming Te T'ang has been seen to do. Trusts created in the name of a long dead ancestor are intended primarily to cater for ritual; but trusts created by or in the name of a man alive or only recently deceased may be said to have the purpose uppermost of avoiding the dissipation of wealth. In this latter case the trusts become a source of income for the immediate descendants, who share the revenue of the trust, but it is only the small numbers of the beneficiaries which make the sharing of income a viable proposition. As generation succeeds generation so the number of trust beneficiaries increases and the amount of the benefit for each decreases,

---

[18] It is probable that some of the other wealthy segments also belong to these lines of descent, but the unfortunate failure to send genealogical information on to me prevents my being certain.

FIGURE 7
Wealthy segment distribution

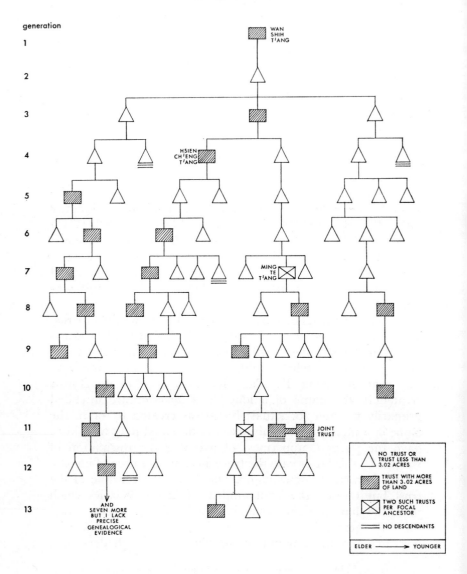

until a point is reached where the trust must either be liquidated and its property shared out between the descendants or pass into the ranks of the older established trusts which exist mainly for ritual reasons. I have suggested elsewhere,[19] that the boundary between individual grave worship and communal grave worship lies somewhere around three or four generations higher than the generation of those who are worshipping: probably the point of decision with regard to trusts is similarly placed (though one informant claimed it to be "too complicated" to divide an estate any older than that of a father or grandfather of the living adult descendants). Up until this point a trust must necessarily have a precarious life—insolvency of one of its members, disputes, or even perhaps the chance to sell land at a high price, all may bring about the dissolution of the T'ang or Tsu. The greatest holdings of land throughout the lineage in 1906 were in the name of the 16th generation I Mao T'ang of the Second Branch. It owned 51·83 acres of land, 4 houses, and shares in various other parcels of land; but at that time the great majority of this was already mortgaged, and a recent letter from an informant in the village translates: "in the last few years they have divided the land up, it has been sold and built on, and doubtless there is very much less now than there was in 1905". Even such a large holding may be divided. But once past the point of decision a trust becomes very much more stable. Personal greed or quarrelsomeness have less scope, for the income from the trust's land is less and less used for benefits to the individuals living, and the difficulty of dividing the trust between a multiplicity of individual claims makes dissolution more unthinkable than conciliation, even were the resultant shares likely to be valuable. The grave rites and feast afterwards may be made to consume the greater part of the trust income by allowing a greater or lesser number of segment members to take part or by decreasing or increasing the quantity and range of foods. Thus some segments permit only men over 61 *sui* to eat at the feast, some allow all men over 21 *sui*, and some provide food for all members of the segment, men, women and children: and while some segments eat only pork, vegetables and rice, others add squid, chicken, duck, salted fish, duck eggs, wine, beer, etc. to the feast. The further the living generations

[19] Above, p. 62.

I

recede from that of the focal ancestor the more living members there are likely to be, and the trust may have to tailor its benefits accordingly. In a sense, then, a trust which is stable in its ownership of land is steadily devalued by its own increasing membership; and in practice most old established trusts seem to be stable, the last sixty years having apparently made little difference in overall holdings to these trusts.

Kinship-ritual trusts are created in two ways: immediately, by setting aside land in the name of a long dead ancestor, and gradually, by evolving a ritual trust from a primarily secular one. The evolutionary process is probably not a straightforward one whereby all the property of a secular trust becomes the endowment of a ritual one: it is more likely that as the point of decision is reached, so the major portion of a secular trust is shared out, perhaps on a *per stirpes* basis among the segment, forming a new series of wealth-preserving trusts—and an endowment sufficient to meet expected ritual needs goes forward as the ritual trust. The I Mao T'ang, mentioned above, seems to be an example of this kind of evolution. It and the Kwang Te T'ang (also extremely wealthy) are formed around two brothers as focal ancestors, the wealth having presumably come down from the also wealthy Yün Sheng T'ang formed around their father. Certainly, where a trust is formed from the property of a recently deceased man, it does not follow that all his property will be put into trust. It is clear from the two sets of land records that the trusts formed during the last sixty years have not all used all the property which their focal ancestor owned when he was still alive in 1906. Once a ritual trust is well established it is extremely stable and it is normally only external events, such as Government resumption of its land for some purpose, or a radical change in land values, which can destroy it. Of course the trust may be augmented from time to time by donations or by accident of inheritance. In 1960 a dispute arose over the property of two Second Branch brothers of the 16th generation who had died without heirs. The various claimants to the property were genealogically linked so tenuously that the Village Council, which arbitrated the dispute, decided in the end to give only a portion of it to one group of claimants, the rest was to be added to the endowment of a 9th generation Tsu, which was the smallest segment to which the deceased men had belonged, and of which all claimants to the property were members.[20]

Ritual segments are defined by Tsu and T'ang, whose primary purpose is the provision of expenses necessary to segment worship. Without a trust there can be no ritual segment. Nor are the segments necessarily of importance outside the ritual sphere, being for the most part groups which have cohesion and identity only in the worship of their focal ancestors. Only where a trust is wealthy enough to have a large surplus of income over ritual expenditure is there much material advantage in the funnelling of inheritance into narrower channels by this segmentation, and it has been shown that such segmentation is mainly of necessity short-lived. Most long-established ritual trusts may be considered to be the skeletons of earlier living material trusts (though these too of course worship their focal ancestors), and it is to be expected that the paths of descent of many wealthy living segments will be littered with such skeletons. The amount of land tied up in trusts must increase year by year, since old-established trusts are from time to time augmented in number and in holdings, but the increase is not as great as would have been the case had not newer segments been unstable, so that land in these newer segments is constantly changing hands as they are dissolved.

VI

At the Branch level ritual segmentation is important, as we have seen; and at a much lower level ritual segmentation serves to hold accumulations of wealth together and thus to assist materially members of wealthy segments. There are segments, however, which are unimportant ritually and may not in fact have a ritual basis at all, but which have great importance politically in the village. To retain the dualistic terminology which we have been using, they may be called community segments as opposed to ritual segments.

The division of the lineage into three Branches stemming from the three grandsons of Chung-chieh is on the face of it a reasonable one, and certainly it is acceptable ritually, as

[20] This settlement was later again disputed, and the case had been re-opened when I left the village.

witness the emphasis on the leaders of the three Branches in lineage ceremonies. However, the Second Branch has expanded at a much faster rate than either the Senior or the Third Branch, and is now, as indeed it must have been for many generations, larger (and therefore not surprisingly wealthier) than the other two together. Ritually some attempt to redress the balance seems to have been made in the formation of the joint Kuei Pi Tsu, so that the Senior and Third Branches might hope jointly to compete on a par with the Second Branch in ritual observances—note the ostentatiously donated couplet-board in the Ming Te T'ang. But in community matters it is clear that the Second Branch, by its superiority of numbers and wealth, must be able to dominate the lineage and the village. Short of an artificial merging of the Senior and Third Branches by genealogical manipulation—a device not unknown to the Chinese lineage[21]—a method of neutralising the potentially overweening power of the Second Branch had to be found.

The problem of the Second Branch domination did not of course arise until the amalgamation of the lineage late in the Ming dynasty, for the descendants of Chung-chieh were living scattered throughout the Sheung Shui plain in several settlements, as we have seen. (I believe the account in the genealogy of this scattered settlement to be substantially correct, present-day land-holdings[22] and the two Branch temples lending credence to the tale.) The amalgamation was presumably the work of an astute brain, the geomancer Nan-sha being given the credit for the conception of a united lineage, but whether the solution to the problem of segmentary imbalance was his, or whether it was arrived at slightly later when the village was walled, it is not possible to say. The genealogy seems to suggest the latter: "It was decided to build a defensive wall. The work . . . was finished in 1647, whereupon the walled area was divided into four quadrants."[23] The four quadrants (tou) were

---

[21] See Freedman, *Lineage Organization*, pp. 70–1. Hu Hsien-chin, *The Common Descent Group in China and its Functions*, New York, 1948, p. 19, says: "To take the *tsu* of T'an as an example: The several lines of descent having become greatly differentiated not only in the number of members but also in wealth, their heads were unable to fulfill the functions of manager of the common property. So the *tsu* was reconstituted by common consent and the one *fang* which had developed far beyond all the others was subdivided into five *fen*, or 'parts', while the rest formed two 'parts'."

[22] See Chapter Seven.   [23] *LSTP*. Historical Movements.

known by the quadrants of the compass which they occupied, thus North Tou, East Tou, etc., as in Figure 8.[24]

FIGURE 8
Walled Hamlet Quadrants

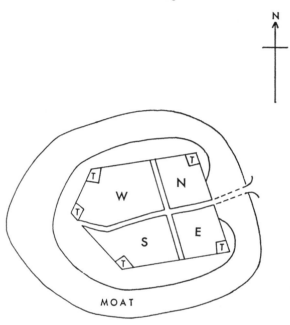

T = TOU

Each of these quadrants was occupied by the descendants of one man, and thus became a kinship-residential (kinship-community) unit. The division into four residential sections and the particular four kinship-defined groups chosen to fill them were no doubt conceived as deliberately and consciously as was the original uniting of the lineage. Figure 9 shows the genealogical basis of quadripartite residence.

[24] I was much puzzled at one stage by hearing the phrase "Four Tou, five Tou", and was uncertain whether it might not refer to a fifth segment not now in evidence. Under the lead of the village school headmaster, I have decided that "five Tou" is probably a reference to the five watch-towers which were placed one at each of the five corners of the hamlet wall. They do not stand now.

Of the 4th generation of the lineage, Ying-wu is said to have returned to Fukien with Chung-chieh, while Ying-chi apparently had neither offspring nor wife.[25] The occupants of the quadrants came to be known by the directional quadrant names, and became in fact well-recognised residential segments focused on the four 4th generation ancestors. The residential segments came also to be political segments, and their names have been perpetuated despite the later residence of the majority of the lineage outside the walled hamlet.

FIGURE 9
Quadrant residents

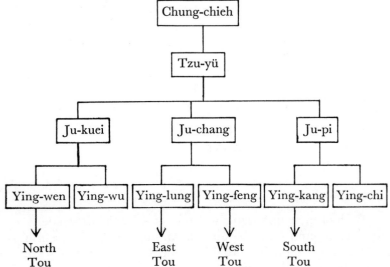

It is of course immediately apparent that the occurrence of four ancestors in this 4th generation conveniently divides the Second Branch, while leaving the Senior and Third Branches intact.

[25] There is one reference in the genealogy to "the descendants of Ying-chi", but there is every reason to believe that this is a mistake.

Reference to Figure 7 above will show how the division also splits the two wealthiest lines of the Second Branch.

I have called these 'community segments', but segmentation is very much unlike that of ritual segments. There is no organisation of the segment, no recognised leader, no worship of a focal ancestor (though the segments are obviously only defined by reference to a focal ancestor), and, above all, no property endowment. (It may be pointed out that there are trusts for two of the four segments—the East and the West Tou—but that these must be considered accidents of the ritual segmentation pattern which happen to coincide with the community segmentation, especially as the Ying-feng Tsu is so small as to be non-viable as an operational trust.) The four segments in fact exist only as names for the four kinship groups, but none the less they play a vital role in village affairs, colouring the outlook of villagers in such a way that the East and West Tou, which make up the Second Branch, are considered to be as much diametrically opposed as are, for example, the East and the North. The Second Branch has indeed been bifurcated in all but its ritual functions by the division of the lineage along these four lines. Yet, with the exception of some now disregarded tablets in the Wan Shih T'ang, the only physical expression the quadrants find is in patterns of residence.

The walled hamlet's division into four quadrants has persisted in general until the present. The picture has been blurred by the arrival of outsiders on the scene (though of course they do not own the houses in which they reside), and by a certain amount of infiltration of quadrants by men of other Tou buying into them, but by and large the Tou still occupy their respective quadrants. The two lineage-owned temples of the walled hamlet are both situated in the South Quadrant, and it may be that the small size of the south segment meant that more room was available here for this purpose than in the other quadrants. There is a third temple in the hamlet: it is a small building in the West Quadrant, dedicated to the Goddess of Mercy, Kuan Yin, and used apparently by all the hamlet residents, though owned by the West Tou. West Tou bridegrooms worship there jointly with their brides on the first day of marriage. The reading-room of the Ming Te T'ang is also, of course, situated in this quadrant.

VII

When expansion of the lineage outside the walled hamlet took place, the new pattern of settlement was strongly influenced by the Tou segmentation system, and the majority of hamlets are each owned and occupied by members of one Tou only. Table 11 gives the hamlet occupants, population 1961, and probable Liao population 1965 (based on the estimated growth rate of 13·4 per cent.,[26] and the percentage of Liaos of 67·5 per cent.).[27] From this we can extract rough figures for the sizes of the four Tou in 1965, as in Table 12.

TABLE 11
Hamlets and Tou

Hamlet	1961 Population	Estimated 1965 population	Tou	Estimated 1965 Liao population	
Wei Nei	564	591	N	30	
			S	77	
			E	125	
			W	167	399
Pu Shang	1453	1665	E		1124
Men K'ou	524	601	N	203	
			S	203	406
Chung Hsin	135	155	S		105
Shang Pei	241	276	N		186
Hsia Pei	396	454	N	153	
			S	153	306
Ta Yüan	826	947	W		639
Hsing Jen	271	311	N		210
Total	4410	5000	—		3375

These figures give some idea of the proportions of the segments, though the North Tou is probably exaggerated in size, especially as Shang Pei Ts'un is inhabited now by many out-

[26] See Introduction, p. 21.
[27] See Chapter Two, p. 47.

siders and very few Liaos. Neither the North nor the South
Tou is as large as either one of the other two, and collectively
the East and West Tou (i.e. the Second Branch) are more
than half as large again as the combined North and South Tou
(2,055 against 1,320).[28] Shared hamlets not surprisingly involve

TABLE 12
Tou population

	North	South	East	West	Lineage
Wei Nei	30	77	125	167	399
Pu Shang	—	—	1124	—	1124
Men K'ou	203	203	—	—	406
Chung Hsin	—	105	—	—	105
Shang Pei	186	—	—	—	186
Hsia Pei	153	153	—	—	306
Ta Yüan	—	—	—	639	639
Hsing Jen	210	—	—	—	210
Total	782	538	1249	806	3375

the North and South Tou, just as the Senior and Third
Branches (which have the same membership) have been seen
to co-operate in the Kuei Pi Tsu.

Each of the hamlets is defined ritually as well as geographically: the ritual involved is not ancestor worship but territorial
deity worship as might be expected since residence falls within
the community sphere. The ritual focus of each hamlet is an
Earth God, a shrine to whom is built on the outskirts of the
hamlet.[29] These Earth Gods are similar in construction and
function to and protect the fortunes of hamlet residents in much
the same way as the God of Earth and Grain, so that just as

[28] The reproductive and economic success of the Second Branch is said
to stem from Tzu-yü's grave, and a geomancer, in talking to me of it,
claimed that its site was particularly favourable to the numbers 2, 5 and 8.

[29] Exceptions to this rule are Hsing Jen Li, where the Earth God is
merely a paper tablet stuck into a niche in the wall of the ornamental
gateway of the hamlet, and Shang Pei Ts'un, where the Earth God of the
hamlet well does double duty as the hamlet Earth God.

there is a hierarchy of ritual segments under the Wan Shih T'ang so there is a hierarchy of residential segments under the God of Earth and Grain. Conceivably this god was the only community-defining god when there was only the walled hamlet in existence, and when he was given added importance by the expansion into other hamlets it became necessary to build a separate Earth God shrine for the walled hamlet. (The date, 1812, on this could hardly, however, be the date of its foundation, for we know that Pu Shang Ts'un was in existence as early as 1688.) The Earth Gods are regularly worshipped on the first and fifteenth days of the lunar month and on other ceremonial or especially auspicious occasions. The bridegroom always announces his marriage to the Earth God on the morning of his wedding day, for instance. The life of a hamlet is so closely identified with its Earth God that, as in the case of the village and the God of Earth and Grain, when the shrine of Chung Hsin Ts'un's Earth God was demolished by typhoon flood-waters, no time was lost in rebuilding and rededicating it.

The analogy of these residential sub-segments to ritual sub-segments is made closer by the fact that trusts were formed around the Earth Gods, the income from the trusts being used for the upkeep of the shrines (though not for their worship, since this was a matter left to individual households of the hamlet), and for the benefit of the hamlet inhabitants, particularly in regard to public works. The trusts were not formed in the same way as kinship-ritual trusts, for since hamlets were not based explicitly on kinship there could be no question of land being set aside in the name of a focal ancestor— some of the hamlets are inhabited by more than one Tou, as we have seen, and even where one Tou is the sole occupant of a hamlet there can still be no founding ancestor, for, to the best of my knowledge, movement out of the walled hamlet into other hamlets was initially haphazard by descent within the Tou segments. The trusts were in fact founded solidly in the community sphere, deriving their income initially from a monopoly of the collection of pig-droppings within the hamlet boundaries.[30] The droppings were highly valued as fertiliser, and by putting the pig-droppings concession out to tender the Earth God was

[30] Pigs foraged freely about the village—as many still do today.

assured of an income. In some cases this income enabled the trusts to invest in land or property, and so both to diversify and to make more permanent their income. Of recent years pig manure has lost its value owing to the introduction of artificial fertilisers and in some measure to decrescent Liao participation in agriculture. Those trusts which relied entirely on the concessions have become defunct, and no more than three landholding trusts, those of Pu Shang, Ta Yüan and Hsia Pei hamlets, survive. The last is of interest in that, since Hsia Pei Ts'un is a mixed Tou hamlet, it cuts across Tou boundaries. It owns one house with an income of $480 per annum, the money being spent on auspicious couplets to be pasted on every house at New Year, on maintenance of the hamlet Earth God, on annual *tso-fu* and *ch'ou-shen* ceremonies, and on well and path maintenance. Of the three, the Tung Ch'ing T'ang of Pu Shang Ts'un and the Chih Fu T'ang of Ta Yüan Ts'un are particularly active. It is to be expected that of all the hamlet trusts these two should be the richest and the longest lasting; for not only are the two hamlets far and away the largest of the eight but they are occupied and owned by the East and West Tou respectively. Thus not only owing to the large size of the hamlets must the number of pigs have been greater and income accordingly higher, but, since these two Tou were wealthy, the proportion of pigs to population was probably higher than in other hamlets.

The Tung Ch'ing T'ang was wealthy enough to donate $3,500 towards the building of the new school (though $500 of this was actually the donation of the Hsien Ch'eng T'ang, as we have seen). It paid out considerable sums in public works while I was in the village, contributing several hundreds of dollars towards the cost of two new wells sunk in the hamlet (the Wan Shih T'ang met the remainder), and several hundreds more towards the cost of the section of new road which gave access to the hamlet. It annually pays for the pumping out and cleaning of the hamlet wells, and paid for an additional cleaning in 1964 when flood-water contaminated all the wells. It pays one man to write out auspicious couplets for the doors of all houses in the hamlet at New Year. When I left the village, a site was being prepared for the building of a community hall for the hamlet, the Tung Ch'ing T'ang owning the land and paying for the building. The Chih Fu T'ang did not contribute to the school building, but is very active in public works in Ta Yüan Ts'un.

Ta Yüan Ts'un is the stronghold of the West Tou. The Ming Te T'ang, which represents all but a few families of the West Tou, is built in the hamlet, and the Chih Fu T'ang uses the hall for its managerial meetings, posting of accounts etc. In this way the Ming Te T'ang becomes drawn further into the community sphere than it might otherwise have been, but it must be remembered that ritually the hall serves a larger group than just Ta Yüan Ts'un. A similar position pertains with the Hsien Ch'eng T'ang, the hall of the trust whose membership is the entire East Tou. The hall is built in Pu Shang Ts'un, the stronghold of the Tou, and the Pu Shang Ts'un trust, the Tung Ch'ing T'ang, has traditionally used the hall as a community hall for the hamlet. However, the Kindergarten has tied up the hall so much that it is rarely available for other uses, and is indeed kept locked when the school is not in session in order to guard against loss of school property: hence the plans to build another hall, for community purposes only, in the hamlet.

Other less serious-minded groups, notably firecracker loan associations, tend to centre on the Earth Gods too, membership being confined to hamlet residents only.

Within the hamlet, residence also is affected by kinship. That is to say, it is likely that two families living side by side will be more closely related within the Tou than two families living separated by several rows of houses. Members of any one segment (actually so constituted, or merely the descendants of one ancestor) are more likely to live in one section of the hamlet than scattered in single households throughout it. Thus, many members of the wealthy Yün Sheng T'ang of the East Tou live in that part of Pu Shang Ts'un immediately adjacent to the T'ang hall itself. The row of six houses in one of which I lived was owned and occupied by the descendants of one man of the 16th generation, though no property-owning segment held the group together. Figure 10 illustrates the situation in simplified form.[31]

---

[31] Basically there was a simple *per stirpes* inheritance pattern following a division of the property in the 18th generation, but other factors had arisen to complicate the picture.

Figure 10
Residence and kinship

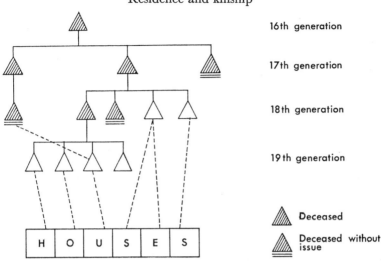

16th generation

17th generation

18th generation

19th generation

△ Deceased

△ Deceased without issue

| H | O | U | S | E | S |

Residence by kinship necessarily confines the sphere of normal contacts of lineage members within close limits. The result is an intense hamlet (and indeed sub-hamlet) parochialism, which is alleviated more or less for each individual according to the nature of his occupation and to his involvement in ritual (and to a certain extent politics) on a scale larger than the hamlet. In women, for most of whom business, ritual on an organised basis, and indeed most recreations are not a part of life, this parochialism reaches its greatest intensity. Normally confined to a narrow sphere of home, immediate neighbours, market, Earth God shrine and grass-cutting, a woman may get to know little of matters outside this sphere.[32] An old woman of Hsia Pei Ts'un was asked in my presence by an employer to go to the T'ien Hou Temple in the walled hamlet on a task for him. She had to enquire the way, though she had been married into the village for some thirty years and Hsia Pei Ts'un is not a quarter of a mile from Wei Nei. Yet even men of some standing in the village display similar ignorance of much that is outside their own immediate hamlet sphere. I found no one

[32] Older women cannot read or write either, which narrows their interests still further.

who was able or prepared to list the Tsu and T'ang even of his own Tou; very few knew more than the names of the trusts of which they themselves were members; a man of the East Tou who prides himself on his knowledge of lineage ritual was quite unable to tell me on what day of the year the Spring Rites are held in the West Tou Ming Te T'ang . . . the list could be extended, but it is sufficient here to say that where close kinship and residential proximity are coincident, spheres of contact are drastically limited, and that this in turn has a disruptive effect on lineage unity.

The Tou segmentary system has been seen to be the basis of the residential segmentary system, but it is more than that. A system of political control which has survived in direct and indirect ways to the present was developed from the residential pattern of the walled hamlet.[33]

It is hardly necessary to point out again the essential imbalance of the lineage at the Branch level—only at the Tou level are there roughly equal units poised against one another. The four Tou have become the essential ingredients of village politics in that four managers are required for the Wan Shih T'ang, one from each Tou.[34] Similarly, there seems to be a requirement (or at least an expectation?) that the Village Watch shall be drawn from all the Tou, and the notices posted on the village boards announcing the successful tenderers for the 1966–67 Watch placed each name clearly under the heading of a Tou—there were three from the North Tou, four from the South, three from the East and six from the West. Representation of each individual of the lineage is thus only made on a basis of near equality at the Tou level. Most important of all, the Village Council system which has emerged since the Japanese occupation has rooted itself in the hamlet system, and thus retained the Tou as four basic units of political balance. The way in which this has been managed will be described in the following chapter.

[33] Cf. Gamble, S. D., *Ting Hsien: a North China Rural Community*, New York, 1954, p. 146.

[34] Only one manager (from the East Tou) is regularly given in the 1906 Government records which I consulted, but it is possible that this was for brevity's sake.

VIII

There are, then, in the lineage two basically different kinds of segmentation, both founded in kinship but with differing functions. Kinship-ritual segments make up a pyramidal structure with the lineage, the Wan Shih T'ang, at the top and the most recently formed at the bottom. One man *may* in principle be a member of as many such segments as there are generations from Chung-chieh to his own father, though in practice no line is segmented to this extent. Segments exist with the primary object of worshipping the ancestor on whom the segment is focused, and cannot exist unless there is an endowment of land set aside providing an income sufficient to undertake this. In exceptional cases an 'indirect segment' is formed around a trust in the name of an 'ancestor' who in fact has no descendants: thus, in the name of a childless 12th generation man of the Second Branch there is a substantial trust in existence, the indirect segment being composed of the descendants of his younger brother, who worship his grave once a year: and the 'joint trust' marked in Figure 7 is in the name of two childless men who are worshipped by an indirect segment consisting of the descendants of their older brother. Such a situation is known as *fu-chi* ('next of kin worship') and is so indicated in the genealogy. A constant redefinition of and emphasis on kin relationships is brought about by these ritual segments, while from Branch (*fang*) level down to the newest segment the essential unity of the lineage is demonstrated, for, if focal ancestors may be seen as marking off segments from the rest of the lineage, they may also be seen as the points of junction which tie all segments into one united whole.

Community segments, on the other hand, though they too are based on kinship, draw their strength from undifferentiated kinship but differentiated residence below the level of the 4th generation. A man may only belong to one community segment, his hamlet of residence, defined by reference to the Earth God. Above that he belongs, as do all other members of the lineage, only to the village, defined by the God of Earth and Grain. Thus kinship-ritual segments may be said to be conducive to unity within the lineage by virtue of the pyramidal hierarchy of segments which step by step lead ties of kinship back through an ever-widening membership to the full unity of the lineage T'ang; but community segments are disruptive of unity within the lineage by virtue of their complete exclusiveness, the only point of junction between segments being their common membership of the village as a whole.

Examples have been given to demonstrate the important limitations on contact spheres brought about by the coincidence of close kinship and residential proximity. Other examples could be adduced to demonstrate that it is the factor of residential proximity which seems to carry the most weight in imposing these limitations. Where outsiders have infiltrated a residential area, they seem to become as close-knit with their neighbours as if they had been of the lineage. There are times when women from different households co-operate in certain tasks, notably in the making of New Year cakes. The co-operative groups are composed of close neighbours even where some of these neighbours are outsiders. Similarly, outsiders may worship the hamlet Earth Gods and the God of Earth and Grain (but in the kinship-ritual sphere it would be impossible for outsiders to worship Liao ancestors). The most striking example of the importance of close residence as a separational factor is, of course, the division of the walled hamlet into four. If residence did not create its own exclusive groups, then the division into four Tou would have been meaningless. That it was not meaningless but highly successful is proved by the later growth of hamlets formed separately by East and West Tou members. Paradoxically, we have the joint founding of other hamlets by the North and South Tou; but may not this be understood by reference to the joint Tsu of the Senior and Third Branches—which have of course precisely the same membership as the North and South Tou—and therefore demonstrate the unifying effect of kinship-ritual?

Of course kinship-ritual segmentation and community segmentation run along different lines, so that the effect of these two important types of segmentation, Fang and Tou, is to create a close-knit system of interlocking allegiances in the individual.

In Sheung Shui at least there is little doubt as to the essential unity of both the community segment system and the kinship-ritual segment system. Both find their apices in the Wan Shih

The entrance to the walled hamlet, with fresh 'lucky couplet' for New Year.

The old gates of the walled hamlet.

Autumn Rites at Chung-chieh's grave: clearing up the altar after the ceremony.

Cooking for the grave-side meal after the Autumn Rites for Chung-chieh.

T'ang, which sits supreme over all aspects of lineage life. The choice of tablets on the main altar of the Wan Shih T'ang may now be seen to have great symbolic significance for lineage unity. Figure 11 sets out in genealogical form the seventeen lineage tablets on that altar,[35] and comparison with Figure 9 above shows quite clearly that the tablets cover both Fang and Tou segmentation. In order to define Tou segmentation in this form it was necessary to include tablets of the 5th generation (eldest sons only), for there could be no other indication of how the six great-grandsons of Chung-chieh founded only four Tou.

FIGURE 11
Wan Shih T'ang tablets and segmentation

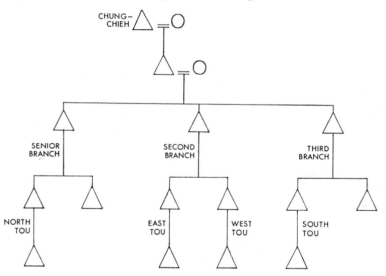

[35] Again, the one 15th generation tablet is excepted. See above, p. 57.

K

CHAPTER FIVE

Leadership

I

IN Chapter Two attention was drawn to differences in coming of elder-age between the Liao lineage and the lineages of Nanching described by C. K. Yang, and it was noted that, while certain privileges and ritual responsibilities were common to elders in both instances, political responsibilities devolved only on the elders of Nanching, where, it was suggested, the small size of the lineages meant less likelihood of there being a literati-pecuniosi group to manipulate political matters.

If a lineage is in most cases the long-term result of expansion from a single family—as it must be where all members trace their descent from one founding ancestor—then it follows that gerontocratic leadership will have been of importance in the early stages of lineage development at least, for the single family is of necessity so led. A lineage which over the generations fails to expand greatly in numbers and wealth is likely to remain under this kind of leadership, for there is probably no other form of social differentiation drastic enough to mark off a clear group capable of leadership. Yang's lineages seem to fall within this category, the most important of them having been founded as long ago as the 11th and 12th centuries.[1] In such a case the gerontocracy are leaders in both the ritual and the community spheres. But a lineage which does contrive to develop considerably in wealth and numbers is likely to throw up a community leadership based not on seniority of age or generation but on wealth, education, and perhaps on sheer ability independent of either of these. Ritual leadership remains in the hands of the aged. In Sheung Shui this division of leadership between elders and literati-pecuniosi reflected in general the

[1] Yang, *op. cit.*, p. 12.

kinship-ritual/kinship-community duality with which we have been dealing.

II

Community leadership before 1899 was largely the prerogative of the educated men of the lineage. It may be called an informal leadership in that it was not formally constituted and that no elections or selection procedures were resorted to. A lineage member who had passed one of the Imperial examinations was certain to be accepted as a political leader, I was told. Such men were doubtless best qualified to represent the lineage in the outside world, where the possession of a degree or official title was a passport giving ready access to similarly qualified men in other communities[2] and in local government.[3] Indeed, several informants stated categorically that it was quite impossible for non-*kung-ming* to achieve entry into the Hsin-an Hsien Yamen. The passing of examinations was not the only way to obtain a degree, of course, and holders of degrees by purchase were also candidates for political power. Similarly influential were men of wealth, many of whom would tend in any case to purchase their way into the degree-holding group.

Amongst the composite group of these influential men certain individuals would stand out as of particularly high calibre on grounds of seniority, or of higher degree passes, or of greater wealth, or perhaps of more forceful personality. Of these, the one man of greatest influence would become recognised as leader of the lineage community *primus inter pares*.[4] He is said to have been referred to by the title *Hsiang-chin*, but the second character of this term seems to be of very doubtful authenticity. Although no formal procedures decided the identity of the prime leader of this lineage community, it may be pointed out that the existence of a title for such a leader served to confirm the position on a man when once he had attained it. Furthermore, there seems to have been a strong correlation between prime leadership and managership of the Wan Shih T'ang, so

[2] Ch'u T'ung-tsu, *Local Government in China under the Ch'ing*, Harvard, 1962, p. 173.

[3] *Ibid.*, p. 181.

[4] Informants said: "There was no way of choosing the leader, but everyone knew who he was."

that of the four managers the *Hsiang-chin* was one, and other leaders of particularly great influence from other Tou filled the remaining three places. In the 1906 land records only one manager is regularly mentioned, and I suspect that he is perhaps the same community leader who earlier had been the instigator of lineage resistance to British rule.[5] A second manager occasionally mentioned in the same records certainly became *Hsiang-chin* in the later stages of his life. Both these men were holders of degrees, the latter by examination, the former by purchase. Thus the positions of the more important community leaders were bolstered by their managership of the Wan Shih T'ang.

The power of these leaders seems to have been strong, and their use of it somewhat arbitrary and largely unquestioned. The lineage possessed only the most sketchy of written rules, and the interpretation of the one rule which dealt with discipline —"If any male becomes an entertainer, or a lictor, or is adopted into another surname group, or becomes a priest, or commits a serious offence against lineage rules, his name should be expunged from the genealogy"[6]—must have varied widely from one leader to another. Community leaders could apparently sit in judgement either singly or as a group when concerned with disciplinary matters. Internal village discipline was not their only concern, however, for as members of a wider society the most important of the leaders were involved in inter-village matters too, no doubt sitting with other *kung-ming* on the council which represented the immediate neighbourhood, the *tung*, and probably on the wider area council, the Tung P'ing Kuk, as well.[7] As managers of the Wan Shih T'ang leaders were able to print their own personalities upon lineage affairs, encouraging projects which appealed to them and refusing money to those which did not. If lineage accounts were not published, as they are not at present, then the opportunities for personal gain must have been many, though no mention of such gain was made to me by informants. In 1724 an 11th generation man, Chiu-wo, donated a large area of 'ancestral trust land' (*chia-ch'ang-t'ien*) to the newly founded Hsien school, the Wen Kang

[5] See Chapter Seven, p. 196.
[6] *LSTP*, Rules for revising the genealogy, Rule 6.
[7] See Introduction, and *Lockhart Report 1898*, p. 45.

Shu-yüan at Nam Tau, the Hsien capital.[8] Chiu-wo was a Salaried Licentiate and certainly of much influence as a leader in the village, where, having been born in 1666, he must have been one of the most senior leaders. It is open to doubt whether anyone other than a powerful community leader could have successfully alienated trust land in this way. (And of course only a literatus would have been interested in or known anything of an institution as remote from the village as the school at the Hsien capital.) The land involved was situated not far from the village, but I could find no trace of it in the 1906 records.

In the Introduction the relatively unchanged composition of unofficial government after 1899 was pointed out: there was little difference, either, in leadership patterns. The number of Imperial examination graduates diminished rapidly of course, but, since the examination system was abolished in 1905,[9] it must of necessity have done so in any case.[10] The old standard which measured the capabilities of leaders may have been abolished, but the same kind of man—that is, a man of outstanding experience, wealth or education—rose to the leadership. The education received by these men came more and more to be of the Western type, some leaders in the early years of the 20th century already having Western training, as we have seen; and the founding of Fung Kai School in the Wan Shih T'ang in 1932, itself the work of these men, accelerated the process of Western educational invasion. The prime leader of the village was known by the term *Hsiang-shen*: it is possible that the old title *Hsiang-chin*, which was told to me by a group of old men, is a confusion of this more logical term. Whereas before 1899 leaders achieved power mostly by their qualifications to have influence and move freely in the outside world of literati contacts, after the British administration commenced a new outlook was called for, leaders requiring the ability to mix with and understand the new Western government more and more as the unofficial government system became weaker. Hence the importance of a Western type of education. If any-

[8] *HAHC 1819*, chüan 23, 'Chi-hsü'.
[9] Chang Chung-li, *op. cit.*, p. 208.
[10] Inexplicably there is an honours board in the Wan Shih T'ang dedicated to a man who became an *en-kung-sheng* in 1909 (Hsüan T'ung 1st year)!

thing, the period between 1899 and the Japanese occupation was one of gradual adjustment to new patterns as the lineage swung southwards to face the Westernising influence of Hong Kong. Innovation in leadership came in only with the Second World War.

The Japanese created the post of *Ts'un-chang* (Village Headman) and required the incumbent, who was 'selected' for the position according to village custom, to act as contact between the government and the villagers. Not surprisingly, the *Hsiang-shen* of the immediate pre-war period continued his leading role in the official position of *Ts'un-chang*, and after the occupation, when the British administration retained the *Ts'un-chang* post, the same man remained in office until his death in 1953. This last period of his life was a fruitful and important one. He it was who began the annual public meetings in the Wan Shih T'ang on the day of the Winter Solstice (*tung-chih*), thus creating for the first time in lineage history a vehicle for the direct and open confrontation of the villagers and their leaders: and it was under his leadership that the community was guided within the new framework of local government in 1949. The policy of the administration was rigid only in that it required villages to appoint representatives to serve on Rural Committees and to act as contacts with the District Offices.[11] The method of appointment was a matter left to the villages to work out, and as a consequence there is a wide variation in practice between different villages. The method promulgated by this leader, and later elaborated upon by others, was one of the most democratic and advanced of any village in the New Territories.

The quota of representatives (*Ts'un-tai-piao*) for Sheung Shui was fixed by Government at three, of whom two are considered to be Assistant Representatives (*Fu-tai-piao*). They are always referred to and addressed by the villagers as *Ts'un-chang*, a term which in many villages is certainly a much closer reflection of the function which they perform—that is to say, they lead rather than represent their villages—but which in Sheung Shui is only partly applicable. It was decided that not only these three positions should be filled, but that the three men should be drawn from a Village Council (*Ts'un-wu wei-yüan-hui*) of twenty-one members, of which they would compose the Execu-

11 See Introduction.

tive Committee. All positions were to be filled by secret ballot elections. The electorate consisted of all lineage males of 21 years old (according to Western reckoning) and over, any one of the electorate being eligible for election. The twenty-one Council members were not to be elected at random from the village as a whole, but each hamlet was given a quota of representatives roughly proportional to its lineage population, as in Table 13.

TABLE 13
Village Council Representation

Hamlet	1961 population	Tou	Quota
Wei Nei	564	N.S.E.W.	5
Pu Shang	1453	E.	7
Men K'ou	524	N.S.	2
Chung Hsin	135	S.	1
Shang Pei and ⎱ Hsia Pei ⎰	241 ⎱ 396 ⎰	N.S.	1
Ta Yüan	826	W.	4
Hsing Jen	271	N.	1
Total	4410	—	21

As a result of the Liao depopulation of Shang Pei Ts'un, this hamlet was combined for election and representation purposes with Hsia Pei Ts'un. It will be seen that this system of hamlet representation results in representation on the Council of the four Tou roughly in proportion to their size, but that the representatives per hamlet are not in proportion to the size of the hamlet populations. Thus, if the fifth seat of Wei Nei is taken by the West Tou (as in fact it mainly seems to be) and other shared hamlets divide their representatives among their Tou, then if the percentages of seats per Tou on the Council are applied to the assumed lineage population of 3,375 the resultant figures correspond quite closely with those already worked out in Table 12. Table 14 demonstrates this. It is clear that the system was devised with Tou groupings in mind, for there could otherwise be no reason for the disproportionately high number of representatives allotted to Wei Nei.

TABLE 14

Tou quotas and populations

Tou	Council quota	% of quota	Quota % applied to lineage popn.	Tou popn. figs. in Table 12
N	3·5	16·7	563	782
S	3·5	16·7	563	538
E	8	38·1	1287	1249
W	6	28·5	962	806
Lineage	21	100·00	3375	3375

Lists of the electorate in each hamlet were compiled, each hamlet list was distributed to all electors in that hamlet, and they were required to tick off as many names as the hamlet quota allowed. The quota number of most ticked names were considered elected to the Village Council. A second ballot was then held, the whole electorate being asked to tick three names from the twenty-one already elected, the man with the most ticks becoming Village Headman (or Village Representative in Government's terminology) and the two runners-up Assistant Village Headmen.

The Council and Headmen were elected for a term of two years. The Fourth Council, however, which should have been in office from 1955 to 1957, remained in office an extra year so that the terms of office were brought into line with the Sheung Shui Rural Committee and the Heung Yee Kuk, and the possibility was averted of discontinuity of representation on these bodies through a change of village election fortunes.

The Fourth Council was remarkable also in that it inaugurated a change in the original pattern of council elections, the first change since 1949. During the term of office of the Third Council it was mooted that the hamlet quota system of representation was working to exclude able men from the village government merely because the quotas for their hamlets were inadequate. The matter is said to have been raised as a direct result of the imminent retirement from Government service of one of the richest and most influential men of the lineage. His hamlet, Hsing Jen Li, had a quota of one Councillor only, and the incumbent, his own younger brother, was able enough and popular enough to be well entrenched in the position. Increase in the quotas of the smaller hamlets would have affected the proportional representation system, and would not necessarily have solved the problem. It was decided that there should be an additional ten Council seats created, the ten to be elected by the whole electorate from all the lineage after the twenty-one original seats had been filled. This meant that a small hamlet with a large number of able men could supply a high number of representatives to the Council, but, in practice, the strength of ties of residential proximity works against the underlying purpose of this additional quota, so that the larger hamlets may be expected to benefit more from it than the smaller. Thus, in 1958, and again in 1960, five of the ten seats went to Pu Shang Ts'un. In 1964–66 of the total thirty-one seats the East Tou had fourteen, the West nine, and the North and South Tou four each. It is true, however, that probably no man of outstanding ability who desires to be on the Council is denied a place under this system.[12] The man whose exclusion was the original cause of the change has been elected to the Council under the supplementary quota continually from 1955 to the present. The change meant, however, that it became necessary to run the elections in three stages, one to elect the twenty-one Councillors, the second for the ten, and the third for the election of the three Headmen. The three elections were held at short intervals— 11th December, 15th December and 22nd December in 1955,[13] and at similar intervals in after years. This tripartite system still obtains, creating a large amount of work for the sub-

[12] Of course, under this non-nominational system men who do not wish to serve may be elected. Such a case occurred in 1958, one man resigning his seat as soon as elected (Shang Shui Ts'un-kung-so, *1958 ti-wu-chieh hsüan-chü wei-yüan-hui chi-lu*, MS, 1958), his place being taken by the man with the next greatest number of votes. In general, however, the close knowledge which the electors have of their fellow hamlet dwellers obviates such occurrences.

[13] Shang Shui Ts'un-kung-so, *1955 Hsüan-chü wei-yüan-hui chi-lu*, MS, 1955.

committee of the Council which runs the elections—the ballot papers alone require a considerable expenditure of time, for at the first stage each elector must be provided with a list of all electors in his hamlet, and at the second stage a list must be prepared of all electors in the village minus the twenty-one already elected. It has already been noted that the large hamlets, and in particular the largest of all, Pu Shang Ts'un, stand to benefit by the extra quota of ten seats on the Council. It should be remarked that the free vote for the Village Head-men also gives advantages to the larger Tou. Thus, since 1949 the Chief Headman has been either of the East or the West Tou, and since 1955 the Headman and first Assistant Headman have been of the West and East Tou respectively, the third position changing hands between the North, South and East Tou. But the traditional leadership system gave much the same advantages to the bigger Tou, and, as far as I can ascertain, the prime leadership of the village has not passed out of the hands of the East or West Tou during the whole course of this century.

Only lineage males are eligible to become Councillors and only lineage males have the vote. (In practice, this means only lineage males at the time resident in or constantly present in the village.) The political leadership system in fact takes no account of the large non-lineage minority which now lives in the village. The implications of this will be further explored in a later chapter, but it must be pointed out here that the situation is fast growing ludicrous, for not only are the numbers of out-siders mounting rapidly, but the numbers of lineage males actually present in the village have been diminishing at a very fast rate owing to the attraction of work overseas and in the cities—the electorate shrinks while the village expands. In 1955 there were 643 men on the electoral roll,[14] in 1958[15] the number had fallen to 507,[16] and by 1960 the roll could boast only 484.[17] I was unable to obtain figures for later years, but was told on good authority that by the 1966 elections there were likely to be less than 400 men voting. The progressive and democratic

---

[14] *Ibid.*
[15] The 1955 Council held office for 3 years, of course.
[16] Shang Shui Ts'un-kung-so, *1958 ti-wu-chieh, etc.*
[17] Shang Shui Ts'un-kung-so, *1960 ti-liu-chieh hsüan-wei-hui*, MS, 1960.

system of 1949 threatens to become an inequitable parachronism by the 1970s.

The kind of man who becomes a Councillor has changed somewhat from the pre-war and pre-British political leader. Education has ceased to be the most important factor in selecting leaders, partly owing to its less prestigeful nature, which, no doubt, is in turn due to the raised level of education in the lineage (and society) as a whole. Instead, wealth has become the dominant factor, its possession at once enabling a man to make his way in a highly materialistic society and proving to others his ability to do so. Businessmen of one kind and another make up the majority of the Council, and it is reasonable that they should do so, for almost invariably their commercial interests lie outside the village in Shek Wu Hui, in other market towns of the New Territories, or in the cities; and compared with the village-oriented man, they have consequently more practice at dealing with outsiders and Government, not to mention a greater sophistication and worldly wisdom. The Eighth Council (1964–66) included twenty-one practising businessmen, two retired businessmen, and two retired Government employees, all of whom had the requisite kind of contact outside the village. Of the remaining six Councillors, one was a headmaster and one a school-teacher (both working in schools outside the village), one was a very old retired man (a farmer?), one was a landlord and paid official of the Council, and two were clerks in businesses in Shek Wu Hui. Some of these Councillors were very wealthy men indeed—one was away on a world tour for most of my stay in the village, and another is to do likewise in 1967. Twenty-one of them had donated a total of $11,130 as individuals to the school building. Almost all the thirty-one had incomes considerably above average for the village (eleven of them managed to maintain a concubine in addition to a wife, and a twelfth had three concubines and a wife), but educational attainments varied considerably, the average length of study of 6·6 years disguising extremes of 2 years and 10 years. The average age of the Council was 52 in 1965.

Freedman has quite rightly pointed out the shift in qualifications for community leadership: "the old scholar-gentry has no cultural successors. Leadership and learning have been divorced, for, although there are some schoolmasters among the New Territories élite, the predominating element is commercial."[18] But he does not draw attention to the fact that basically the same kind of leadership has emerged from these new qualifications as was in power before. The essential unity of leadership type lies in its ability on behalf of the lineage to face and extract advantage from the outside world. In Imperial China this meant that the leadership must if possible largely belong to the literati class, which had the greatest and most prestigeful spread of contacts. Under British rule a period of re-orientation, in which the literati tradition faded from importance and the new influences from Hong Kong and the West were savoured, was succeeded by the emergence after the war of a leadership which again had maximum contact with and influence in the outside world.

To the villager it is apparently important that the lineage should be represented in the outside world to the maximum advantage; that is to say, that the lineage must be represented wherever possible by someone of high prestige attainments who will both cast maximum reflected glory on to the lineage and be in a position to obtain maximum advantages for it. To this end it may even happen that a leader will continually be re-elected despite his lack of interest in and lack of attention to the internal affairs of the lineage. There are probably few such men in Sheung Shui, but some do exist. In a similar situation in another village, one of the most universally disliked of men has been chosen year after year to represent his village, although it is well known that he will not lift a finger to run it—but he is the richest man of that village and has a commercial life based on a market town. In these circumstances it is necessary to ask why a man should seek to be, or consent to be, on the Council.

We may assume that all those on the Council are there because they want to be there, for all have the opportunity to resign. There are disadvantages to being a Councillor in that a certain amount of time has to be given over to meetings and that it is necessary from time to time to do work on behalf of one's hamlet 'constituents' and perhaps for the village itself.

---

[18] Freedman, Maurice, 'Shifts of Power in the Hong Kong New Territories', *Journal of Asian and African Studies*, Leiden, Vol. I, No. 1, January 1966, p. 10.

Advantages are the prestige of being a recognised leader of the community, the fairly frequent social events, mainly banquets, to which one is invited as a Councillor, and the opportunity to mix with a wider and wealthier circle of contacts, which must be attractive to the businessman at least. In practice these advantages attract a number of 'passengers' who are quite content to bask in the glory of deeds done in the name of the Council by a few of its members only. At the same time the disadvantages are sufficient to discourage some able men from participating in the leadership. It is safe to say that as the number of available lineage males decreases so it becomes easier to gain admission to the Council, and that at present there are probably few men with an unrequited desire to serve on it. It is likely that it will become increasingly more difficult to find men of high calibre who are willing to work on the Council and whose living is earned in a manner which allows them to spare time for Council work. At the present time the sparsity of able men has already resulted in a tendency to stagnation in Council membership. Thus, in 1964–66 the average Councillor was serving on his fourth or fifth Council. The average age of the Council is also likely to rise as the years go by.

The advantages and disadvantages are magnified for the three Village Headmen, and in particular for the Chief Headman. It is for these positions that there could be something in the nature of a struggle, for the rewards in terms of prestige at least are high. But the Headmen must be free to devote much time to their task and must at the same time be wealthy enough to keep up a front of respectability and display commensurate with their standing as chief representatives of the lineage outside the village. The Chief Headman, who has held the office since 1955, runs a smart saloon car and a well-kept concubine in Shek Wu Hui. His solid income is derived from some company board positions and a photographic studio which is run for him by trusted relations. His business interests give him contacts with the market towns of the New Territories and with the cities. His photographic exhibits carry him into the international field. His concubine, a Teo Chiu, links him with the crescent fortunes and powers of the very wealthy Teo Chiu community in Shek Wu Hui and elsewhere. His wife enables him to keep one foot firmly anchored in the Walled Hamlet. His position as

Chief Headman is apparently unassailable, especially as he combines these qualifications with a personality, knowledge, diligence, experience, skill in compromise and mediation, and success in office which make him the obvious leader of the village from any point of view. A comparatively young man (he was 48 in 1965) there is no reason to suppose that he will not retain his position for many more years. His invariable runner-up at the Headman elections is not particularly wealthy. A school-master, who perforce is out of the village a great deal at his work, he seems to be elected primarily owing to the massive vote of the East Tou, and in particular to that of his own hamlet of Pu Shang Ts'un, where he is popular for his assistance in clerical matters. The third position was held in 1964–66 by a recently retired Government hospital administrator, who brought much energy, wealth and a knowledge of English to the post.

If the traditional leadership of the village was largely in the hands of one recognised leader, there is little doubt that the present-day leadership rests heavily on the one recognised leader too. The old *Hsiang-chin* may by right have had virtual say in all that happened in village politics—the present *Ts'un-chang* has a similar amount of control by virtue of his position and his own personal powers of leadership.

The community leaders, working through the offices of Village Councillor and Village Headman, control all aspects of community life in the village.[19] In the Village Council Hall is a framed diagram of the organisational structure of the village government. I reproduce it in translated form in Figure 12.

[19] In addition to those aspects already mentioned in Chapter Three, attention must be drawn to the role of the leaders as mediators in disputes. In 1965 a case was brought before the Council (or, rather, before one well-respected member of it) in which a non-Liao tenant wished to make repairs to the house which she rented from a lineage member. She feared, not without good cause if reports of similar situations are to be believed, that having undertaken the repairs she might not have her tenancy continued; and the landlord refused to grant her a long-term lease on the grounds that he did not know when he might require the use of the house for his own family again. The mediator heard both sides with patience, then suggested that the disputants come back in 24 hours having worked out a compensation agreement to cover the eventuality of the landlord's not renewing the lease within a fixed number of years from the repairs. He, the Council member, would then draw up a written agreement and have it witnessed by Council members. See also above, p. 116.

FIGURE 12
Village Chain of Authority

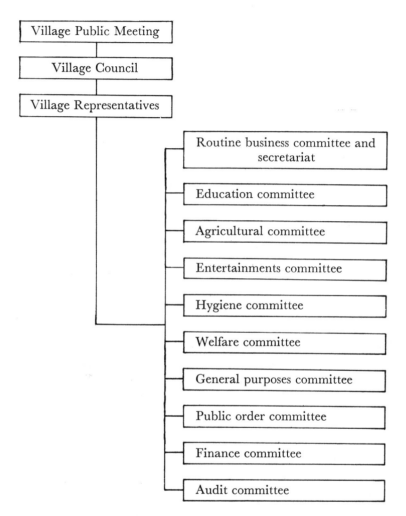

Its order of precedence is correct, though the Village Public Meeting on the Winter Solstice is perhaps not really taken seriously enough by the bulk of the electorate to fulfil its important role in the system, so that a clearer order would have been headed by the 'People of the Village', who take precedence through the election system. The impressive array of sub-committees of the Village Council is a sign of good intention rather than good practice, for the majority of the sub-committees existed only in name while I was in the village. As an informant, himself a Council member, said: "Just look at the Hygiene Committee. Who's done anything about hygiene in this place?"

In general the Council discusses village affairs and takes decisions without reference to the public. Its meetings are held once a month in the Village Council Hall, and presided over by the Village Headman, of course. Since it is responsible for the administration of all lineage funds, the accounts of the Wan Shih T'ang are presumably made available to the Council, but they are not published outside the meetings. The three Head-men hold Executive Committee meetings more frequently than once a month, usually in response to the arising of a matter of some urgency. They have fairly wide powers of decision and are authorised to spend sums up to $50 without prior reference to the full Council. Most of the schemes which are approved by the Council seem to originate with the Executive. Decisions are transmitted to the public via the notice boards which are placed at central points in the village.

Members of the Council form the majority of really able men of the lineage who remain village based and relatively leisured. Not surprisingly their names recur in other community projects. The School Board of Directors, for instance, is entirely made up of Council members, including all three Headmen. The final section of this chapter will show the way in which they also dominate the ritual sphere.

III

Community leaders owe their positions to the undifferentiated kinship system in the sense that only lineage members may become leaders. Ritual leaders, on the other hand, come to the fore not through personal qualities or attainments but through accident of birth in the generation-age hierarchy of the kinship system. One rule holds good for the leadership of any ritual unit below the full lineage: the leader is the oldest man of the senior surviving generation of that unit. Thus, all kinship-

Worship at the rebuilt shrine to the God of Earth and Grain.

Inscribed granite slabs, the base supports of flagpoles which bore the honours of the *chü-jen* Yu-chih. A duplicate set nearby has all four slabs complete.

Music for a segment's grave rites.

Autumn Rites at Chung-chieh's grave in 1965: the important occasion of the first Rites after restoration of the grave.

ritual segments, from the smallest and newest up to the level of the Branches, have recognised ritual leaders.

The chief ritual leader of the lineage as a whole is the Lineage Headman (*Tsu-chang*). Like the segment heads he comes to his position by virtue of being the oldest man of the senior surviving generation of the lineage. The present incumbent was 82 years old in 1965, a West Tou man of the 17th generation. He leads the lineage worship at the Spring and Autumn Rites and on the birthday of the founding ancestor. At New Year he leads the *Tso-fu* worship, and is chief supplicant on other special occasions, such as the rededication of the God of Earth and Grain. His qualifications for lineage headship must also qualify him for leadership of all other segments of which he is a member, multiplying the number of occasions on which he is required to lead in ancestral worship, but, as has been pointed out in a previous chapter, he is of an impecunious descent line and belongs to no segment below one of the 9th generation. His ritual duties are already heavy enough, particularly at the Autumn grave-worshipping period, when long hill walks in order to reach the graves are added to his tasks.

The Lineage Headman is the chief ritual leader, but not the only one. The man next in the generation-age order is considered his deputy (or perhaps his 'trainee successor' is a more fitting description), and as such is given the title Second-in-the-Lineage (*Erh-tsu*). Furthermore, the Branch Headmen are also an integral part of the lineage ritual leadership, so that at all major lineage ceremonies there is a nucleus of four ritual leaders present—the Lineage Headman, the deputy headman of his Branch, and the two other Branch Headmen. One of the latter three must by definition be the *Erh-tsu*. (While I was in the village the *Erh-tsu* came from the East Tou, so that by a happy accident each of the Tou was represented among the four ritual leaders, but of course this is not necessarily always the case—the Tou are not ritual units.) This quadripartite leadership is the only exception to the general rule of ritual leadership, for these four are by no means certain to be the four oldest men of the most senior surviving generation of the lineage. The Lineage Headman and the *Erh-tsu* of course do fulfil the conditions of usual leadership, but the Branch or Branches which

L

do not contain either of these two men may well be headed by a much younger man of the senior generation or even by a man of quite another generation. The ritual leadership of the lineage is thus shaped to lay emphasis on the Branch segmentary system.

As minor ritual leaders all elders are entitled to worship the lineage ancestors and the ancestors of their own segments, but they do so only after the lineage or segment headmen have worshipped, and they do so without regard to precedence of age or generation amongst themselves. As ritual leaders they are almost disregarded, and many do not now trouble to attend lineage or segment ceremonies.

There is another kind of ritual leadership working alongside the ritual headmen, but not composed of elders and not owing its place to either the generation-age hierarchy or material success. These leaders are perhaps best described as 'ritual officiants'. They are the repositories and interpreters of ritual knowledge, men who, by virtue of an idiosyncratic interest in ritual, devote themselves whenever necessary to the task of organising ceremonies, and make themselves familiar with the forms of service, learning the complicated patterns by heart. Such men are neither elected nor chosen nor given official position, but, having the spare time, do the work for its own sake. Their numbers are unfixed, and more are required for some ceremonies than for others. A notice on the public boards in 1965 gave the names of fourteen men who would officiate at the lineage Spring Rites in capacities as Altar-server, Wine-bearer, Master of Ceremonies, Address-deliverer, Drum-beater, etc. A similar notice for the Ming Te T'ang listed eleven names. Many of these men, but not all, are Village Councillors, as might be expected since the Council mostly consists of public-spirited men of some leisure. The Village Headmen are not amongst the officiants, but it is said that the *Ts'un-chang* who devised the election system regularly acted as Master of Ceremonies until his death in 1953. An officiant reaps little reward other than the satisfaction of his own interests and perhaps a certain amount of prestige from being in the public eye in the execution of the job. Probably because of the scant rewards it is becoming increasingly more difficult to find the necessary volunteers. Only two men officiated at the Spring Rites in the Hsien Ch'eng T'ang in 1965, and only ten people (including the Segment Head and the anthropologist) were present altogether.

IV

The two major kinds of leadership in the village—the community type and the ritual type (discounting the officiant ritual leaders, who have authority only in a minor sphere of ceremony)—have so far been depicted as quite discrete in nature and in function. In nature it is unlikely that the two types could become confused, for ritual leaders come in general from poor sections of the lineage, while community leaders tend to come from wealthy (as they almost certainly did also in pre-British times, when educational prowess, itself dependent largely on wealth, was the determinant). Furthermore, there is a marked tendency for both kinds of leadership to adhere to certain lines of descent.

A man whose father was Lineage Headman is himself likely to succeed to the headmanship several incumbents later, because he will have been born correspondingly later than others of his generation number. The son of the present Headman told me that he fully expects to come into the position in due course. The Headmanship, then, is likely to pass down the generations through a limited number of descent lines only.

The community leadership also tends to be vested in a limited number of wealthy families. This must especially have been the case in the days when an agricultural economy and the system of trust endowment kept opportunity for betterment of economic circumstances to a minimum, so that wealth was confined to the few (as Figure 7 has shown). Even today a leadership position can materially assist a man by broadening his business contacts, giving him better market information, etc., so that he will have more wealth to hand on to his sons as their qualifications for leadership. The present Village Headman has held the office since 1955. The man who was Headman before, throughout, and after the Japanese occupation up until 1953, when he died, was his first cousin, the son of his father's elder brother, and this last man, his uncle, was Headman for many years in the 1920s and 1930s. From his uncle on, then, three of the five men who have held office as Village Headman have come from one restricted descent line.

In function the same discreteness of leadership is not apparent. It was earlier suggested that gerontocratic leadership based on the generation-age hierarchy must be the dominant one in an embryo or poorly developed lineage. The survival of this leadership in the kinship-ritual sphere has been noted, but it must be added that some vestiges of community power remain to it. Most important of these is the idea of the Lineage Headman as head of the lineage in all its aspects. Until the Japanese occupation the Lineage Headman and the elders composed the only formally constituted leadership group in the lineage, and as such probably did wield some authority, if only enough to preserve the illusion of their power. Certainly older informants frequently remarked that when they were young the elders were not only listened to with respect by all but also had a say in village government. Now, of course, the community leadership is on an official footing and all other illusion is shattered; but the Lineage Headman has retained some semblance of authority. Like the Wan Shih T'ang he symbolises the essential unity of the Liaos by heading both the ritual and the community spheres—he is at once Archbishop of the lineage church, worshipping on behalf of the whole, and Constitutional Monarch of the lineage state, signing the minutes of the Public and Council Meetings. In both capacities he signs the certificates of lineage membership at the New Year *K'ai-teng* ceremony,[20] the only occasion when the rest of the elders clutch the sad shreds of their authority to them.

If the ritual leaders still have one toe in the door of community power, it is certain that the door of ritual authority is firmly jammed open by the community leaders. The ritual leadership in fact only has authority in the narrow sphere of actual worship, and even here there is intrusion by the community leaders, who worship the ancestors in the same way as (and usually in greater numbers than) the elders at major ceremonies. The community leaders control the income, expenditure and very existence of the ritual segments through their management of the trusts round which the segments are formed. All long-established trusts have as managers men of the same type who make up the community leadership: indeed, many of the community leaders themselves are to be found as

[20] See above, p. 48.

managers. In 1906 the 158 kinship-ritual segment trusts were managed by 111 men. Some of these 111 men managed only one trust, and some had only a part share in the management of one trust: but the community leaders of the day stand out by their control of numerous and important trusts. The prime leader who was leading manager of the Wan Shih T'ang[21] also managed either wholly or jointly thirteen other kinship-ritual trusts, as well as three community trusts and an inter-lineage trust (which will be discussed in a later chapter). The second manager of the T'ang,[22] who later became Village Headman in the 1920s and 1930s, managed wholly or jointly ten other kinship-ritual trusts and another inter-lineage trust. Thirty-three men were managers or part managers of more than one trust each, and between them they had control of 104 of the 158 ritual trusts, including almost every one of the wealthiest trusts. Doubtless a similarly stark pattern of concentrated managership could be found in the present-day land records. Controlling the finances of the trusts the managers control the ritual aspect too.

The Wan Shih T'ang has a pattern of management which differs from other trusts only in being more complex. It has four managers, one from each of the Tou. Three of these men are the Village Headmen, the fourth is not on the Village Council, but is a lineage member of very high standing, being headmaster of a school in Kam Tin (the stronghold of the powerful Teng 'lineage') and a high official in the Hong Kong Boy Scouts' Movement. In addition to the managers there are five treasurers, a chief treasurer and one assistant from each Tou. All five men are Village Councillors, and one of them is an Assistant Headman and therefore both a manager and a treasurer. The important posts as far as the T'ang is concerned are those of the treasurers, who must manage the finances correctly. The management of the T'ang is merely a puppet of the Village Council, for the Council controls the activities of the T'ang and in fact uses it as little more than a convenient name for a bank account.

---

[21] His tablet in the Wan Shih T'ang gives him the degree of *En-chin-shih*, while that in the Hsien Ch'eng T'ang refers to him as a *Kuo-hsüeh-sheng*. Presumably both titles refer to the lowest purchased degree (?).

[22] He was an *I-hsiang-sheng*, according to the genealogy.

It is known that the Wan Shih T'ang has always been for all practical purposes the concern of the community leaders of the lineage in their capacities as managers. The ritual leadership has not had control of the funds without which ritual itself cannot go forward, and has had authority virtually on sufferance of the community leadership of the village. On the face of it, then, the Village Council's acquisition of control over the Wan Shih T'ang is merely a recognition that the Council is the natural successor to the old informal community leadership, and, indeed, since the Councillors are all lineage members, there is little significance in the change at the present. None the less, this change is potentially a very serious one for the lineage, and could lead to much friction in the community in certain circumstances.

CHAPTER SIX

The Lineage and Resident Outsiders

I

THE lineage had relationships of various kinds with other groups both inside and outside the village. The factors which determined the kind of relationship between the lineage and another group were numerous and inconstant, but a broad distinction may be drawn between relationships within the village and those outside it.

The hub of lineage settlement was and is the eight hamlets, all of which are built on the same large area of raised and agriculturally inferior land, the sum of the hamlets composing the village of Sheung Shui. The clearest picture of settlement of the village is provided by the 1906 land records, since at that time the pattern had not been disturbed by the subsequent revivification of Shek Wu Hui, nor by the even more drastic effects of the post-war wave of immigration from the Chinese mainland and the associated vegetable-growing revolution centred on nearby Fanling, both of which have combined to blur village boundaries, to the extent that it becomes increasingly more difficult to say where the village ends and Shek Wu Hui begins. In 1906, however, the village was clearly a discrete settlement. At that time it consisted of 724 building lots,[1] of which 614 were houses (including 12 broken-down houses), 16 were temples, halls or 'reading-rooms', 4 were shops, and the remainder were sheds and other non-residential buildings. Scattered amongst the houses were many threshing-floors and plots of land, all poor, third-class land suitable only for growing vegetables such as sweet potatoes and peanuts.

[1] I have omitted from the reckoning the two temples which are included with the village in the records but which are in fact situated far away near Red Bridge.

The village was clearly marked off from any other settlement, but it did not occupy the entire area of the raised, non-paddy land: there was in fact ample room for expansion in this less valuable land to the east and south-east of the village. All land and buildings within the area occupied by the village (and probably, I suspect, all the rest of the raised area as well) were considered sacred to the lineage in that they might not be sold to outsiders, a stipulation which the lineage leaders are said to have supported wholeheartedly. Today, the village precinct (but not the remainder of the raised land, because buyers and Government have been too pressing for lineage owners to resist) is strictly preserved as an area for Liao owners only, and it is true to say that the lineage fears the possible consequences of a lapse from this policy, believing that effective control over village residents can only be maintained through control of property owners, which itself can only be done through common kinship. In explaining this to me, an informant said: "There would be no control over the outsiders, and they might be in some way undesirable; they might, for example, open a brothel or an opium den: besides, the village itself is above all the place which belongs to the lineage, and it would be hurtful to our pride if we were to dispose of what our ancestors have handed down to us." It follows that, since anyone not of the lineage can be neither owner nor potential owner of land or property within the precinct, residents in the precinct who are not lineage members have not equal rights with lineage members, and are, in fact, considered to be of lower standing than Liaos. It is in this that the distinction in relationship lies— relationships with outsiders within the village tend to be ones of superiority-inferiority, while lineage members outside the village may expect to have all kinds of relationships with others, depending on occupation, prestige and other factors, as well as on a today less important 'sphere of influence' factor, which will be discussed in the following chapter.

II

Despite the prohibition on non-lineage ownership of land and property within the village precinct, the 1906 records show that twenty of the 614 houses were owned by people of

other surnames. Since it is certain that there was strict observance of this prohibition, these twenty houses can only have
belonged to *hsi-min* ('minor people'), servile families bound to
their masters in perpetuity.

Chen Han-seng mentions servile families under the name
sia-wu,[2] and Freedman cites Professor J. M. Potter's mention
of them in the New Territories village of Ping Shan by the
Cantonese term *ha-fu*,[3] which may well be the same term.
Ha-fu I have myself heard used in other villages as a synonym
for *hsi-min*. Chen's *sia-wu* were "subjected to a sort of extreme
exploitation":[4] they were "hereditary tenants who look upon
the members of the clans that harbour them as their masters
and who, in addition to farming the fields assigned to them,
render additional services as labourers, servants, and watchmen, for which they are paid no wage, though here and there
their wretched condition is occasionally alleviated by perquisites
of various kinds".[5] He goes on to detail the high rents which
were demanded of these 'hereditary tenants'. In Sheung Shui,
the *hsi-min* were tenants in the sense that they held land from
their masters, but not in the sense that they paid rent as such
for their fields. The *hsi-min* fell between the two terms which
Chen uses, not really being 'hereditary tenants', nor being
'slave clans' (as he quite rightly points out, they had the right
to private property and could not be sold). Perhaps the term
'hereditary servants' best describes them.

At the outset a rich household would purchase a boy from
poor parents (but not from within the lineage under any
circumstances)[6] and raise him as a servant of the family, in rare
instances using him as a study companion to their sons. In
treatment and status the boy probably was on a par with the
female *mui-tsai* servant, of whom much has been written,[7] and,

[2] Chen Han-seng, *Agrarian Problems in Southernmost China*, Shanghai, 1936,
pp. 57–8. (Spelt *siao-wu* in the index.)
[3] Freedman, *Lineage and Society*, p. 10. I have not seen Potter's thesis.
[4] Chen, *op. cit.*, p. 57.
[5] *Ibid.*, p. 58.
[6] Many *hsi-min* in Sheung Shui and other villages of the New Territories
seem to have come from the relatively poor valleys which now lie on and
near the Anglo-Chinese border.
[7] For a brief summary, see, for example, League of Nations, Commission
of Enquiry into Traffic in Women and Children in the East, *Report to the
Council*, Geneva, 1932, p. 132.

indeed, one informant described the *hsi-min* boy as a "male *mui-tsai*". When in due course the master family married off a *mui-tsai*, she became free of her servitude, but when the master family paid the expenses of a *hsi-min's* wedding, no such freedom resulted: the wife and children also became servants, and agnatic male descendants were servants in perpetuity. The *hsi-min* family would be given by their masters a house to live in and fields to till. Unlike the *sia-wu*, they were not required to hand over any part of their crops to their masters, nor were they charged rent for the house and fields, but, as a return, the *hsi-min* were supposed to give their services to the master family whenever required, and especially on ceremonial occasions such as weddings and the Autumn Rites, when they performed all the most menial of tasks, carrying the bridal sedan-chair, carrying the pigs to the graves, cutting up the food, washing the dishes, etc. Their children (I assume) continued as household servants in the places vacated by the fathers. In practice, however, the *hsi-min* were exploited rather more fully than the above indicates, for they came to be at the beck and call of the entire lineage. While the master family had first call on their services, anyone of the lineage would give them orders without asking the leave of the masters, and no payment was necessary, though it was in undertaking tasks for these other lineage members that the *hsi-min* were occasionally able to come by the 'perquisites of various kinds'—"Perhaps a meal or a few copper cash", said one informant.

The position of a *hsi-min* was a peculiar one. On the one hand, he was provided with a wife at master family expense, he was guaranteed a house and fields sufficient to support his family, and he was allowed to marry off his daughters and female descendants as he wished (to other servants or to free men of other villages). Thus, economically he was better placed than many poorer members of the master lineage, because his livelihood was virtually guaranteed by his wealthy masters. On the other hand, he, his wife, unmarried daughters, sons and agnatic male descendants were all at the command of the entire lineage, and were expected to perform the most degrading and laborious work without additional remuneration in most cases. His wife (and, if he were unfortunate, his unmarried daughters too) was liable to be used sexually by less scrupulous members of the lineage.[8] In general, the position of the *hsi-min* was unpleasant because of the treatment which they received as a distinctly inferior and politically impotent class. The terms of address used by lineage members to them were universally degrading. Until about the age of fifty all *hsi-min* were called by their personal names, regardless of the age or standing of the lineage member addressing them. After that age males were known by the term "*a–(personal name)–po*" and females by "*a–(personal name)–wu*". The advantages of this hereditary servitude must have outweighed the disadvantages, however, for it is said to have been open to *hsi-min* to run away at any time once the first period of premarital servitude was over, and no form of punishment or attempt at capture would result.

For the master families the advantages do not seem to have been very great. True they received regular service from the *hsi-min* initially and spasmodic service afterwards whenever their need of it was greatest, but, to offset this, they lost the use of houses and fields without financial return. A large part of the benefit of 'owning' such servants must have come from the prestige which this display of wealth gave, and which accrued as a result of being able to benefit the lineage as a whole through their work. In one example quoted by Chen, about 30 per cent. of one village's population were *sia-wu*. Quite clearly, in the Sheung Shui situation, where no financial benefit in the way of rent came to the masters, it would have been impossible for the lineage to support such a large percentage of *hsi-min*. They were in many ways a luxury, a symbol of wealth obtainable only by the very wealthy.

Indeed, verbal evidence and the evidence of the 1906 records point to the possession of *hsi-min* by only a few of the wealthiest families of the lineage. Of the twenty houses, thirteen were situated in Pu Shang Ts'un (five of them close to the Yün Sheng T'ang), and four were close to the wealthy Yi Lan T'ang of Chung Hsin Ts'un. It is probable that many of these *hsi-min* may have been owned in common by members of a trust (for

---

[8] "If you wanted her, you merely had to tell the woman to leave her door open that night", I was told by a group of old men, and (drily): "They were supposed to gain face by having the master lineage men as their sleeping partners."

hereditary servants would seem to require hereditary masters, and the problem of dividing an inheritance of this nature must have been otherwise extremely difficult, whereas a *hsi-min* family farming trust land can readily be available to serve all members of the trust), though informants said that none were owned by the Wan Shih T'ang. All twenty houses were of inferior quality, as is shown by the low Crown Rent which was required for them in 1906—50 cents each; but did they really belong to the *hsi-min* whose names are in the records? The basic intention of the prohibition on ownership by non-lineage members would not be violated if the *hsi-min* did own them, for they were given no political rights with their houses; indeed they received the houses as a direct result of their rightless circumstances. It seems more likely that houses and fields were 'given' to *hsi-min* for their use in servitude only, and that the permanent ownership remained in the hands of the master families. It was quite clear from informants' statements that a *hsi-min* who ran away forfeited his claim to house and fields. It is perhaps surprising that the real owners of the houses should have allowed the *hsi-min* to register them in their own names, but probably the master families were confident of the strength of their claims within the village. No record was found of agricultural land (which also is said to have been given to these servants) registered in the name of a *hsi-min*.

The *hsi-min* are all said to have been freed "about 30 years ago", many men still being able to remember the days when they could shout to a *hsi-min* to do something for them. What it was which brought about the manumission at that time is not quite clear. Certainly it was due to no kind of intervention by Government, who were apparently unaware of the existence of the institution. A report to the Governor in 1935 stated: "There is no evidence of slavery among Chinese males",[9] and Appendix No. 12 to the same report quotes an 1886 report by J. Russell:

> "The most careful inquiry shows that no male children are bought and sold here as slaves or servants, and confirms the statements in the Blue-Book that 'Boys are sold to be sons not slaves'

[9] 'Mui Tsai in Hong Kong: Report of the Committee appointed by the Governor', *Sessional Papers 1935*.

and 'that no such thing as a slave-boy exists in Hong Kong'. It might too with truth have been added 'nor in Canton'."

Hsi-min had always been redeemable either by parents in the initial stages or by the servants themselves, if they managed to save up the price of their repurchase. In some cases faithful service was rewarded with freedom, and in others (but this does not seem to have applied to Sheung Shui) the master lineage would absorb *hsi-min* by adoption. But there seems no reason why these factors should have combined at that time to sweep away the institution not only in Sheung Shui but in all other *hsi-min*-owning villages which came to my notice. Perhaps world economic depression played some part in the change: at any rate, the only explanation advanced to me by informants in the village was: "No one could afford to have them any more."

Three *hsi-min* surnames are remembered generally in the village today, and fifteen of the twenty houses are registered in the names of one or another of the three. (Each of the other five houses is registered in a different surname.) *Hsi-min* of one of these predominant surnames moved out of the village on manumission, gradually acquired wealth, bought fields, and set up a small settlement a few miles away on the outskirts of Shek Wu Hui, where now their descendants are said to be flourishing. All contact with the Liaos was cut off by the move. Their old houses in Sheung Shui stand ruined in Chung Hsin Ts'un. I was unable to discover what had become of the other surnames, with the exception of one, some descendants of which still live in Pu Shang Ts'un, in the same house which their parents occupied as *hsi-min*. I do not know whether or not they pay rent for it. What is certain is that they are considered to be privileged *above* the common run of non-lineage inhabitants, so much so that those of their children who attend the Kindergarten in the Hsien Ch'eng T'ang are charged the $12 fee which the lineage children pay, instead of the $15 outsiders' fee.

The position of *hsi-min* descendants must be something of a problem for all lineages. While these people were still acting as servants there could be no problem about their treatment; the situation was structured in terms of superiority-inferiority, the *hsi-min* were denied the rights and privileges of lineage members, and were politically ignored. Freed, there could no longer be justification for a superiority-inferiority relationship between them and the lineage, and an immediate threat to lineage monopoly of its village territory was posed, for the *hsi-min* were 'owning' houses and yet had lost the bonds which controlled them and made it acceptable for them to 'own'. From the *hsi-min's* point of view, the village of his servitude might constitute the only home he had known, especially where he was not a 1st-generation servant, and quite possibly he identified the village as his *hsiang-hsia* ('native home'), a concept of much importance to the individual in this area of China at least. The ways in which this problem was solved seem to vary from village to village. We have seen that the bulk of Sheung Shui's *hsi-min* descendants chose to leave the village which had known their degradation, and this perhaps is the simplest of the solutions adopted. In Kam Tin, a large village of the Teng lineage, *hsi-min* descendants of two different surnames, who had moved out of the village on manumission, later donated money to one of the village schools,[10] perhaps an indication that for them Kam Tin is still their home, and a possible threat of their future return to it. In the small Hou lineage village of Ping Kong some of the *hsi-min* moved away from the village immediately they were freed. Those who did not were almost all adopted into the failing Hou lineage, assuming full and equal rights of inheritance with blood descendants of the lineage; "their names could be entered in the genealogy and their tablets could be placed in the ancestral hall when they died".[11] "When the *hsi-min* were freed, of those who did not become Hous, the majority returned to their 'native homes' or went elsewhere to make a living, for otherwise their descendants might have been imposed upon and despised by the lineage."[12] Clearly the *hsi-min* descendants who remain in Sheung Shui are in an anomalous position. The lineage finds difficulty in fitting them within the normal category of 'outsiders', and so feels bound to extend the Kindergarten privilege to them; but, on the other hand, strict rules of

[10] See my 'Five Great Clans', p. 36.
[11] Private communication from Mr. Leung Kwok-wai, Headmaster of the Ho Kai School in Ho Sheung Heung, dated December 1965.
[12] *Ibid.*

adoption preclude their absorption into the lineage. It is probably only because the problem is so small in extent that no decisive policy of treatment of these people has been evolved.

III

It seems safe to assume that, with the exception of the *hsi-min*, the vast majority of persons living within the village before the Japanese occupation were lineage members. The four shops were all owned, and presumably run, by Liaos; and most occupational specialists which the lineage itself could not supply probably appeared in the village only for work purposes, being resident elsewhere. Those who did live in the village, and I know only of school-teachers in this connection, were of course precluded from buying houses, and had to rent. No doubt then, as now, a small perishable goods market was held early each morning for two hours in the centre of the village, outside the gates of the walled hamlet, and hawkers and beggars would constantly be circulating through the village: all these people being outsiders as far as I know.

But after the Japanese occupation, the flood of immigrants caused by the Communist–Nationalist fighting in China, and particularly in Kwangtung, swiftly changed the picture of settlement. Sheung Shui, being the first major village on the main exit route from the mainland, was heavily influenced by the demand for accommodation, and empty houses were let to outsiders at rents which, while not exorbitant when compared with the extremely high rents charged in the cities, were high enough to make a considerable difference in the income of the landlord. Fields, of course, were similarly rented out. Since that time the demand for accommodation has flagged little, as the pressure on urban housing has caused a back-wash into the rural areas, and as the extremely rapid rise of Shek Wu Hui has had an effect on nearby villages too.

Some of the outsiders, not unnaturally, have been families of Liao women married to men of villages across the border, the whole family fleeing to Sheung Shui when the civil war approached. In the walled hamlet in 1965 seven of the 116 households (a total of forty people) were composed of families taking up matri-local residence for this reason; in five of the

cases the husband resided with the family, in a sixth the husband
was working in France, and I have no information on the
seventh husband. If this position is reflected in other hamlets of
the village, and I do know of other instances, then the number
of outsiders in the village who can trace kinship or affinity with
the Liaos must make up a considerable part of the whole mass.
Undoubtedly such people would have had priority in the
renting of available accommodation.

If 3,375 inhabitants of the village were lineage members, then
there must in 1965 have been some 1,625 outsiders living in
Sheung Shui, nearly one-third of the population. In dress,
customs, income, and occupation (with the exception of
government service, agriculture and overseas jobs, in each of
which the lineage has many more men involved) there is little
difference between lineage members and outsiders. In speech
there is a recognisable Sheung Shui accent and certain pe-
culiarities of vocabulary, but in general there is again little
difference. The outsiders live, not in any particular section or
sections of the village, but intermingled with the lineage. As
individuals outsiders may be very well liked and respected,
and we have seen that non-lineage neighbours are completely
accepted into lineage residential groupings. But as a class (they
are too amorphous to form a group) outsiders are treated with
much the same lack of consideration as were the *hsi-min*; that
is to say, they may not own land or property within the village
precinct, and consequently they are politically ignored, for they
may have no share in a village government entry to which is
dependent on land ownership or potential land ownership.
"All outsiders are only temporarily resident", to quote a
Village Councillor: but some of them have already been there
for fifteen years or more! In that fifteen years the only change in
attitude has been the gradual acceptance by the lineage of the
fact of a village in which they are not the only residents. An
informant living in Shek Wu Hui told me that when he first
came out of China he went to live in the walled hamlet, but
that the attitude of the Liaos was so haughty at that time and
their behaviour towards outsiders so fierce that he had found it
more congenial to move out again. That was in the early
1950s. "But they are not like that now", he added, and rightly.

When I left the village there was no sign either that the

lineage had plans to expand the electorate or give the outsiders some representation on the Council, or that the outsiders were in any way disturbed by their lack of political representation at this and higher levels of the local government hierarchy. The very diffuseness of outsider settlement, of course, prevents the formation of residential groups of outsiders, and we have seen that near residence is one of the most cohesive of factors in village life. Again, the outsiders arrived as single families, they are of many surnames and different areas (but mostly from Kwangtung), and they have no lineage organisations or district-of-origin associations of their own round which to build any movement for political representation. Furthermore, pressure on accommodation both in the cities and Shek Wu Hui is still such that it would be foolhardy in a tenant to jeopardise his rented home for the sake of what must seem to the majority at best a rather empty privilege.

The outsider pays his rent and his contributions to the Village Watch. True some of that money goes on lineage ritual and display, from which he derives neither advantage nor pride, but at the same time the village as a community is advancing rapidly. The recent installation of electricity in the houses, the building of roads to replace the muddy paths, the incipient installation of piped water, the building of public toilets and so on, all these may be taken advantage of by the outsider as much as by the lineage member. The Village Headman, backed up by the Council and the District Office, is endeavouring to make Sheung Shui a 'model village', a concept which perhaps means little in itself, but which does seem to have had the effect of ensuring for Sheung Shui a large share of Government development funds. The outsider is living in a village which has as many advantages as perhaps any other village of the New Territories. Small wonder that he is not at present concerned at his lack of participation in the government of the village.

M

CHAPTER SEVEN

The Lineage and its External Relationships

I

THE external relationships of the lineage are characterised by a lack of kinship-ritual ties with other Liao lineages, whereas in other similar instances in the New Territories there were such ties.[1] The lineage as a kinship-community group and as a collection of individuals, however, has relationships of many different kinds outside the village precinct.

In the previous chapter the extent and nature of the precinct were analysed, and it was seen that the village marks the limit of absolute Liao dominance. It is now necessary to look outward from this hub of settlement at a wider area of lineage influence, for, clearly, the absolute mastery of a village area of inferior land cannot explain the wealth and power which the Liaos came to possess. The picture of land ownership is today so blurred by recent changes that it is necessary to look again at the land records for 1906 in order to gain an insight into the traditional patterns of settlement and land ownership, patterns largely determined by the strength of lineage organisation, for in 1906 the heyday of lineage power in the New Territories had not yet passed.

The land outside the village precinct was not inviolate, but there was a large area of land adjoining the village which was almost exclusively owned by the Liaos, and this area composed a Liao 'territory' or 'sphere of influence'. Within it there were no settlements other than the small cluster of buildings which made up the market of Shek Wu Hui.[2] Of the 973·33 acres of

---

[1] See, for example, Freedman, *Lineage and Society*, p. 19.

[2] In Chapter One we have seen that the population of this market place was very small indeed—120 in 1898 and 43 in 1911.

land which the Liaos owned in 1906, almost two-thirds—
635·23 acres—was in this territory.[3]

North-east and east of the village the border of the territory
was fixed by the hills. In all other directions geographical
features were the main delineators of the territory's border,
but the reasons for the delineation were political rather than
geographic; that is to say, in any one direction, the comparative
distances of the border from the village and from the nearest
settlement in that direction were a measure of the importance
of the lineage vis-à-vis the occupants of that settlement. The
nearer the border to another settlement the less powerful the
occupants of that settlement must have been. To a certain
extent the border was influenced by geographical features, so
that, within the general area which the border must occupy
according to the relative importance of the lineage and a
particular neighbour, the exact border line probably depended
upon the convenience of a stream or hillock. But not only were
the distances of settlements from the border indications of the
relative power of their occupants, the sharpness of the border
line was also of significance. Where a powerful neighbour's
territory was next to that of the Liaos, the border was distinct,
land on one side being virtually 100 per cent. Liao owned, and
on the other side equally fully exploited by the neighbour.
Where the neighbouring settlement was less powerful, much of
the land on its side of the border might also belong to the Liaos.

Map II shows the Liao territory as I have reconstructed it
with the aid of the 1906 land records and the Hong Kong
Government's original Demarcation District maps. To the
north and north-north-west of the village, the nearest parts of
the Sha Ling Valley, from the Indus River to the headwaters
of the valley streams,[4] are Liao territory, and part of the rest of
the valley has Liao land-holdings interspersed with others,
chiefly those of the weaker Yüan lineage of Lo Wu, a village
on the other side of the Anglo-Chinese border.[5] To the north-

---

[3] This figure includes the agricultural land but not the building land
within the village precinct.

[4] The valley is part of two different river systems, as the map shows.

[5] I am less clear about the border in this valley than elsewhere and
suspect that on the map I may have been a little sanguine about the extent
of Liao territory. My confusion emphasises the point made about blurring
of borders in such circumstances.

west and west, a major tributary of the Indus River, the aptly named Sutlej, serves as the sharply defined border between Liao territory and that of the Hou lineages of Ho Sheung Heung, Yin Kong, and Kam Tsin. From south-west to south-south-east the Sutlej continues as the border of Liao territory, and beyond it are quite extensive Liao holdings reflecting the relative weakness of the mixed lineage village of Tsung Pak Long and of the small Chien lineage village of Tai Tau Leng. The rest of the border follows small streams dividing off Liao territory from that of the P'eng lineage of Fanling in the south-south-east to east-south-east and the Teng lineage of Lung Yeuk Tau in the east-south-east up to the hills in the east.

The size of the territory was at once an indication of the power and wealth of the lineage and the prime factor in the acquisition and maintenance of that power and wealth. It included one of the largest areas of first-quality land in the New Territories.[6] Demarcation District 52, which covers 258·24 acres[7] of the territory contiguous to the village itself, in 1906 was more than half made up of first-class land, thus:

1st class land	133·54 acres in 472 lots.
2nd class land	33·32 acres in 135 lots.
3rd class land	91·38 acres in 502 lots.

The territory was extremely well served by streams and rivers, as Map II shows.

Public works within the territory would be undertaken by the lineage. An important aspect of this was, of course, irrigation—all the three dams mentioned in the 1819 edition of the *Hsin-an hsien-chih*[8] were situated within the territory. The lineage was prepared to spend money on irrigation projects within the territory, because virtually all the benefit must go to lineage members: and here it must be stressed that land near the village was not only owned by Liaos, but, where rented out, it was leased to Liaos too, as has already been hinted in Chapter Three. If this was true of the Liao territory, it was probably also true of the territories of other powerful lineages. Less powerful lineages and settlements, whose territory was

---

[6] See Grant, *op. cit.*, figs. VI (o) and (p), and Pocket Sheets 1 and 2.
[7] Exclusive of the four lots owned by outsiders.
[8] See above, p. 45.

small or whose surrounding lands were much encroached upon by owners from other lineages and settlements, were probably neither able nor willing to afford the expenditure on irrigation systems which would benefit more than themselves. Large lineages, then, must have been better equipped than small to improve the fertility of their fields and to maintain their wealth.

Within the territory, also, there could be no serious irrigation disputes, for all the users of the system were both dependent on the lineage-controlled dams and subject to lineage authority. By contrast, irrigation of land elsewhere was a fertile source of disputes. In a social context in which powerful lineages were poised against each other in rivalry and a delicate but never constant balance of power, irrigation disputes must have been both a recurring cause and a result of friction. Informants, indeed, frequently mentioned the importance of irrigation matters in sparking off inter-lineage fighting.

In 'The Five Great Clans of the New Territories' I have tried to demonstrate the dominance of the New Territories by five different surnames. One of these was the Liao lineage of Sheung Shui. It is worthy of note that three of the four other surnames have settlements the territories of which have common borders with the Liao territory, and it is precisely where the territories of these three (Hou, Teng and P'eng) are contiguous with that of the Liaos that the border is sharp on the map. Borders of this nature, once arrived at, must have been extremely stable, and not normally amenable to encroachment from either side. On one occasion while I was in the village I was regaled by some old men with tales of the fights which had taken place with other lineages. One of the stories concerned the P'engs of Fanling, and, at the time, I put down to my mishearing a reference to "the mud rampart dividing Sheung Shui from Fanling" over which threats and missiles were hurled; but it now seems less improbable that such a concrete and permanent mark of division should have existed—perhaps at that point on the border where no stream makes a boundary, or perhaps for even a greater distance.

If the common borders of powerful lineages' territories were relatively stable, the rivalry for power and influence must have found expression elsewhere, in the areas where weaker, poorer lineages and settlements were unable to retain full control of all the land immediately around them. It must be expected, then, that a map of the land-holdings of the agricultural countryside would show a series of almost exclusive territories, the property of powerful lineages, and kaleidoscopic patches of mixed owners outside those territories. Such certainly seems to be the case in the New Territories.

The Liao land-holdings may in fact be divided into three major sections: the village precinct, the territory, and the scattered holdings. This last section demonstrates quite clearly that, outside the territory, amount of land held did not decrease in proportion with distance from the village, and that political and historical rather than purely geographic factors were of importance in acquisition of land.

Land was acquired along the lines of least resistance in two directions from the village—that is, north-west towards Lo Wu, where the Yüan lineage's power was most extended and therefore least effective, and south towards and around the relatively impotent settlements of Tsung Pak Long and Tai Tau Leng. In the former case acquisition of land was made easier by the lack of settlements in the Sha Ling Valley (or do I perhaps confuse cause and effect?—we have seen that the Chien lineage could be driven out of Sheung Shui); in the latter, the Liaos had pushed their holdings out to meet the borders of the territories of the Hou lineage villages of Kam Tsin and Ping Kong. The borders of the territory and of this potential extension to it were thus in contact on all sides with those of other major lineages, or with the hills which define the plain. No further lineal expansion was possible. There were, however, greater or lesser holdings in areas separated from Sheung Shui by the territories of these other major lineages or by the hills.

Over the hills in the Ta Kwu Ling Valley, some $2\frac{1}{2}$ miles to the north-east of the village as the crow flies, the Liaos owned 18·62 acres of land, and a further 16·44 acres some 2 miles from the village to the north-north-east in the same valley. On the far side of the Hou lineages' territories, the Liaos owned 73·09 acres in the Tsiu Keng Valley (part of which is shown in the bottom left-hand corner of Map II). It was characteristic of both these valleys that they were occupied by many small lineages and settlements, and that Cantonese and Hakka were found living side by side, sometimes in the same village. (In

1961 the largest village of the Ta Kwu Ling Valley numbered 561 people, and that of the Tsiu Keng Valley 706,[9] but, in this latter case at least, the population had been greatly swollen by recent immigration.)[10] None of the lineages resident in these valleys was big enough or powerful enough to own a large territory, and the strong lineages of the New Territories and of the Mainland competed in buying land in the valleys. In the Ta Kwu Ling Valley the Liaos competed principally against the Huang lineage of Fuk Tin and the very powerful Chang lineage of Heung Sai, both on the Mainland side of the border. In the Tsiu Keng Valley the chief rivals were the same Chang lineage, the Hou lineage, and the Wen lineage[11] of San Tin. In these competitive areas there was very little zoning of lineage holdings, and land was apparently bought by any of the contenders wherever it was available, so that the holdings were well scattered. It was probably in areas such as these that irrigation disputes were most common. In effect, large lineages competing for land in areas of this nature stood to gain not only wealth, in the increased income from extra land, but also influence, in that the land must in many cases have been rented out to the inhabitants of the areas, making them dependent for their livelihood upon the goodwill of their landlords.

An expanding lineage, then, sought to push its territory to the furthest extent, and then to acquire land in areas where by doing so it could broaden its sphere of influence. It might be expected that in such areas other powerful lineages would also be competing for the land, for it would be against their interests to allow one lineage to acquire control of another area and so to change the balance of power. It would certainly be more rewarding for a lineage to seek land in one of these areas than to buy lots within the territory of a neighbouring large lineage, for to do so (were it in any event possible) would be to invite retaliatory measures against the lots—by cutting off irrigation, for example—whenever inter-lineage disputes flared up. Indeed, few of the non-Liao owned lots in the territory belonged to immediate neighbours. In the Tsiu Keng Valley, the Liaos

[9] Unpublished 1961 Census material, kindly made available by the New Territories Administration and the Commissioner of Census.

[10] Cf. *A Gazetteer of Place Names*, p. 202.

[11] The fifth of the major surnames of the New Territories.

were strong, but they were not strong enough to prevent the valley's being exploited by the Wen lineage of San Tin, which exacted an annual 'protection' fee[12] from its villages until the Japanese occupation.[13]

Comparison of territory land-holdings and of scattered land-holdings was made by collecting more detailed information on Demarcation District 52, already mentioned, and on Demarcation District 100, which covers part of the Tsiu Keng Valley. The results are shown in Table 15.

TABLE 15
Territory and scattered land-holdings[14]

D.D.	52		100	
Class of land	Tsu and T'ang	All Liaos	Tsu and T'ang	All Liaos
First	61·33	133·54	11·33	21·55
Second	16·49	33·32	6·90	13·08
Third	30·59	91·38	2·97	5·36
Total	108·41	258·24	21·20	39·99

Two major differences emerge from these figures. First, the proportions of good and poor land differ in the two Districts. In D.D. 52, 35 per cent. of the Liao holdings was made up of third-class land, but in D.D. 100, where buyers could be selective (not having to take up all the land of a territory), only 13 per cent. of the Liao holdings was third-class land. By taking up the better land in these other areas the powerful lineages not only received high incomes, they also confined the weaker lineages to the worse land and thus kept weak or weakened their positions, making their reliance on the strong

[12] Cf. Hu, op. cit., p. 91.
[13] This I was told by some old men of the village of Tsiu Keng. I did not discover when the fee paying had started.
[14] The measurement is in acres throughout.

lineages greater. Second, 42 per cent. of the total Liao holdings
in D. D. 52 was owned by kinship-ritual trusts (Tsu or T'ang),
but in D.D. 100 Tsu and T'ang owned 53 per cent. of the total
Liao land. In short, the further away from Sheung Shui, the
more likely were Liao holdings to be trust ones—and this was
the very type of holding which was most rented out for cultivation, a convenient vehicle for the subjugation of other areas.
Of the total 973·33 acres which were owned by the Liaos,
503·64 acres (52 per cent.) were owned by kinship-ritual trusts.
Since, as we have seen, nearly two-thirds of the Liao holdings
were within the territory, and since within the territory the
percentage of trust holdings was comparatively small, the
percentage of trust holdings outside the territory must have
been well above 50 per cent. in order to result in an overall
percentage of 52.

The constant search for more land and larger spheres of
influence gives a political reason for the holdings of the Liaos
in areas away from their village and territory. In common with
Freedman, "I think we must assume that the desire to form a
single lineage in one village territory is a motive given in the
system",[15] and the more successful a lineage was in expanding
its territory, the more prosperous and numerous became its
members, and the more land was required for the greater
number of their descendants—a revolving sequence of cause and
effect. But there must have been a historical factor which
determined some of the holdings, just as the very reasons for
the initial wealth of lineages may in many cases be traced to
accidents of history.[16]

At this point it is worth while looking again at the account
of early lineage history contained in the genealogy.[17] Before the
lineage came together to settle in the present site, segments
lived at Ping Kong, Kak Tin, Lung Ngan Yuen, Ha Shui,
Wang Mei Shan, Sheung Shui, Siu Hang and Ling Ha. Of
these, Lung Ngan Yuen, Ha Shui, Sheung Shui and Ling Ha
were certainly within what is now Liao territory—indeed we
have seen that temples survive at two of the sites—and Kak

[15] Freedman, *Lineage and Society*, p. 8.
[16] See 'Five Great Clans', pp. 27–31. Also Freedman, *Lineage and Society*, p. 36.
[17] *LSTP*, Summary of Historical Movements.

Tin may also have been in the same area.[18] Siu Hang survives as a settlement east of the village (marked 'A' on the map), but away from the Liao territory in the Teng sphere of influence. It is now neither inhabited nor owned by Liaos. Wang Mei Shan is now known as Wa Mei Shan and is situated at the southeastern extremity of the Sheung Shui/Fanling Valley at the place marked 'B' on the map. A few scattered lots of land are still owned by the Liaos in this area, but the chief survival of Liao occupancy is the very important grave of Chung-chieh's son. Ping Kong, south of Sheung Shui, has been a Hou lineage settlement for many years, but there are still many Liao land lots in the vicinity, and particularly east of Ping Kong in an area, marked 'C' on the map, which may well have been the old site of the Liao Ping Kong settlement.

An anomalous land-holding is connected with the grave of Chung-chieh. This grave, marked 'D' on the map, is situated close to the village of Kam Tsin in the Hou lineage territory. It is protected from interference by flanking strips of Wan Shih T'ang owned land, land which is not farmed and certainly has not been farmed for many years.

All land-holdings mentioned so far have been within three or four miles of the village, but in the past the Liaos have owned land elsewhere. The 1906 records do not show land north of the Anglo-Chinese border, of course, but informants told me that there were at one time Liao holdings many miles away on the Mainland. Furthermore, there appear to have been extensive Liao holdings on the Sai Kung peninsula, in the extreme east of the New Territories. I am indebted to Mr. James Hayes for a copy of a document, dated sixth year of T'ung Chih (1867), which records the lease by a Tsu of Sheung Shui of an area of hill land on the peninsula to a local man surnamed Li. The land was at the village of Long Keng, which is 12½ miles from Sheung Shui as the crow flies, and many more miles by the most direct human route. All these more distant holdings have now been sold or abandoned—"It was too troublesome to collect the rents", said one informant—and, indeed, few people in the village even knew that they had existed.

[18] But there is a Huang lineage village of this name near the Huang village of Fuk Tin (or possibly they are the same village under two names?).

The weakening of a lineage by virtue of failing manpower or misspent wealth must have been marked by the gradual collapse inwards of its land-holdings, more distant ones being sold first. I mentioned above the relatively stable territories of powerful lineages, especially where they touched the territories of other similar lineages. The intention was not to make such lineages seem statically powerful. There must have been lineages which descended from power to weakness and perhaps extinction. The Teng lineage of Lung Yeuk Tau seems to be a case in point. At one time powerful enough to produce major scholars (a *chü-jen* of A.D. 1258, one *sui-kung-sheng* of the late Ming dynasty, and others of 1728, 1740, and 1765)[19] and to play the main role in establishing a market town,[20] it has declined during the last century until now its village is no longer sacrosanct.[21] The borders of the territory of such a lineage must gradually have shrunk, retreating little by little to geographic frontiers closer to the village.

The Liaos seem to have succumbed in precisely this way to the recent wave of immigration and the changes it has made in land values, occupations, etc. More distant holdings have been sold or abandoned, land nearer the village has been sold or rented out, and the territory itself has been much invaded by immigrants to whom the land has been rented and occasionally sold. Almost all land south of a line drawn east–west through the walled hamlet is now growing vegetables under the hands of immigrant farmers. The line of inviolability has collapsed inwards stage by stage until now only the village precinct is left untouched, and even there the number of outsiders admitted on a tenant basis threatens the foundations of lineage solidarity. The process is only at an early stage, the Liaos still owning much land, but it is likely that more and more land will be sold, by individual members at least, leaving islands of inalienable trust land, the majority of which, unless a pattern of selling some land and buying other develops, will be situated paradoxically in areas away from the village.

[19] *HAHC 1819*, chüan 15, Examination Tables.
[20] Groves, Robert G., 'The origins of two market towns in the New Territories', *Aspects of Social Organization in the New Territories*, Hong Kong, 1965, p. 17.
[21] Ingrams, Harold, *Hong Kong*, London, 1952, p. 169.

II

The pattern of Liao land ownership was and is to a great extent determined by the overall system of land ownership in the area. Paramount in the system are the major lineages of the New Territories; but until the closing of the Anglo-Chinese border in 1949 the system included important lineages of the Mainland side as well. We have seen that four of the five major New Territories lineages and lineage groups shared common borders in the Sheung Shui/Fanling Plain, and that the fifth was in contact with some of them in the Tsiu Keng Valley at least. In their dominance of the best agricultural land and the wealth which this brought them, these major lineages, together in the past with those of the Mainland, formed an élite group centred on the intermediate market town of Sham Chun, which lies a few miles the other side of the border.

The exclusiveness of this élite was reflected in many other aspects of the social structure of the area. As far as I was able to ascertain, it was only the élite lineages which could afford to be served by *hsi-min*—and, of course, members of élite lineages did not become *hsi-min* either in their own or in other lineage villages. Similarly, the markets of the New Territories, with the exception of Sha Tau Kok market, which is situated in an area of heterogeneous settlement, were controlled originally at least, by one or another of the major lineages.[22]

One of the clearest indications of the extent of the élite group is given by the marriage system. Surname exogamy was the strict rule in the area—and remains as strict today, for the Liaos at least—so that it was necessary for lineages to draw their wives from other surnames. For élite lineages, wives were to a large extent taken from other lineages of the élite. Of the 113 wives and concubines mentioned in the Liao genealogy, ninety-eight were of the nine surnames Teng, Hou, Wen, Ho, Huang, Cheng, Ts'ai, Yüan and Chang; and, while the villages of origin of the women are rarely given, there is no doubt in my mind (or in my informants') that they came from the villages of the élite lineages. None of the component genealogies has been brought up to date within at least the last thirty years, so

[22] 'Five Great Clans', pp. 31–2.

that the cross-Tou sample[23] may be taken as the pattern of traditional marriage. Table 16 demonstrates that there is little significant difference between the four Tou as regards marriage

TABLE 16

Tou and élite marriage according to the genealogy
(e = élite, o = others)

Tou	N		S		E		W		Lineage		
Wives	e	o	e	o	e	o	e	o	e	o	Total
Generation											
1	—	—	—	—	—	—	—	—	1	—	1
2	—	—	—	—	—	—	—	—	—	2	2
3	—	—	—	—	—	—	—	—	2	1	3
4	—	1	1	—	1	—	—	1	2	2	4
5	—	1	1	—	1	—	2	—	4	1	5
6	3	—	1	—	2	—	1	—	7	—	7
7	2	—	1	—	2	—	1	—	6	—	6
8	1	—	1	1	1	1	1	—	4	2	6
9	4	—	1	—	2	—	2	—	9	—	9
10	3	1	1	—	4	—	1	—	9	1	10
11	—	1	1	—	1	—	1	—	3	1	4
12	1	—	1	—	5	—	1	—	8	—	8
13	2	2	1	—	1	—	1	—	5	2	7
14	3	—	—	1	1	—	2	—	6	1	7
15	6	—	1	—	3	—	1	—	11	—	11
16	11	2	1	—	1	—	1	—	14	2	16
17	—	—	1	—	2	—	1	—	4	—	4
18	—	—	—	—	—	—	3	—	3	—	3
Total	36	8	13	2	27	1	19	1	98	15	113

[23] I was able to track down only four genealogies of the lineage, each of the four, by a coincidence which is perhaps not remarkable, detailing part of a different one of the four Tou. A rudimentary fifth genealogy (of part of the East Tou) is contained in Liao Shao-hsien, *op. cit.*, but not only is it skeletal, it is also wrongly headed 'Genealogical tree of the Third Branch'. No wives are noted in it.

with women from élite lineages, but it should be noted that the proportion of non-élite wives is slightly greater in the cases of the less wealthy, less successful North and South Tou.

If there is no significant difference between the Tou, then it is safe to take the one Tou on which there is a greater amount of information as representative of the pattern for the lineage as a whole. In Table 17 the results of analysis of the ancestral tablets in the Hsien Ch'eng T'ang (of the East Tou) have been added to those obtained from the genealogy, to give a breakdown by élite lineage and non-élite of 366 wives and concubines. It will be noted that a tenth élite lineage, the P'eng, has been added to the list compiled from the genealogy, it not having appeared in that sample. Addition of one more, the Chung lineage, would seem justified on grounds of frequency of occurrence of marriage with the Liaos, and indeed of wealth and quality of land-holdings, but for reasons which will become clear later, I have considered this lineage not to be of the élite. The last time that tablets were added to the Hsien Ch'eng T'ang was in 1923, so that the tablets complement the genealogical information in showing the traditional pattern of marriage.[24] This table makes it clear that the overwhelming majority of marriages (86 per cent.) were traditionally arranged with women of other élite lineages. (There seems to have been no significant differences between first marriage, second marriage and concubinage—all types were equally likely to come from the élite.)

Map III plots the villages of the élite in their geographical situation. Geographically, the area as a whole is made discrete by the hills and sea which surround it, but breaks down into three sub-areas served by different river systems. Politically, the area was a unity in its dependence on Sham Chun as an intermediate market and as the headquarters of the Tung P'ing Kuk. Map III and Table 17 in conjunction demonstrate the extent of élite lineage connections, and it has already been stated that these connections coincide with the Sham Chun intermediate marketing area.

But it is possible that the sample of wives, reasonably large though it is, is not a fair one. The majority of the data come from the tablets of the Hsien Ch'eng T'ang, and the qualifications

---

[24] Care has been taken to avoid counting twice those women whose names appear both on the tablets and in the genealogy.

TABLE 17

Elite and other marriage

| Gener- ation | New Territories | | | | Mainland | | | | | | Total | Others | Total |
	Teng	Hou	Wen	P'eng	Ho	Huang	Cheng	Ts'ai	Yüan	Chang			
1	—	1	—	—	—	—	—	—	—	—	1	—	1
2	—	—	—	—	—	—	—	—	—	—	—	2	2
3	1	1	—	—	—	—	—	—	—	—	2	1	3
4	—	—	—	—	—	—	2	—	—	—	2	2	4
5	1	—	1	—	1	1	—	—	—	—	4	2	6
6	5	—	—	—	—	1	—	1	1	—	8	—	8
7	4	1	1	—	—	1	—	1	—	—	8	—	8
8	4	—	1	—	1	1	—	—	—	—	7	2	9
9	5	1	1	—	1	3	1	—	—	—	12	—	12
10	9	1	2	—	—	4	—	1	1	—	18	3	21
11	2	—	—	—	1	2	2	—	—	—	7	5	12
12	13	1	1	—	—	3	1	—	—	—	19	4	23
13	27	1	1	—	1	2	—	4	—	—	36	4	40
14	25	3	2	—	2	4	1	—	1	—	38	4	42
15	9	2	7	1	3	2	2	3	5	4	38	4	42
16	19	5	6	4	3	5	1	5	3	10	61	7	68
17	10	1	3	7	1	4	3	—	2	6	37	9	46
18	2	—	1	—	—	2	2	1	2	3	13	2	15
19	1	—	—	—	—	1	—	—	—	2	4	—	4
Total	137	18	27	12	14	36	15	16	15	25	315	51	366

which ensured entry of a tablet into that hall were largely connected with wealth: that is, with the élite stratum of the élite lineage. To offset this there is the evidence of the genealogy, two of the lines of descent traced in it being by no means wealthy, and yet showing the same pattern of élite marriage. Freedman asks, "Is it not possible that in a highly differentiated lineage the marriages of the humbler families or segments will take a different direction from those of the more powerful and ambitious families or segments?"[25] I cannot give a categorical answer to this question, but, on the evidence of the genealogy and of the frequently expressed conviction of informants, I would suggest that the *majority* of lineage marriages were traditionally arranged with women of the intermediate marketing area élite, and that, therefore, it is possible to say that, by and large, in respect of marriage, social differentiation within a lineage was not of as much importance as social differentia-

[25] Freedman, *Lineage and Society*, p. 103.

KEY TO MAP III

No.	Village/Town	Lineage	Remarks
1	Ha Tsuen	Teng	
2	Ping Shan	Teng	
3	Yuen Long	Teng	
4	Kam Tin	Teng	
5	Tai Po Tau	Teng	
6	Lung Yeuk Tau	Teng	
7	Loi Tung	Teng	
8	Tai Hang	Wen	
9	San Tin	Wen	
10	Fanling	P'eng	
11	Ping Kong	Hou	
12	Kam Tsin	Hou	
13	Yin Kong	Hou	
14	Ho Sheung Heung	Hou	
15	Tai Om Shan etc	Chung	Not of the élite.
16	Sun Kong	Ho	
17	Mui Lam	Huang	
18	Sha Tau	Huang	
19	Fuk Tin	Huang	
20	Sheung Po	Cheng	Another Cheng lineage
21	Choi Uk Wai	Ts'ai	lived at San Tong?/Tsui
22	Lo Wu	Yüan	Tong? but I cannot locate
23	Heung Sai	Chang	this village.
24	Wu Pui	Chang	
25	Shui Pui	Chang	Exact location uncertain.
26	Wong Pui Ling	Chang	
27	Kong Ha	Wen	

tion between lineages. (The smallness of differentiation within the lineage sample which we have may be demonstrated by examining the marriages of the fifty-three of the 101 *kung-ming* of Figure 1 about whom such information is available. The fifty-three men between them had eighty wives and concubines. Of these, eight were of non-élite surnames. In contrast with this 10 per cent. non-élite figure, the non-élite wives for the remainder of the lineage—43 out of 286—made up 15 per cent. of the total. Table 17 yields a lineage-wide average of 14 per cent. of non-élite wives.)

The fact that it was the intermediate marketing area which determined the élite marriage area meant that it was not necessary for the Liaos to confine their wife-seeking to the immediate vicinity of the village, and it is clear from Table 17 that the closest élite lineages, that is, those with common borders with the Liao territory, were at best only averagely favoured in this respect. Indeed, it seems not unlikely that contiguous territories would cause lineages to tend to avoid marriage ties. Lineages in such a close territorial relationship were almost unavoidably in a state of rivalry, and were potential opponents in battle: such conditions could hardly be conducive to desire for marriage links. Where there were marriages between neighbouring élite lineages, a dispute could result in hardship and divided loyalties. A story is told in the village of one occasion when fighting was going on between the Liaos and the P'engs of Fanling: a Liao woman married to a P'eng was seen to be praying to Heaven (*T'ien*) for a 'double-headed victory' (*liang-t'ou-sheng*). It may be noted that the P'eng lineage which has a long common border with the Liao territory, is represented by fewer wives than any other of the surnames in Table 17. At the same time it is the one lineage with which the Liaos are said to have been in almost constant conflict. (Perhaps this explains the lack of P'eng wives for so many generations.) Similarly, when the Liaos were involved in a dispute with the combined Hou lineages in circa 1880, the latter used cannon to bombard Sheung Shui,[26] and it is said that a Hou woman married to a Liao smuggled spent cannon-

---

[26] One of the cannon still lies hidden in an ancestral hall of Kam Tsin, and an old hall in Sheung Shui still has a hole in the wall where (it is said) it was struck by a ball.

balls back to Kam Tsin for re-use. The stories are trivial, but their survival suggests that the difficulties of this kind of situation were appreciated, and therefore perhaps avoided, by neighbouring lineages.

The figures show a high percentage of inter-élite marriages right through the generations, but probably of greatest significance is the rise in proportion of non-élite wives in the 11th generation, followed by the increased percentage of élite wives thereafter. According to the dates as shown in Table 8, the 11th generation would have reached marriageable age roughly at the time when the lineage was evacuated from the area (1662–69)[27] and so was out of touch with the élite: hence, possibly, the greater number of marriages to other surnames. After the return to Sheung Shui, the Liaos, as has been suggested in Chapter One, must have been confirmed as a long-established élite lineage, in common with those other major lineages which had returned to their homes. The percentage of élite wives rose accordingly.

The Chang lineages were very rich and powerful. I cannot explain their failure to appear in the table before the 15th generation, though it is possible that their prosperity was a comparatively recent development. Certainly the Heung Sai lineage owned much land in the Ta Kwu Ling Valley, in the Tsiu Keng Valley, and even in the Sheung Shui/Fanling Plain. Two of the four plots of non-Liao owned land in D.D. 52 belonged to Changs, and the area of scattered Liao landholding immediately south of the territory was quite liberally sprinkled with Chang holdings. It is possible that distantly based élite lineages of this nature performed a buffer function between neighbouring élite lineages, not only in physical terms, by owning land between them, but also perhaps metaphorically, by using their interest in the area to give them a standing as mediators in disputes, but I have no information on this point. What is of significance is that many Changs fled into the New Territories as a result of the civil war in China in 1949, and that their wealth and, no doubt, their close relationship with the Liaos enabled them to gain a firm foothold in the rising town of Shek Wu Hui, where in 1965 a Chang was not only Chairman of the Sheung Shui District Rural Committee, but Chair-

[27] See above, pp. 30 and 42.

man of the Heung Yee Kuk too. According to one informant, a third of Shek Wu Hui now belongs to the Changs. (But not to a Chang *lineage*, of course, for it was as individuals that they came to the Colony.)

The most striking feature of Table 17 is the very large number of Teng women married into the lineage. The Tengs, as well as being the largest lineage group with the most settlements in the New Territories, were the most powerful and wealthy of its élite. Their long history has seen a marriage connection with the Imperial house of the Sung dynasty, and they boast the only *chin-shih* graduate of the New Territories.[28] According to the tablets of the Hsien Ch'eng T'ang, all of the Teng lineages have provided wives for the Liaos, but the majority of wives whose Teng lineage of origin is identified on the tablets came from Kam Tin, the original and largest of the lineages. The Tengs having an indisputable claim to the highest position among the New Territories élite, their numerous marriages with the Liaos give an indication of the important place which the latter also attained in the area. A further indication of the importance of the Tengs is that 45 per cent. of the wives of the 53 *kung-ming*, mentioned above, were Tengs, while only 35 per cent. of the remainder of the lineage wives were of this surname. Table 17 shows that an average 37 per cent. of lineage wives were Tengs.

That there was not a 'one-way system' of bride-taking is apparent from the few genealogies of other élite lineages which I have seen. Élite lineages in fact exchanged brides with each other. Thus, one genealogy of the Kam Tin Teng lineage shows thirteen Liao wives, two of them married to *kung-ming*;[29] a genealogy of the Teng lineages of Lung Yeuk Tau and Tai Po Tau gives ten Liao wives;[30] a Wen lineage genealogy from Tai Hang includes the names of twenty-one Liao wives;[31] and the

---

[28] For these and many other details of Kam Tin, the main settlement of the Tengs, see Sung Hok-p'ang, *op. cit.*, Pt. III, 'Kam Tin'.

[29] *Pao-an Chin-t'ien Teng-shih tsu-p'u*, MS, Kam Tin, Hong Kong, no date (c. 1920?). Unfortunately many wives are not given in this genealogy. The percentage of élite wives of those given, however, does not appear to be as high as that in the case of the Liaos.

[30] *(Teng) Yao-lin Chia-p'u*, MS, Tai Po Tau (?), Hong Kong, no date. Many wives came from the Wen lineage of Tai Hang.

[31] *T'ai-k'eng Wen-shih tsu-p'u*, MS, Tai Hang, Hong Kong, no date. A large number of wives came from the various Teng lineages.

genealogy of the Ho Sheung Heung Hou lineage yields three Liao wives.[32] From all these lineages it is known that the Liaos in turn took wives.

The pattern of marriage seems fairly clear. The élite of the Liaos were almost certain to marry women from other élite lineages. Many of the remainder of the Liaos followed the same pattern, perhaps utilising élite wives as bridges. Some, probably the poorest, would have found wives from lesser lineages and settlements in the smaller standard market area. Liao daughters would be married out following a similar pattern. The pattern was not in any way institutionalised or bound by rules. There seems in general to have been no bar on marriage either of men or women to Hakkas, for instance; and indeed the Chung lineages of Lam Tsuen, some of which were Hakka, certainly supplied wives to the Liaos, though I do not know whether Liao women were married to the Chungs. Similarly there seems, with one exception, to have been neither prohibition nor encouragement regarding marriage with particular lineages—in fact, if it is necessary to explain the traditional marriage area of the lineage, it is perhaps enough to say that the pattern which evolved out of historical accident (the juxtaposition of major lineages with common features of long settlement, wealth, and high prestige attainments) persisted and flourished because those features continued to be important, and because of precedent and of the ready-made contacts which precedent afforded.

The one exception to the rule of uninhibited choice of marriage partners was the Wen lineage village of San Tin. Almost every informant who talked of marriage to me mentioned this exception, or knew of it if I spoke of it. The Liaos did not in general marry with the Wens of this particular village, though they had many links with the closely related Wen lineage of Tai Hang. The reasons for the exception fell into two categories, one connected with the nature of the Wen men, and one with that of their land. According to the Liaos, the Wens were too fierce, too ignorant and too lawless to be married.

---

[32] *Hou Shan Hsing T'ang tsu-pu.* The early generations of this lineage do not seem to have married élite wives, but from the Yuan dynasty onwards the great majority of wives were from the élite. This genealogy is only very short and sketchy in nature.

We have already seen that they were engaged in a 'protection racket' directed against lesser lineages of the area,[33] and their genealogy throws fascinating sidelight on a mode of life which was consistently swashbuckling and violent. In 1851, at least one of their men was killed in battle (*hsieh-tou*) against the Hou village of Kam Tsin. In 1851 again, another man was killed when the Wens fought beside the Shap Pat Heung[34] of Yuen Long against the Tengs of Ping Shan, and in the same year yet another death resulted from the Wens helping the Tengs of Ha Tsuen, again against the Ping Shan Tengs. In 1862 cannon-fire killed one of their men in a battle in which San Tin were aiding their fellow Wens of Kong Ha.[35] Their genealogy is replete with such examples, with others of Wens dying in the Hsien gaol, with poisonings, with punishments by drowning, and so on. There was no doubt much truth in the accusations which my informants made.

Reference to Map III will give point to their criticism of the Wen land. Much of it is either marsh or recently reclaimed land,[36] and the Liaos claim that working such land is arduous, unrewarding and degrading, and that to marry their women into such 'slavery' would be a reflection on their pride.

The combination of violence and bad land is the apparent cause of an unusually large number of women *remarrying* out of San Tin after (and sometimes it seems even before) the death of their husbands.[37] Of the many hundreds of wives and concubines recorded in the Wen genealogy, only nine are Liaos. There was a corresponding dearth of Wen women married to Liao men, though, unless reciprocity of wife-giving was a requirement of the system, the reasons for this are not apparent. Strangely, no history of fighting between the Wens and the Liaos was known in Sheung Shui, the only comment of the old men being: "There must have been some." (The antipathy towards the Wens does not seem to have been felt

[33] See also 'Five Great Clans', p. 40.

[34] An alliance of villages (formed expressly to counteract Teng power in the area?).

[35] All these examples are taken from the *Wen-shih tsu-pu* (*hsia chüan*), MS, San Tin, Hong Kong, 1938.

[36] The western side of the New Territories is emergent, adding rapidly to the land area. See Grant, *op. cit.*, Fig. 1 (c).

[37] The *Wen-shih tsu-pu* records several tens of such cases. The *LSTP* records none for Sheung Shui.

by other élite lineages. The Tengs, for instance, are represented by at least sixty wives in the Wen genealogy.)

The traditional marriage pattern was not fixed and un-alterable, of course, and indeed Table 17 shows the tardy introduction of the Changs and the P'engs to the Liao marriage circle, but probably changes were only slight over the period from the return from evacuation in 1669 until the second quarter of the 20th century. The lease of the New Territories to Britain in 1898 made little or no difference to marriage patterns, because the border with China was an open one and did not interfere with the marketing patterns which the marriage patterns emulated. Indeed, it was not until the 1920s and 1930s that the effects of the propinquity of Hong Kong and its tentacles of communication, the railway and the roads, began to take a toll of the traditional orientations of the village. We have already seen, when considering leadership, that the period between 1899 and the Japanese occupation was one of adjustment to the influences of Hong Kong. This adjustment was aided by the disorders which rent the Chinese side of the border, where warlordism was rife, and where the Kuo Min Tang was gathering its strength for the northward march. It was no doubt largely because of the comparative good order on the British side that it was possible for the market of Shek Wu Hui to be restored to healthy life in 1925, dealing the first blow to the stability of the marriage pattern. With the Japanese occupation and the subsequent closure of the border with Communist China, the influence of Sham Chun as the centre of a market and marriage area was removed from the Liaos, and Shek Wu Hui and urban Hong Kong took pride of place.

The replacement of Sham Chun by Shek Wu Hui and the cities must itself have affected the traditional marriage pattern, but other factors connected with the political changes and with the re-orientation of the lineage also played parts in changing the pattern. The same change of government in China which led to the closure of the border caused a great wave of im-migration into the Colony, and the immigrants changed settlement patterns rapidly and drastically. Almost overnight Shek Wu Hui became a major population centre, and Sheung Shui and other villages were filled with immigrant tenants and robbed of physical discreteness by litters of temporary buildings which sprang up around them. The old pattern of settlement was swamped. Wealth tended increasingly to concentrate in the towns and cities. On a lineage-wide scale there was little which connections with other lineages could offer above those with any other group or class. Kinship as a basis of community organisation was fading from the scene. Lineages themselves became less important as their numerical dominance of the general population was lost, and as their fields were sold. In addition, the growing Westernisation of the lineage had been striking at another pillar of the traditional marriage pattern, the institution of arranged marriage. Young men and women who had received a modern education in the lineage's fine school and elsewhere were no longer content to have their marital future dictated to them by others. Marriage according to 'romantic love' and 'free choice' gradually became more important, until at the present it is the dominant form. This has had the result of bringing into being a new pattern of marriage. For the poor, the farmers, and those who work in the village or in Shek Wu Hui, the marriage area is limited to the standard market town, with the possibility of a wider choice according to the area from which school classmates are drawn.[38] For the rich, the well educated, and the businessman the cities provide a much wider field of choice. The whole Colony of Hong Kong has replaced the Sham Chun marketing area as the area from which wives of the élite may be drawn.

The questionnaire administered to households of the walled hamlet in 1965 attempted to provide statistical backing for the above general account of change in marriage patterns. The results, while broadly reflecting the account which has been given, are not as clear-cut as perhaps might have been expected. Ninety-one wives and concubines of Liaos gave the dates of their marriage, surname and village of origin. It is unfortunate that in many cases this last item of information was not given in specific enough terms for my purposes;[39] however, on the basis of surnames and general area of origin in such cases and of the full information supplied in the remainder, I have con-

[38] Some of the Fung Kai pupils came as much as twenty miles to the school.

[39] Terms such as 'Pao-an Hsien' (the more recent name for the old Hsin-an Hsien) or 'Sham Chun'—the latter apparently meant to describe all the Sham Chun Plain—were given in many cases.

structed Table 18, which must be taken as only a very rough indication of recent marriage patterns. It does seem to show that the 1920s and 1930s swung the pattern decisively away from the traditional, and that the effects of post-war events have been as indicated above. In the 1950–65 marriage category, the main figures are those for the élite of the New Territories only (i.e. those which were still available for marriage connections), the bracketed figures show the difference when wives by village of origin (but not of course by then place of residence) are included. Traditional connections die hard, and it appears that refugee members of élite lineages may, by virtue of old ties, still in many cases be married to Liaos. And, of course, many such refugees have settled in the Shek Wu Hui area—we have already seen the strength of the Changs in that town—and thus are now resident within the new marriage area.

TABLE 18
Recent marriage trends

Year of marriage	Numbers of wives	
	Élite	Others
1900–1910	5	2
1911–1920	5	3
1921–1930	5	7
1931–1940	12	14
1941–1950	10	12
1951–1965*	4 (9)	12 (7)
	41 (46)	50(45)

* In fact 1962 was the last date involved.

Information required concerning married Liao daughters by an oversight did not include date of marriage, but the results show a roughly similar ratio of non-élite to élite husbands, thirty-two and twenty-two respectively. Whereas only one Liao man had married a Hakka woman, seven Liao women were married to Hakkas: an interesting but as far as I know not particularly significant proportion.

III

Marriage relationships with other lineages seem to have made little difference to relationships of other kinds with those lineages (they were apparently no brake on inter-lineage disputes and fighting, for instance), but the marriage area did coincide with the area within which the lineage had external relationships of various kinds. Outside the Sham Chun marketing area virtually the only relationships which the lineage had were with the representatives of the Central Government at Nam Tau—and only the élite members of the lineage, the *kung-ming*, were involved personally in these relationships.

In an earlier section of this chapter I spoke of a 'balance of power' between lineages. The term was not used loosely: an important aspect of the external relationships of a lineage of the area was its alliances and enmities, traditional and *ad hoc*, the sum of which determined, and to a large extent kept stable, the broad outlines of its sphere of influence. From my observation of the Liaos and of other lineages it appears that alliances can be broadly divided into two types—those of weak lineages and non-lineage settlements, and those of the élite and strong lineages.

The most important characteristic which singled out the strong lineage was the ability consequent upon its wealth and numbers to be self-sufficient in land-holdings and defence—to have an inviolate territory and to be able to keep it. A secondary characteristic was the expansionist tendency which was the concomitant of the growth in wealth and numbers—a tendency 'given in the system'. But this tendency was common to all strong lineages (and indeed in some degree to all lineages), so that conflict must have arisen as expansionist interests clashed. Temporary alliances between lineages might be made in order to achieve an immediate bellical or territorial aim; or long-standing alliances might serve to offset the overweening strength of a neighbouring lineage. Enmities, of course, followed the same pattern, being either temporary (with a specific cause) or of long standing (where initial causes, right and wrong were of little account in a general welter of antagonism).

The traditional antagonists of the Liaos were the Hous, the P'engs and, to a lesser extent, the Tengs of Lung Yeuk Tau, the three lineage groups which barred the way to expansion of Liao territory. Indeed, if expansion was an essential part of lineage function, then strong lineages with territories must surely have been constantly antagonistic towards neighbours of their like. An alliance with a neighbouring strong lineage would have been a contradiction of expansionist tendencies. Certainly the Liaos seem never to have been allied with any of these three groups. The P'engs and the Tengs, whose territories were contiguous, were certainly at loggerheads, and the P'engs joined with the Wens of Tai Hang to oppose the Lung Yeuk Tau Tengs and the Tengs of Tai Po Tau (whose territory bordered that of the Wens) in the formation of the new Tai Po market in 1893.[40] Similarly, the Wens of San Tin and the Hous, whose territories touched, were constantly at odds—some examples have already been given. Indeed, it seems that the expansionism of powerful lineages was so strong that not even common agnatic descent could prevent antagonism between neighbouring powerful lineages. Thus, the Ha Tsuen Tengs were frequently fighting with their kinsmen of Ping Shan, as we have seen in connection with the Wens of San Tin in the previous section: and even the Hou lineages seem to have had their unity endangered by internal quarrelling.[41]

Strong neighbours could not be allies, but this did not mean that powerful lineages at a distance were necessarily allies, or that they were not occasionally fought with. The Liaos were in general on good terms with the Changs, but on one occasion ("about a hundred years ago", said my informants) an irrigation dispute arose with the Changs of Wong Pui Ling. A pitched battle was fought at Man Kam To (on the Sham Chun river, roughly midway between the two villages), from which the Liaos retreated to Sheung Shui, where at Red Bridge they had a position prepared complete with cannon loaded with grape-shot. The Changs, however, were by then reinforced by their kinsmen of Heung Sai and Wu Pui, and the Liaos judged it expedient to retire into the walled hamlet without further fighting. This retirement constituted recognition of defeat, the

[40] For some details see Groves, *op. cit.*

[41] In their village of Yin Kong stand two walls of an old ancestral hall. The Hou villagers said that it had been the main hall of the Hous, but that the other stronger Hou lineages had 'refused to allow it to be rebuilt' lest its *feng-shui* benefited Yin Kong at the expense of the other three villages.

Changs withdrew immediately, and the irrigation dispute was accordingly considered to have been resolved in their favour.

The above was the only instance of which I heard of actual fighting between the Liaos and more distant lineages, but alliances with other lineages and groups certainly existed. I have already mentioned that the Liaos were allied from time to time with the small settlements of the Tsiu Keng Valley. Further away still from Sheung Shui, and to the south-south-west, the villages of the Pat Heung alliance[42] lay at the upper end of the Kam Tin valley. The alliance was composed largely of small Hakka settlements, and came into being, so far as I can tell, in an attempt to counteract the great influence of the supremely powerful Teng lineage of Kam Tin. With this alliance the Liaos were closely associated, according to my informants, on the grounds that they themselves were originally Hakka. Common origin may have been one reason for the interest of the lineage, but it is perhaps no coincidence that the Pat Heung area covers the entrance to the pass through which an expanding Teng lineage might work its way towards the Tsiu Keng and Sheung Shui Valleys.

The Pat Heung alliance illustrates the difference between powerful and weak lineages, for it is an alliance of small lineages and settlements which are situated close together. Weak lineages, far from automatically repulsing their neighbours, were constrained to join with them as protection against more powerful lineages. In marriage ties they were confined no doubt to the standard marketing area; thus the whole range of their contacts and relationships operated within a small radius. Powerful lineages, on the other hand, as we have seen, tended to have few relationships in their immediate neighbourhood, but many outside it. Strong lineages could fight in their own defence and in offence: weak lineages had to content themselves with resignation to their impotence, or with a nominal revenge. During the last century the weak Lin lineage of Chek Mei were in dispute with the neighbouring Huangs of Kak Tin (= Fuk Tin?), for whom they were by no means a match. They came to the Liaos for assistance, but received neither the men nor the arms they sought, and were lent only some metal helmets.

[42] Not to be confused with the Shap Pat Heung alliance mentioned above.

Against the Huangs they probably had neither victory nor redress, but they did take a measure of revenge on the Liaos by not inviting the Liao unicorn dance team to their village the following New Year.

With more distant lineages relationships were much more changeable than with powerful neighbours, a generally peaceful atmosphere being occasionally broken by short-lived antagonisms. To this the only known exception was the relationship of the lineage with San Tin, which was one more of open indifference than hostility. The greater part of the lineage's antagonism was directed towards its nearest neighbours, the P'engs, Hous and Tengs. It could not have been, of course, that constant warfare reigned, the antagonism could only have occasionally shown itself in this way,[43] but rivalry was always present, manifesting itself in economic warfare (particularly over control of markets) and in conspicuous consumption.

I was told by men in a village situated roughly between Ho Sheung Heung and Kam Tsin (both Hou villages) that they still turned up with the plough many relics of an old market town called Kak Chun Hui, and many pieces of broken pottery, tiles, etc. were produced as proof. They claimed that this town had died about 300 years ago, but knew no more. The existence of the town, or at least of a village, on the site indicated is confirmed in the 1688 edition of the *Hsien-chih*, where 'Kak Chun Tsuen' is shown next to Ho Sheung Heung in the list of settlements.[44] The 1819 edition contains no mention of the place. If it is true that there was a market on the site, then the foundation of Shek Wu Hui must represent an economic victory for the Liaos over the Hous, for it is said to have been founded 300 years ago.[45] Revenues from markets were large, and we have seen that Shek Wu Hui even today, when its periodic market is fading in importance, yields some $70,000 per year. For the Liaos, who formerly received all its income, the market is no longer as profitable, only a one-third share remaining to them. The income is shared out thus:

---

[43] But it is said that until the last decade the youths of Sheung Shui and of the Hou lineages used to meet regularly at New Year to fight with stones over the border of their territorics.

[44] *HAHC 1688*, chüan 3, Tu-li.

[45] *Shih Hu Hsü, Ch'ung-chien, etc.*, Chairman's speech.

Sheung Shui Village	8/24
Sheung Shui Rural Committee	8/24
Sheung Shui St. John Ambulance Group	3/24
Sheung Shui Land Investment Company	1/24
Shek Wu Hui Chamber of Commerce	4/24

Quite how their share has been whittled down so much I did not discover, but suspect that it has to do with modernisation of market facilities over the last decade. The Hous, though they have used and still use the market, had and have no share in its income. It is probably true to say that, until recent changes made such rivalry rather less important, the Liaos were well ahead in the battle for economic success and consequent prestige.

The system of Rural Committees has divided the New Territories (somewhat arbitrarily in some cases) into separate areas. The P'engs and the Lung Yeuk Tau Tengs find themselves together in one district centred on Luen Wo Hui, and the Hous and the Liaos are together in another centred on Shek Wu Hui. Both pairs contain traditional enemies. In the case of Shek Wu Hui, the rivalry between the Liaos and the Hous shows itself only occasionally, and the only indication of it which I saw was during the 1964 celebrations of Shek Wu Hui's rebuilding. Both the Liaos and the Hous erected ceremonial arches for the occasion; each paid the same amount for its arch—$3,300; but the Liaos considered themselves the winners of the match, for, their arch partially blowing down on the day before it was due to be demolished, they received a rebate from the builder.

Traditionally one of the most important occasions for showing the strength of the lineage was at the autumn grave rites. By what is probably only a curious coincidence, the grave of the Liao first ancestor is in Hou territory, and the Hou first ancestor's grave is in Liao territory. (It seems far-fetched to postulate a system of 'hostage graves', but it might be a point worth investigating in other instances.) Both the Liaos and the Hous use the occasion to process in strength to the graves. The Liaos pass right alongside the Hou village of Kam Tsin, banners flying and roast pigs much in evidence. The Hous usually honour the Liao procession with a string of fire-crackers. The Hou procession does not pass quite so close to Sheung Shui, and seems largely to be ignored by the Liaos. When asked about the effects of inter-lineage strife on these processions, the old men of Sheung Shui denied that their procession had ever been interfered with; but there has certainly been trouble at some time in the past. The Hou first ancestor "is said to have been buried in the pine grove of Sheung Shui. He is the ancestor called Lin-yu who is buried in the right-hand tomb of Cho-feng's grave. His remains were dug up by mistake when the site was restored for Cho-feng, so his name was changed to Lin-yu; and . . . because we were in a legal dispute with the Liaos over the Kam Tsin village territory, the names of the first ancestor and his wife were put upon silver plaques which were buried together beside Kam Tsin village . . . where now they are lost and so not worshipped."[46] The account is not clear, but obviously at one stage the Hous found themselves unable to go to the grave because of Liao interference. Whether or not the Liaos were similarly prevented from worshipping must have depended on the relative power of the Hous and the Liaos at that time.

The grave of Chung-chieh's son lies in an area of mixed ownership, where the P'eng lineage has not been strong enough to push its territory to its geographical limit. The Liao procession on the second day of the Ch'ung Yang celebrations passes the P'eng village of Fanling on its way to this grave. Again, the lineage must gain face by its display of wealth and numbers. The Tengs of the Lung Yeuk Tau complex might also have been expected to watch the procession, which passes not far from them. In 1963, Liao women married to P'engs provided tea for the procession as it returned from the grave, and this was not, I know, the first occasion on which it had happened. I suspect, however, that the institution was a fairly recent one, probably starting after the war. In 1964, the women did not provide tea, and the packets of roast pork which had been prepared for them as a gift were carried back to Sheung Shui. Little was said about the omission, and I detected no more serious feelings than ones of slight disappointment and mild surprise.

On both days of these grave rites the processions pass

[46] *Hou Shan Hsing T'ang tsu-pu*, Biography of first ancestor.

through Shek Wu Hui. Wealthy Liaos resident in the town, or with businesses there, greet them with long strings of fire-crackers, the largest outside the shop of the chief Village Headman. Shek Wu Hui is left in no doubt about the wealth of the Liaos, their circuitous route being marked by one long chain of noise and smoke. None other of the local strong lineages can boast such a procession or such a reception.

The Liaos were known throughout the New Territories (and in parts at least of the Sham Chun Plain, if not in the whole of the market area) for their unicorn dance team. During the first month of each lunar year a team of about one hundred young men would tour the area giving performances at any village which would feed them and give them shelter for the night. In the Village Council Hall are some scrolls presented to the team by the community of the island of Cheung Chau over twenty miles to the south. The tours finished in about 1960, when the number of young men available for and willing to take part in the team had fallen too low. In any event the tours would probably have ceased, where the prestige of a lineage is no longer of much account in a society which increasingly adopts modern urban values.

IV

In two exceptional cases the Liaos joined forces with neigh-bouring lineages irrespective of traditional enmity or friend-ship in the face of an external threat to or stimulus acting on the geographical area as a whole.

In Chapter One the existence of a temple-owning group of élite lineages was mentioned. After the evacuees had returned to their homes in the coastal strip in 1669, temples were founded in many places to house the images of the two deified officials who had been instrumental in bringing about their return—Chou Yu-te, Governor General of Kwangtung and Kwangsi, and Wang Lai-jen, Governor of Kwangtung. The *Hsien-chih* of 1819 mentions three such temples under the name Wang Hsün-fu Tz'u (Temples to Governor Wang)—one at Sai Heung, one at Sha Tau Hui, and the third at Shek Wu Hui.[47] In addition, both the men were deified in the Ming Huan Tz'u

[47] *HAHC 1819*, chüan 7, Temples.

(Temple to Famous Officials) in the Hsien capital, Nam Tau.[48] Apparently none of these deifications had taken place by 1688, for I found no trace of them in the *Hsien-chih* of that year. The three temples mentioned in the 1819 edition are not an exhaustive list, for there still survives a fourth one at Kam Tin,[49] and it is said that another lies just over the Anglo-Chinese border in Sha Tau Kok (but this may be a confusion with the Sha Tau one). I do not know whether Sham Chun was in fact evacuated, but the temples seem to have been built for the use of areas smaller than the intermediate marketing sphere.

The Shek Wu Hui temple was burned down in 1955, and has not yet been rebuilt. It is not certain when it was first built, nor by whom, but it seems likely that the Liaos, the Hous and the Lung Yeuk Tau Tengs were the prime movers in its foundation, and most of the land with which the temple was endowed was under the managership of these three surnames in 1906. At the same time the Tengs of Tai Po Tau, the P'engs, and the Wens of San Tin and Tai Hang apparently had an interest in it too. It is hardly possible to be more definite than this. In a dispute over the temple property in 1960, the former group clashed with the latter over the rights to management of the property and to receipt and control of its income. Government arbitration eventually found in favour of the combined group, and arranged for formal registration of the temple and its land in the name of the Chau Wong Yee Yuen Limited.[50] The first board of directors consisted of four Liaos, two P'engs, three Tengs, three Wens and two Hous.[51] The membership of the Company is open to any member of twenty-one years of age and over of the Liao Wan Shih T'ang, the Liao Yün Sheng T'ang, the P'engs, the Tengs of Lung Yeuk Tau, the Wens of Tai Hang, the Tengs of Tai Po Tau, the Hous, and the Wens of San Tin.[52] The Liaos, it will be seen, had and have a double share in the temple: informants said that the Yün Sheng T'ang bought the

[48] *Ibid.*

[49] See 'Five Great Clans', p. 38 and notes.

[50] I am most grateful to the New Territories Administration for permission to see their files on the dispute. I have refrained from giving more details of it for fear of abusing this confidence, but a little more information (not taken from this source) may be found in 'Five Great Clans'.

[51] Wong, Peter C., and Co., *Memorandum and Articles of Association of Chan Wong Yee Yuen Limited*, Hong Kong, 1963, p. 17.

[52] *Ibid.*, p. 12. The lineages are all given under their T'ang names.

share of the Wens, who had been founder members, and certainly the only land record of 1906 which I found to be different from the above pattern showed the existence of two lots of land with a Wen as co-manager with men of the other three surnames.

The grouping of these joint owners is interesting, for they are spread geographically over three standard marketing areas. In marketing area terms only the first of the contending groups in the dispute makes a cohesive unit, and on these grounds there would seem to be justification for its claim to ownership of the temple (after all, it was built for people to worship in, and if the other lineages did not use the market, they would have had no chance to worship there). But there was a complication of groupings involved. The semi-official administrative area, the Sheung U Tung, included all the above lineages, with the possible exception of the Wens of San Tin.[53] Certainly the *kung-ming* of the lineages were the ones who ran the temple—"the gentry of all these surnames meet for worship and feasting on the first day of the sixth lunar month"[54]—and these would also have been implicated in the semi-official administrative system.

The significant point is that these powerful lineages were able to subjugate their differences and rivalries to found the temple, and, furthermore, to keep it alive over a period of probably some 250 years; and it was these same lineages which composed the élite of the area. Ownership of the temple was in fact a mark of superiority, at once proving the long history and the wealth of the five surnames. (It is because they were not members of this temple-owning group that I did not consider the Chung lineage of Lam Tsuen as élite. Moreover, I suspect that the strong connections between the Chungs and the Liaos might have been owing to Liao recognition of their Hakka origin, and that the Chungs did not marry so freely with others of the élite lineages.)

The second instance in which the Liaos co-operated with other powerful lineages of the area is connected with the

----

[53] *Lockhart Report 1898*, pp. 58–9. But in *Extension Despatches*, Colonial Secretary to Governor, 26th April 1899, this village too is put in the Sheung U Tung.

[54] *Hsin-yüeh-hui shen-tan: Lung Yüeh T'ou ts'e*, MS, no date, Preamble.

O

assumption of control of the New Territories by the British in 1899. The first resistance to the British was offered apparently by the villagers of the Tai Po Tsat Yeuk alliance[55] (the organisation, including the Tai Hang Wens and the P'engs, which built and controlled the new Tai Po market) in whose area the flag-hoisting party landed. Later resistance was organised mainly by the Tengs, first at Ping Shan and then at Ha Tsuen,[56] and implicated the Kam Tin Tengs, the Pat Heung alliance, the Liaos, the P'engs, the Tai Po Tau Tengs, the Hous, and the Wens of Tai Hang and San Tin.[57] These in turn attempted to bring in other lineages; and the Liaos, it is known from captured letters, sent to the Changs of Wong Pui Ling, Wu Pui, and Heung Sai, to the Yüans of Lo Wu, to the Ts'ais of Choi Uk Wai, to the Chengs of Sheung Po and the Huangs of Sha Tau, as well as to two other settlements not on the élite list which has been given.[58] Thus an attempt was made to bring in on the side of the affected lineages many of those other élite lineages which were connected with them in the Sham Chun marketing area. Partially at least this attempt was successful, for it is known that men from Sha Tau and Sham Chun (as well, surprisingly, as from Tungkwan Hsien) took part in the resistance.[59] Significantly, all communication was in the hands of the *kung-ming*, and the resistance was organised along the lines of the semi-official administrative system, the Tungs ('divisions') of Sheung U (meeting in the Chau Wong Temple in Shek Wu Hui) and Yuen Long leading the way, but reporting to and conferring with the Tung P'ing Kuk in Sham Chun.[60]

From these two instances of inter-lineage co-operation it is plain that in exceptional circumstances rivalry could be set aside. The machinery for co-operation existed in the semi-official administrative system, which paralleled the marketing system in hierarchical form, but which was split into different

[55] *Extension Despatches*, Colonial Secretary to Governor, 5th April 1899, and 17th April 1899.

[56] *Ibid.*, 24th April 1899.

[57] *Ibid.*, and 'Translation of written statement of NG K'i-cheung', dated 21st April 1899.

[58] *Ibid.*, Colonial Secretary to Governor, 11th May 1899, Enclosure No. 1.

[59] *Ibid.*, 'Statement of NG K'i-cheung'.

[60] *Ibid.*, Colonial Secretary to Governor, 11th May 1899, Enclosure No. 1.

geographical divisions. This difference no doubt made easier the process of mediation, for *kung-ming* members of the same division but of different standard marketing areas could take the lead in talking peace and co-operation to lineages which were opposed under both systems.

But under the semi-official system, no less than under the market system, the large élite lineages were at an advantage, for in the majority of cases it would have been only these lineages which were capable of producing *kung-ming* (who alone were eligible to sit on the councils). The Chau Wong Yee Yuen was entirely owned and run by élite lineages. The opposition to the British was almost all in the hands of the élite lineages, and the only non-élite represented were those lesser settlements which had managed to band themselves together in alliances such as the Pat Heung. No wonder that, as the small all-conquering British force strolled blustering through the New Territories, "the elders of the small villages expressed a hope that they would be specially protected from the bullying they have been experiencing from large villages".[61]

V

Traditionally the external relationships of the lineage were for the most part with the other large lineages of the area, but in small degree there was contact with the government too. Land transactions were supposed to be registered with the Hsien Government in Nam Tau (though not all were),[62] and it was from Nam Tau that the official legal system reached down to touch village affairs. The lineage was represented at the Hsien level by its *kung-ming*, who are said to have been the only ones ever to go to Nam Tau on official business; but much of what would have been official business was probably absorbed by the semi-official system, which (supposing Lockhart's account to be correct) in itself was virtually a representation in council form of the large lineages of the area.

After the British leased the New Territories the village was much more closely affected by Government. All land was

[61] *Ibid.*, Colonial Secretary to Governor, 26th April 1899.
[62] See Hayes, J. W., 'The Pattern of Life in the New Territories in 1898', *JHKBRAS*, Vol. II, 1962, p. 96.

required to be registered afresh and all sales and mortgages to be declared thereafter. Police stations were built in strategic spots, one of them on the outskirts of Sheung Shui. The District Officers were found to be approachable and prepared to undertake almost any task of arbitration or mediation without partiality or venality. Furthermore, it was open to all, influential or humble, to go to the District Office and to receive attention. From the days of the *kung-ming* monopoly of government attention this was a far cry, but after the Japanese occupation and the great increase in population of and activity in the New Territories, the District Officers became less approachable and lost their judicial function. The ordinary villager may still take his own problems to the District Office, but he probably finds it easier to ask his Village Representative (Headman) to do it for him, and thus to save himself time and puzzling over unfamiliar forms and procedures.

The Sheung Shui representatives, and in particular the Chief Headman, who is the most active and mobile of them, are as far as I know diligent in fulfilling this part of their task, so that the lineage is well served in its relationships with Government. (But whether the outsiders in the village receive as good attention is a matter for doubt, my own impression being that they do not ask for the help of the Headmen for fear that it should be refused or given only for a consideration.) The Village Headmen not only, as we have seen in a previous chapter, are of the same type as the old *kung-ming*, but they may now be seen to parallel the *kung-ming* in function as well, for if their member-ship of the Rural Committee and the Heung Yee Kuk is the counterpart of the *kung-ming* membership of Tung council and the Tung P'ing Kuk, their growing monopoly of the District Office traffic certainly begins to parallel *kung-ming* exclusiveness with regard to the Hsien yamen at Nam Tau.

VI

The many Teng lineages which inhabit the New Territories not only claim and show proof of common descent from a first ancestor in the Sung dynasty, they also keep alive and give expression to their ties of common origin through combined ceremonies of worship of their early ancestors. The Liaos, on the other hand, stand alone and have no kinship-ritual ties outside the village, despite the existence of two other Liao lineages in the New Territories.

The first of these is about 300 strong and lives in two neighbouring villages (Wu Kai Sha and Cheung Muk Tau, but mainly in the former) on the north-western shores of the Sai Kung peninsula. Neither of the villages is exclusive to the lineage. The Liaos of Sheung Shui barely knew of the existence of this lineage, and claimed that there was no demonstrable kinship between them, they were just of the same surname. I visited both Wu Kai Sha and Cheung Muk Tau, and had a long conversation with the Village Representative of the former on another occasion. Their oral history (they have no genealogy) holds that either "several hundred years ago" or "a hundred or so years ago" (depending on which of the versions I heard is to be believed—I incline towards the latter) their first ancestor, his wife and three sons came down to the area from another part of Kwangtung Province. They went first to Sheung Shui, where the wife and two younger sons settled down, [63] the eldest son accompanying his father to found Wu Kai Sha. Tenuous links with Sheung Shui were maintained and, until some eighty years ago, Wu Kai Sha sent representatives to the Autumn Rites of Sheung Shui—a kinship-ritual tie of a weak kind. The tie was allowed to lapse and has never been remade.

Differences between this lineage and the Sheung Shui Liaos are great. The Wu Kai Sha Liaos have no genealogy, no ancestral hall, no communally owned land (no Tsu or T'ang), no Lineage Headman, and no detailed knowledge of their ancestors (all tablets are of the 'all our ancestors' type). They come together as a lineage on one occasion only each year, when men, women and children go to worship at the grave of their first ancestor. The organising of this ceremony rotates annually among the three branches of the lineage, but the cost of it is met by donations from the entire lineage. The name of the first ancestor is known (I am not sure which of the two versions of the name I was given is correct), but I suspect that the names and generation numbers of the three branch focal ancestors are not known. Nor do the living seem to know to

[63] I found no trace of them, but it is possible that the sons were adopted into the lineage.

which generation they belong, though the Village Representative claimed to be of the 14th generation. Poorly landed, lineage organisation has not developed from the simple form which characterises the behaviour of very minor kinship groups in Sheung Shui, who also tend to rotate organisation of worship *per stirpes* among the immediate descendants of a recently dead trust-less ancestor. The lineage has probably only survived because it is in a remote area of the New Territories.[64] Such a poor lineage can have had nothing to offer Sheung Shui,[65] and its remoteness no doubt contributed to the withering of the initial tie.[66]

The other Liao lineage is a very different case. In 1929 a small group of Hakkas surnamed Liao came to the New Territories from Waichow in Kwangtung Province, having fled the depredations of Kuo Min Tang soldiery in the area, according to their descendants. They lived first on the other side of Shek Wu Hui, but quickly made themselves known to the Sheung Shui Liaos, who recognised them as kin on the basis of the genealogy which the newcomers produced showing a common ancestor in Liao Min of the 23rd generation from Tzu-chang according to the Sheung Shui genealogy (but of the 21st generation according to the other one).[67] This common ancestor almost certainly lived at least as long ago as the Sung dynasty, and the immigrants were Hakka, but neither of these facts seems to have prevented the claiming or recognition of kinship, an indication of the strength of the Sheung Shui belief in their Hakka origin.

The result of this recognition was the presentation by the Sheung Shui Liaos of land within their territory to the Hakkas, who built a village, called Wa Shan Tsuen (marked 'E' on

[64] Communication with it is impossible without a boat or a very arduous hill walk.

[65] There was no connection between this lineage and the areas of the Sai Kung Peninsula where Sheung Shui owned land, as far as I know.

[66] Without evidence, I suspect that Wu Kai Sha's standard market was Taipo, but that its intermediate market may have been reached by sea to the north-east, thus effectually cutting it off from Sheung Shui in this respect too.

[67] The two genealogies, while basically similar, show many differences. In this case the Sheung Shui genealogy inserts three blanks for the generations between the 16th and the 20th, but the other version inserts one generation between the 11th and 12th and has no blank spaces.

Map II) to the north-east of Sheung Shui. The granting of this land, and especially of land within the territory, must be considered a highly anomalous action on the part of the lineage. True the land was not of good quality, being too near the hills and yet subject to summer flooding, but why was not the same privilege extended to the ancestors of the Wu Kai Sha Liaos when they came to the area? The only possible clue which I obtained to the reason was the presentation of a large sum of money to the foundation of the Fung Kai school in 1932 by one of the Hakka Liaos. He had apparently won a considerable amount in one of the *pai-ke-piao* lotteries, for which at that time Sham Chun was the centre, and it is I suppose conceivable that the land grant was a condition of or return for the donation of the money to the school. (His photograph is among those of the other benefactors in the Wan Shih T'ang.) I was unable to discover the details of the transaction. The Wa Shan Liaos (second generation) were not themselves clear about them, knowing only that the land had been given and that the main benefactor was a particular man of the Third Branch, but this man's son knew no more details than that his father had given land. I understood from Wa Shan that the lineage as a whole had given some of the land, but hearing no corroboration of this from Sheung Shui I must doubt it. In short, the reasons for the grant are obscure.

The Wa Shan Liaos said that they were six families when they arrived in 1929. They have flourished in their new surroundings and have bought more land in the area. Some 200 Liaos, still speaking Hakka, now live in Wa Shan Tsuen, the majority of them remaining farmers. Their genealogy gives no indication of the kin-relationship of these six families one to another, and has not in fact been brought up to date since 1943, at which time the only entry made was to record the biography of the man who "uprooted his family and moved from Hsia Ching in Hui Yang to live in Wa Shan",[68] but it seems that this man is to be treated as the founding ancestor of a Wa Shan lineage, whether or not he was the biological ancestor of all the Hakka Liaos of the village. The two ancestral halls were destroyed by typhoons before I arrived in the field.

The increase in size and cohesion of this Wa Shan community

[68] (*Hua Shan*) *Liao-shih tsu-p'u*, Biography 21st generation.

apparently affected the Sheung Shui Liaos no more than did the original grant of land. The Hakkas do not seem to have been placed in any strong kind of superior-inferior relationship with Sheung Shui, though it might be expected that they would side with the Cantonese Liaos in the event of disputes, and they are almost certain to vote with Sheung Shui in Rural Council matters. No kinship-ritual ties have been created between the two lineages, the Hakkas, as far as I know, not even sending a representative to the Spring Rites in the Wan Shih T'ang, despite the existence there of the tablet of Liao Min,[69] the ancestor who marks the juncture of the two ancestral lines. The only contacts which I found between the two villages was at the Village Representative level, where the Sheung Shui Village Headman was seen to lend his experience to a Wa Shan scheme to build a junior school and a road to their village.

With the Wu Kai Sha and the Wa Shan Tsuen Liaos, then, Sheung Shui is not particularly intimate, in spite of the close proximity of the latter. In both cases unconcern succeeded an initial display of warmth. The same sequence of attitudes has occurred in Sheung Shui's connection with a third organised body of Liaos, the Liao Surname Association (*Liao-shih tsung-ch'in tsung-hui*). When in 1955 this Association was formed in Kowloon, many of the leading members of the lineage were involved in its organisation. The Association had ambitious plans, bought rooms for a meeting place, tried to build its own school, set up welfare committees, produced a printed brochure in 1960,[70] and began to make contacts with similar associations elsewhere.[71]

Over 300 men and women from Sheung Shui joined the Association, paying a $5 joining fee and a monthly $1 membership fee. The majority of the 300 were elderly, attracted by the Coffin Club (*Ch'ang-shou-hui*) to which members automatically belonged. The Club was to provide a sum of $500 upon the death of any member, but I was told that it soon began defaulting on the payments, and that Sheung Shui rapidly lost interest in the Association, which had little else to offer members

---

[69] One of the six pre-Chung-chieh tablets.

[70] See Liao Shao-hsien *et al.*, *op. cit.*, for many details.

[71] See Chiang Wan-che *et al.* (eds.), *Chang Liao Shih tsu-p'u*, Taiwan, 1965, pp. B. 3–5.

of a large, wealthy, settled community. In 1965 it was estimated that only about sixty Sheung Shui people were left in the Association. For its part, the Association has not allowed contacts with the lineage to lapse, and there are regularly ten or more Association members present at the Sheung Shui Spring and Autumn Rites, some of them in an official capacity, some by their own desire. But up to the present at least, this kinship-ritual tie is of the weakest nature, for the Association members are there on sufferance as guests of the lineage, not by right as co-authors and co-financers of the ceremonies.

CHAPTER EIGHT

The Process of Change

I

Description of the lineage in the preceding chapters has perhaps given the impression of a virtually static and unchanging institution set in an equally immutable society. It would be wrong to suppose that the lineage either in its internal organisation or in its external relationships was ever constant; none the less, from the return from evacuation in 1669 until the leasing of the New Territories in 1898, change was apparently in degree rather than in kind—that is to say, the lineage may have seen changes in its internal balance, as wealth and fertility saw fit to confer their favours, and its position of power in relation to the outside world may have fluctuated from time to time, but in large it still retained the same attributes of internal organisation and it still pursued the same policies of aggrandisement which were determined by its standing as a single-lineage settlement in a wider society which continued to be composed primarily of other similar settlements.

It is not possible to detail this change in degree, for there is no real evidence to draw on. In general though, the lineage must have grown steadily more powerful, until the first half of the 19th century saw its greatest academic successes, and, judging by the amount of building and restoration which is known to have taken place then, probably its greatest wealth too. The greatly disturbed second half of that century was not necessarily worse for the Liaos than for the area in general, but certainly there seems to have been a decrease in scholastic successes. As regards wealth and power, it is not easy to say whether the lineage was expanding or losing during this period. My impression is that, in the local situation, it was probably benefiting from the decline of its neighbour the Lung Yeuk Tau Teng lineage, and perhaps too from the weakening powers of the Hou Ping Kong lineage.[1] In any event, change in degree fades into unimportance beside the change in kind which has taken place since 1898.

The leasing of the New Territories brought the lineage for the first time into direct contact with the West. It is probable that a few men had found their way to the cities of Hong Kong and Kowloon before 1898, but a small trickle of men began to flow out of the village in search of work when once communications had made the cities more accessible. The majority of these seem to have found work as seamen, signing on with ocean-going ships calling at Hong Kong, but some worked in the cities themselves.[2] It was typical of this early emigration from the village that it was temporary and confined to males—the men left their families in the village and themselves expected to return to the village either on retirement or, perhaps, on acquisition of wealth—and, since the numbers involved were small, the lineage was not radically affected by the change, beyond an increase in wealth.

The revivification of Shek Wu Hui in 1925 may be seen to be a result of differences between the two sides of the Anglo-Chinese border. Disorders on the Chinese side probably made marketing in Sham Chun both unpleasant and unsafe, so that the relatively peaceful Hong Kong side became better patronised. Further, the good communications which by this time Shek Wu Hui had with the cities by road and rail no doubt contributed to its increasing independence of Sham Chun. The revivification, in fact, may be taken as a stage in the gradual re-orientation towards Hong Kong of the village and of the greater part of the New Territories. Increased rents for the land on which the market was built and on which housing sprang up, plus the new and expanded commercial opportunities which were opened to lineage members, meant a higher income and diversified employment for the Liaos. Some members of the

[1] An exhaustive (and exhausting) perusal of the 1906 land records might possibly reveal information on the crescent or decrescent state of the various lineages at the time through the details of mortgaging of land which are often given.

[2] The son of the donor of land to Wa Shan Tsuen ran a restaurant in Kowloon until his retirement a few years ago. I am sad to say he has died since I left the village.

lineage took up residence in Shek Wu Hui, but, it being so close to the village, they did not lose their contacts with the lineage, in most cases probably maintaining their village houses as well as the new town premises.[3]

The opening of the Western-oriented Fung Kai School in the Wan Shih T'ang in 1932 laid the foundations for later educational changes which affected the lineage drastically, but until after the war the standard of education offered was not high enough to have this effect. A few students, however, did graduate from the school to higher establishments, and in one case at least this removed a man completely from the lineage sphere of influence.[4]

The Japanese occupation was another factor setting the stage for drastic change. The three years were hard ones for the lineage, and through scarcity of food and luxuries many of the traditional ritual observances lapsed, while those which were retained were truncated and simplified. This period accustomed the villagers to change, breaking the continuity of tradition: at the same time the reduction in number and complexity of religious ceremonies deprived the Liaos of some of the customary outlets for surplus income. It was perhaps the most important harbinger of far-reaching change, change which finally came in with the tide of immigration in the late 1940s and 1950s.

The immigration caused by civil strife in China coincided with the opening up of opportunities for Chinese workers overseas, and particularly with the boom in the Chinese restaurant trade in Britain and Western Europe. Lineage members, like other indigenous New Territories people, were eligible for British passports, since they were born in British territory, and consequently they had no difficulty in getting overseas to engage in this trade. (Immigrants, who had not this advantage and who were for the most part without passports of any kind, were seldom able to win entry to overseas territories.) Estimates of

[3] A pattern of plural marriage emerged whereby the first wife lived in the village and a concubine in the market town, and this is still fairly common today, but of course it was by no means the invariable rule.

[4] I refer to the present headmaster of the school, who became a graduate of a Shanghai university, and afterwards taught in a school in Kowloon, being away from the village for over thirty years until accepting the headmastership in the 1960s.

numbers of Liaos working overseas ranged from 100 to over 200, the latter being, I believe, nearer the truth. For the most part it has been the young men who have been attracted to this employment, and in general they have left their families in the village, sending back remittances regularly to support them. Such a system *per se* does not necessarily affect lineage solidarity adversely, for it does not remove the men permanently from the lineage, but that it has had such an effect will be seen below. Moreover, there has of recent years been a tendency for men to send for their wives and families to join them overseas, and if this should become the general rule it will add substantially to the decline of the lineage.

The vegetable-growing revolution which succeeded the wide-scale immigration rapidly affected Sheung Shui. In material respects it has been of service to the lineage, for Liaos have been able to rent out (or in some cases to sell) their land to immigrant vegetable farmers very profitably—vegetables paying much better than rice at this time—and themselves to take other employment either in the cities or in Shek Wu Hui. And where men were in any case going overseas and into other employment, the land would otherwise have lain idle. The boom of Shek Wu Hui, which was another effect of immigration, also aided the Liaos materially, for not only did their holdings in and around the town rise in value, but greater commercial opportunities were opened to them, and they were able to rent out any spare accommodation which they had in the village. Without evidence other than informants' words, I feel secure in saying that incomes and standards of living have risen considerably for the Liaos since 1949.

II

Material prosperity, the influence of the West, and the swamping effect of immigration have combined to set in motion a process of deterioration which threatens to annihilate the lineage as an effective unit of social organisation.

The wealth of the lineage made possible the building and expansion of the new Fung Kai School. The standard of education offered by the school is so high that the students are educated beyond what is necessary for any work in the village, so that the education which the lineage provides is forcing those for whom it is provided to leave the lineage in search of work elsewhere. Worse, those who take fullest advantage of this education are of course the brightest students, so that the lineage is losing the cream of its youth to the outside world. But not only does this education cause the students to look elsewhere for work, in its orientation it is Western and urban, and it is these values which are adopted by many of the students, with the result that they tend to despise lineage and rural life. Once exposed to the materialism and cynicism of urban life, they quickly learn to look on their village friends and relations as 'country bumpkins' (ta-hsiang-li), and accordingly diminish their contacts with the village. Rejecting arranged marriage, they find their own marriage partners in the cities, and, since these too are for the most part urban-oriented, the break with village and lineage becomes more certain. Paradoxically, those who have left the village for work elsewhere in the Colony are more often lost to the lineage than those who have gone overseas, for the latter have for the most part remained village-based through the families which they have left there.

The movement away from working the land, which has been seen to have contributed materially to the prosperity of the Liaos, has at the same time been a movement towards urban occupations, and the attitudes which these engender have just been detailed. Moreover, urban occupations tend to be strictly regulated by time, and to run throughout the year. The lineage and village way of life, with ceremonies held at all times of day, and with important ritual occasions timed for those seasons of the year when rice farmers are at leisure, is not consonant with a wage-earning economy, where individuals cannot afford or beg the time for such events.

Ritual, already truncated by economic hardship during the Japanese occupation, has been no better served by material prosperity. Not only has wage-earning deprived individuals of much opportunity to engage in ritual observances, but the growing materialism and opportunities for investment of capital have succeeded in diverting money which erstwhile would have been spent on ritual. There is a growing feeling that money spent on expensive ritual ceremonies is money wasted.

III

In the kinship-ritual sphere there has been a steady deterioration in observance of traditional forms and ceremonies, and since kinship and ritual are in this case mutually reinforcing, it follows that a decline in one must affect the other—a blow to ritual is a blow to kinship solidarity.

The use of an extensive kinship terminology is dying. Young people educated in the school have little time or inclination to worry over precise degrees of relationship, and in any case their increasing concern with the outside world prevents their having the same wide circle of acquaintance amongst kin in the village that their parents had. My next-door neighbour's 16-year-old son knew a much narrower range of terms than his father, and, while youth may have been a factor in his ignorance, it was my impression that he was typical of the whole younger generation. Even the Village Headman, who was in his forties, laid himself open to public rebuke at a meeting by innocently using a wrong term of address to an older man of the lineage. (The rebuke raised laughter from most men present, and dismayed the Headman not at all.)

Adoption rules have been relaxed, as demonstrated in an earlier chapter, and it is now easy to adopt almost anyone as a son. In some measure this is probably owing to the breakdown of the old stable society, where it was comparatively simple to check on the birth and ancestry of any local man. The mass of immigrants in the area now have cut themselves off from their pasts, and almost any one of them might pass as a Liao for the purposes of adoption.

Generation names (*p'ai-ming*) are now the exception rather than the rule (certainly in any sphere wider than the children of one father), though the genealogy seems to indicate that they were never of great significance in the lineage.[5] Similarly, there no longer seems to be care taken that the same name should not be given to more than one member of the lineage. Some names recur not only where an ancestor and a living member have the same name, but even where more than one living member bears it.

[5] By contrast, the genealogy of the Wa Shan Tsuen Liaos uses them consistently throughout.

Ritual ceremonies are short and badly attended. Only nine people were present at the Spring Rites of the Hsien Ch'eng T'ang in 1965. The combined Autumn Grave Rites of three important ancestors of the East Tou (including the geomancer who was responsible for the unification of the lineage) were attended in 1964 by about forty of the eligible men of 51 years and over, no more than four or five of whom bothered even to watch the ceremony (which lasted a total of only 6½ minutes, divided between two separate graves), the rest talking or sleeping while they waited for the graveside feast to be prepared. Even the lure of the feast is no longer so effective, where meat is now a common item of diet for nearly all.

Ritual constantly loses ground to more material considerations. The Wan Shih T'ang and the Hsien Ch'eng T'ang have not only been converted into schools, the conversions flying in the face of the dictates of *feng-shui* by letting windows into the side walls, but women teachers and girl students have been allowed in as well. In the Hsien Ch'eng T'ang the lower tablets of the central altar have been defaced (in some cases to the point of illegibility) by exploring, childish fingers, which have rubbed off the paint,[6] but no loud protests are to be heard from the East Tou. In 1965 the School objected to the closing of the Hsien Ch'eng T'ang on two days in succession (the first a general holiday to mark the lineage Spring Rites and the second for the holding of the East Tou Rites in the hall), and it was agreed that, starting in the following year, arrangements would be altered so as to close the hall for only one day. Both halls are normally lost to the kinship-ritual sphere for six days of the week, and even in a case where someone wished to hold a birthday feast in the Wan Shih T'ang on a Sunday it was the headmaster whose permission was sought, not the managers of the T'ang.

Where kinship is often not as strong a tie as residential proximity, the presence of outsiders in the village also strikes at lineage unity. In any event, solidarity of the kinship group is no longer necessary in the same way that it was prior to British rule, for the protection from external threats which the united lineage afforded is now guaranteed by a government system which seriously attempts to control society even at the level of the

[6] Cf. above, p. 62, footnote 27.

smallest village, and which has a police force capable of so doing.

That the leadership is aware of the implications of the changes which have been taking place in the kinship-ritual sphere, and that it tries to counteract the deterioration in lineage solidarity may be demonstrated by two instances. In August 1964 the Extraordinary Public Meeting of the lineage was addressed by the Village Headman on the subject of the restoration of Chung-chieh's grave. A précis of his speech which I made at the time runs:

"Last year it was noted that the grave was getting very dilapidated. The Village Council feel that it ought to be restored. It is important that things like this be kept up. Our ancestors worked hard and we owe much to them. We must keep our realisation of what we owe to history and to our ancestors. Our young people now are modern educated, some even with University degrees, but, perhaps because of this, they know nothing of the history of our lineage and village. Here is our friend Mr. Baker come to study what none of us has studied—I am going to ask him to write out a history of Sheung Shui, ask the headmaster to translate it, and then have the two versions printed and distributed to all in the village, so that everyone can know our history."

Here, very clearly, was a reasoned attempt being made to call back the attention of the lineage members to their essential unity. The second instance is also connected with ancestral rites and the first ancestor. A few years ago the leadership deliberately started the practice of including all the lineage school-children in the processions and ceremonies of the Autumn Rites at the graves of Chung-chieh and his son. They also made it the rule that all middle school and university graduates of the lineage were eligible to take part in the feasts after the Spring and Autumn Rites. Thus not only have they attempted to keep the young people interested in and based on the lineage-village (even if facing towards the cities), but they have also tried to bring back into lineage affairs the brightest of the youth who, as mentioned above, are the very members whom rural society is most likely to lose. There is little doubt in my mind but that these efforts are unavailing: the two days of procession can hardly be expected to counteract the rest of the year's urban-oriented education.

In perhaps one of the saddest paradoxes of the contemporary

P

situation, the men who as community leaders strive hard to make the school as successful as possible are the very men who attempt to undo the results of that success by calling the attention of the students to the existence of the failing kinship-ritual group. In the educational field, as elsewhere, the lineage as a community is triumphing over the lineage as a kinship-ritual group. The leadership continues to press for better living conditions, for better facilities, for a 'model village', for factories even; and every success which they have seems to weaken still further the lineage on whose behalf they are working.

IV

The institutionalisation of the political leadership in the form of the Village Council and of the Village Headmen must surely be seen as of great importance in the process of change which began in 1898 and has still to reach completion, for, for the first time, the community and kinship-ritual aspects of the lineage were formally and permanently separated. The event marked the reaching of a point in the process at which lineage members were prepared to deny the theoretical right to over-lordship of the kinship-ritual leadership, and hence is an indication of the decline of loyalty to the kinship-ritual group.

But the creation of a formal community leadership was not only an indication of the failing strength of kinship and ritual ties, it was also a factor which contributed to the decline of these ties. The acquisition of control over the finances of the Wan Shih T'ang was probably the greatest single blow dealt to the strength of the kinship-ritual group. As stated in an earlier chapter, this acquisition was on the face of it no more than a recognition that the Council is the natural successor to the old informal community leadership, especially as all members of the Council are of the lineage—that is to say, the community (the village) and the kinship-ritual group (the lineage) are the same, and therefore change of control can mean little. But, of course, the lineage and the village are no longer the same. Two-fifths of the population are now outsiders. True they have no say in the spending of village money, and no political representation of any kind, but they do benefit from the spending of village money.

Moreover, the length of time during which the outsiders can be kept out of village government must surely be limited. While their numbers increase, the lineage numbers decrease. The Liaos in pursuit of prosperity are abandoning their village homes to live overseas or in the cities. The electorate diminishes election by election, and the expanding village is being run by a contracting government. As the election situation grows more ludicrous, and as the percentage of outsiders enlarges, so surely must the desire for a share in village government begin to move the non-represented. A flash-point for an outsiders' revolt seems ready-made in Shang Pei Ts'un, where so few Liaos now live that it has to share a representative on the Council with Hsia Pei Ts'un. How could the leadership justify this situation in terms of hamlet population figures?

If outsiders are admitted to the Council, then the full significance of the change of emphasis from kinship-ritual group to community will become apparent, for it will make clear the fact that the community leadership is not the same thing as the lineage leadership, and the kinship-ritual trust, the Wan Shih T'ang, will be seen to be, in part at least, in the hands of outsiders. And will outsiders be willing to have what they must see as *community* funds (the Wan Shih T'ang income) spent on *lineage* ritual? The split between lineage as community and as kinship-ritual group is incomplete so long as the Wan Shih T'ang serves both as exchequer. At some stage the finances must be divided, and the longer this is left undone the smaller the eventual share of kinship-ritual promises to be. But even supposing the division has been made before outsiders gain a share in village government (as surely they must), the share of the community will still have been taken from what is unquestionably Liao property held in trust for the benefit of Liao descendants. Will the Liaos not stand out against the entry of outsiders to the Village Council for this reason? The alternatives to submission to their entry seem to be either steadily less representative village government, with the possibility of consequent intervention by the British administration, or the withdrawal of all Wan Shih T'ang funds from the community sphere, with the cessation of community activity which that would entail. Perhaps there is indeed no real alternative to submission.

V

That there can be such a smooth development from community based on kinship-ritual principles to non-kinship community (from lineage village to village) indicates an underlying unity of structure, which previous chapters have attempted to describe. *There is, in fact, latent in the lineage village the full apparatus and basis of the non-kinship community.* Real leadership of the lineage village has been seen to have been in the hands of men who would have been leaders in any community; the ties of close residence, which in the non-kinship community are of importance, have been seen to have been developed and institutionalised in the form of Earth Gods, despite and as well as the ties of kinship; community temples unconnected with kinship-ritual matters flourish beside ancestral halls; community defence institutions of the nature of the Village Watch can work as well in a non-lineage environment as they have in the lineage past.

But it has been suggested that residential groupings tend to be disruptive of unity. *The importance of the kinship-ritual aspect which overlies the community aspect in the lineage village is its unifying power.* A lineage community is able to act as an undivided unit vis-à-vis the outside world; it can throw its full strength into offence, defence or public works; it can build up and invest capital (mainly in land) without internal dissension; it can command its members without fear of refusal . . . but it apparently cannot compete effectively against an urban economy which offers its members a greatly enhanced standard of material prosperity.

If the progression from lineage village to village is to be thoroughly worked out, it will surely not be for many years to come. At present Sheung Shui is in a transitional stage, where the unity and strength of the lineage as a kinship-ritual group is losing ground before the lineage as a community group. It cannot be said when the lineage as a community group will eventually give way to the non-lineage community, but it will no doubt be a slow process of attrition which brings it about. The Liaos should by then have had ample time in the process of weaning from the lineage breast to accustom themselves to less sheltered conditions.

List of Works Cited

Sessional Papers = *Papers laid before the Legislative Council of Hong Kong.*

JHKBRAS = *Journal of the Hong Kong Branch of the Royal Asiatic Society.*

BAKER, HUGH D. R., 'The Five Great Clans of the New Territories', *JHKBRAS*, Vol. VI, 1966.

BARNETT, K. M. A., 'The Peoples of the New Territories', in Braga, J. M. (ed.), *The Hong Kong Business Symposium*, Hong Kong, 1957.

—— (Census Commissioner), *Report of the Census 1961*, 3 Vols., Hong Kong Government Press, 1962.

—— 'Hong Kong before the Chinese', *JHKBRAS*, Vol. IV, 1964.

BURKHARDT, V. R., *Chinese Creeds and Customs*, 3 Vols., Hong Kong, 1953, 1955, 1958.

CARRIE, W. J. (Superintendent of Census), 'Census Report 1931', *Sessional Papers 1931*.

CHANG CHUNG-LI, *The Chinese Gentry*, Washington, 1955.

CHANG SHU, *Hsing-shih hsün-yüan*, 2 Vols., 1838.
張澍，姓氏尋源。

CHEN HAN-SENG, *Agrarian Problems in Southernmost China*, Shanghai, 1936.

CHIANG WAN-CHE *et al.* (eds.), *Chang Liao Shih Tsu-p'u*, Taiwan, 1965.
江萬哲，張廖氏族譜。

CHIN WEN-MOU *et al.*, *Hsin-an Hsien-chih*, 13 chüan, 1688. (*HAHC 1688.*)
靳文謨，新安縣志。

CH'U T'UNG-TSU, *Local Government in China under the Ch'ing*, Harvard, 1962.

Ch'un Ch'iu Tso Chuan.
春秋左傳。

Collins, Sir Charles, *Public Administration in Hong Kong*, London and New York, 1952.

'Despatches and other papers relating to the Extension of the Colony of Hong Kong', *Sessional Papers 1900 (Extension Despatches)*.

Donohue, The Hon. Peter (Director of Education), 'Education Department', in *The Government and the People*, Hong Kong Government Press, Vol. I, 1962.

Endacott, G. B., *A History of Hong Kong*, London and Hong Kong, 1958.

—— *Government and People in Hong Kong*, Hong Kong, 1964.

—— and Hinton, A., *Fragrant Harbour*, Hong Kong, 1962.

Extension Despatches: See under 'Despatches and other papers'.

Fitzgerald, C. P., *China: a Short Cultural History*, Revised edn., London, 1961.

Forrest, R. A. D., 'The Southern Dialects of Chinese', Appendix I in Purcell, V., *The Chinese in Southeast Asia*, Second edn., London, 1965.

Freedman, Maurice, *Lineage Organization in Southeastern China*, London, 1958.

—— *Chinese Lineage and Society: Fukien and Kwangtung*, London, 1966.

—— 'Shifts of Power in the Hong Kong New Territories', *Journal of Asian and African Studies*, Leiden, Vol. I, No. 1, January 1966.

Gamble, S. D., *North China Villages*, California, 1963.

—— *Ting Hsien: a North China Rural Community*, New York, 1954.

Gazetteer of Place Names in Hong Kong, Kowloon and the New Territories, Hong Kong Government Press, 1960.

Grant, C. J., *The Soils and Agriculture of Hong Kong*, Hong Kong Government Press, 1960.

Groves, Robert G., 'The Origins of Two Market Towns in the New Territories', *Aspects of Social Organization in the New Territories*, Royal Asiatic Society Hong Kong Branch, Hong Kong, 1965.

HAHC 1688: See under Chin Wen-Mou.

HAHC 1819: See under Wang Ch'ung-Hsi.

Hastings & Company, Solicitors, etc., *Memorandum and Articles of Association of Fung Kai Public School*, Hong Kong, 1961.

Hayes, J. W., 'The Pattern of Life in the New Territories in 1898', *JHKBRAS*, Vol. II, 1962.

Ho Ping-Ti, *Studies on the Population of China 1368–1953*, Harvard, 1959.

—— *The Ladder of Success in Imperial China*, New York, 1962.

Hong Kong Annual Report 1956, Hong Kong Government Press, 1957.

Hong Kong 1964, Hong Kong Government Press, 1965.

Hong Kong 1965, Hong Kong Government Press, 1966.

HONG KONG GOVERNMENT, *New Territories Land Lease Records*, MS, Hong Kong, 1905-7.

HONG KONG AND NEW TERRITORY EVANGELIZATION SOCIETY, *Minute Books, 1904–1932*, Hong Kong. (Part MS, part printed reports. Courtesy of London Missionary Society.)

Hou Shan Hsing T'ang Tsu-pu, MS, Ho Sheung Heung, Hong Kong (1910?).

侯善行堂族簿。

Hsiao Ching.

孝經。

HSIAO KUNG-CHUAN, *Rural China: Imperial Control in the Nineteenth Century*, Seattle, 1960.

Hsin-yüeh-hui shen-tan: Lung Yüeh T'ou ts'e, MS, Lung Yeuk Tau, Hong Kong, no date.

新約會神誕：龍躍頭冊。

HSÜEH, S. S., *Government and Administration of Hong Kong*, Hong Kong, 1962.

HU HSIEN-CHIN, *The Common Descent Group in China and its Functions*, New York, 1948.

Hua-ch'iao Jih-pao, Hong Kong (Daily newspaper).

華僑日報。

(*Hua Shan*) *Liao-shih Tsu-p'u*, MS, Hong Kong, 1938 (with addendum 1943).

（華山）廖氏族譜。

INGRAMS, HAROLD, *Hong Kong*, H.M.S.O., London, 1952.

KRONE, REV. MR., 'A Notice of the Sanon District', in *Transactions of the China Branch of the Royal Asiatic Society*, Pt. VI, 1859.

KULP, D. H. II, *Country Life in South China*, New York, 1925.

LSTP. See under *Liao-shih Tsu-p'u.*

LAM PO-HON, 'Kowloon-Canton Railway', *The Government and the People*, Hong Kong Government Press, Vol. II, 1964.

LEAGUE OF NATIONS, Commission of Enquiry into Traffic in Women and Children in the East, *Report to the Council*, Geneva, 1932.

LIAO JUI-CH'ÜAN (*Shang Shui Liao-shih Chia-li*) *T'ie-shih*, MS, 1946.

廖銳全，（上水廖氏家禮）帖式。

LIAO SHAO-HSIEN, *et al.*, *Liao-shih Tsung-ch'in Tsung-hui Tzu-chih Hui-so K'ai-mu Chuan-k'an*, Hong Kong, 1960.

廖紹賢，廖氏宗親總會自置會所開幕專刊。

Liao-shih Tsu-p'u, combined MS genealogies of the Liao lineage of Sheung Shui, various dates. (*LSTP.*)

廖氏族譜。

LIU WANG HUI-CHEN, *The Traditional Chinese Clan Rules*, New York, 1959.

LLOYD, J. D. (Census Officer), 'Census Report of 1921', *Sessional Papers 1921*.

LO HSIANG-LIN, *K'o-chia shih-liao hui-p'ien*, Hong Kong, 1965.

羅香林，客家史料匯篇。

—— *K'o-chia yen-chiu tao-lun*, Taipeh, 1942.

客家研究導論。

—— *et al.*, *I-pa-ssu-erh-nien i-ch'ien chih Hsiang-kang chi ch'i tui-wai chiao-t'ung*, Institute of Chinese Culture, Hong Kong, 1959.

一八四二年以前之香港及其對外交通。

LO WAN, 'Communal Strife in Mid-Nineteenth-Century Kwangtung', *Papers on China*, Vol. 19, Harvard University East Asian Research Center, December 1965, pp. 85–119.

LOCKHART, J. H. S., 'Report on the New Territory', 7th February 1900, *Sessional Papers 1900*.

Lockhart Report 1898 : See *Report by Mr. Stewart Lockhart*.

MAYERS, W. F., *The Chinese Government*, London, 1897.

MOK, BENJAMIN N. H., *Hong Kong Census 1961; Population Projections 1961–1971*, Hong Kong Government Press (1962 ?).

'Mui Tsai in Hong Kong: Report of the Committee appointed by the Governor', *Sessional Papers 1935*.

NTAR : See *New Territories Annual Reports*.

Nan-hua Wan-pao, Hong Kong (evening newspaper).

南華晚報。

New Territories Annual Reports. (*NTAR*.)

1946–47, by BARROW, J. (District Officer), 1947.

1947–48, by BARROW, J. (District Officer), 1948.

1950–51, by BARROW, J. (District Commissioner), 1951.

1953–54, by TEASDALE, E. B. (Acting District Commissioner), 1954.

1956–57, by BARNETT, K. M. A. (District Commissioner), 1957.

1960–61, by HOLMES, D. R. (District Commissioner), 1961.

1961–62, by ASERAPPA, J. P. (District Commissioner), 1962.

1963–64, by ASERAPPA, J. P. (District Commissioner), 1964.

1964–65, by ASERAPPA, J. P. (District Commissioner), 1965.

NG, PETER Y. L., *The 1819 Edition of the Hsin-an Hsien-chih*, Unpublished M.A. Thesis, University of Hong Kong, 1961.

ORME, G. N., 'Report on the New Territories 1899–1912', *Sessional Papers 1912*.

Pao-an Chin-T'ien Teng-shih tsu-p'u, MS, Kam Tin, Hong Kong (*c.* 1920 ?).

寶安錦田鄧氏族譜。

PLAYFAIR, G. M. H., *The Cities and Towns of China*, Shanghai, 1910.

Report by Mr. Stewart Lockhart on the Extension of the Colony of Hong Kong (Lockhart Report 1898), Oct. 8th 1898, in Eastern No. 66, Colonial Office, 1900.

Report of the Public Works Subcommittee of Finance Committee 1963–64, Hong Kong Government Press (1964?).

SHANG SHUI TS'UN-KUNG-SO, *1955 hsüan-chü wei-yüan-hui chi-lu*, MS, 1955.

上水村公所，1955選舉委員會紀錄。

—— *1958 ti-wu-chieh hsüan-chü wei-yüan-hui chi-lu*, MS, 1958.

1958第五屆選舉委員會紀錄。

—— *1960 ti-liu-chieh hsüan-wei-hui*, MS, 1960.

1960第六屆選委會。

SHEN P'ENG-FEI, *Kuang-tung nung-yeh kai-k'uang tiao-ch'a pao-kao-shu*, Canton, 1929.

沈鵬飛，廣東農業概況調察報告書。

Shih Hu Hsü Ch'ung-chien Hsin-shih Lo-ch'eng: Ta-hui T'e-k'an, Hong Kong, 1964.

石湖墟重建新市落成：大會特刊。

SKINNER, G. W., 'Marketing and Social Structure in Rural China', *Journal of Asian Studies*, Vol. XXIV, Nos. 1–3, 1964–65.

SMITH, A. H., *Village Life in China*, New York, 1899.

SUNG HOK-P'ANG, 'Legends and Stories of the New Territories', *Hong Kong Naturalist*, Hong Kong, 1935–36.

TAGA AKIGORŌ, *Sōfu no kenkyū*, Tokyo, 1960.

多賀秋五郎，宗譜の研究。

T'ai-k'eng Wen-shih tsu-p'u, MS, Tai Hang, Hong Kong, no date.

泰坑文氏族譜。

(Teng) Yao-lin chia-p'u, MS, Tai Po Tau (?), Hong Kong, no date.

（鄧）耀林家譜。

WAKEMAN, FREDERIC, Jr., *Strangers at the Gate*, California, 1966.

WANG CH'UNG-HSI, *et al.*, *Hsin-an Hsien-chih*, 24 chüan, 1819 *(HAHC 1819)*.

王崇熙，新安縣志。

Wen-shih tsu-pu (hsia-chüan), MS, San Tin, 1938.

文氏族部（下卷）。

WODEHOUSE, P. P. J., 'Report', *Sessional Papers 1901*.

—— (Census Officer), 'Report on Census 1911', *Sessional Papers 1911*.

WONG, PETER C., & Co., *Memorandum and Articles of Association of Chau Wong Yee Yuen Limited*, Hong Kong, 1963.

YANG, C. K., *A Chinese Village in Early Communist Transition*, M.I.T., 1959.

YANG, M. C., *A Chinese Village: Taitou, Shantung Province*, London, 1948.

Glossary

A-kung　阿公。

A-name-po　阿⋯⋯伯。

A-name-wu　阿⋯⋯五。

ancestors　祖先。

Chang (lineage)　張。

Ch'ang-shou-hui　長壽會。

Chau Wong Yee Yuen　周王二院。

Chek Mei　赤尾。

Cheng (lineage)　鄭。

Cheng-shih-lang　徵仕郎。

Cheng-Wu tso-wei ta-tsung-kuan　征吳左衞大總管。

Cheung Chau　長洲。

Cheung Muk Tau　樟木頭。

chia-ch'ang-t'ien　家嘗田。

chien　間。

Chien (lineage)　簡。

Chien Kung　簡公。

Ch'ien-hua hsien-ling　虔化縣令。

Chih-hsien　知縣。

ch'ih shan-t'ou　吃山頭。

chin-shih　進士。

221

Ching-che　驚蟄。

Ch'ing-ho t'ai-shou　清河太守。

Ch'ing-ming　清明。

Ch'ing-nien shih-she　青年詩社。

Ch'iu-chi　秋祭。

Choi Uk Wai　蔡屋圍。

Chou Yu-te　周有德。

Ch'ou-shen　酬神。

chu-shu　囑書。

ch'u-shih　處士。

chü-jen　舉人。

Ch'uang-hsiao tsan-chu-jen　創校贊助人。

Ch'un-chi　春祭。

Ch'un-ch'iu　春秋。

Ch'un-fen　春分。

Chün Pin　君賓。

Chung (lineage)　鍾。

Chung Hsin Ts'un　中心村。

Ch'ung-yang　重陽。

en-chin-shih　恩進士。

en-kung-sheng　恩貢生。

Erh-tsu　二族。

Fang　房。

Fanling　粉嶺。

feng-shui　風水。

fu-chi　附祭。

fu-lao　父老。

Fu-tai-piao　副代表。

Fu Te　福德。

Fuk Tin　福田。

Fuk Wing　福永。

Fung Kai　鳳溪。

Fung Shui Heung　鳳水鄉。

ha-fu　下夫。

Ha Shui　下水。

Ha Tsuen　厦村。

Hakka　客家。

hamlet　村。

heung　鄉。

Heung Sai　向西。

Heung Yee Kuk　鄉議局。

Ho (lineage)　何。

Ho A-pa　何亞八。

Ho Sheung Heung　河上鄉。

Hong Kong　香港。

Hou (lineage)　侯。

hsi-min (Cantonese *sai-man*)　細民（？）

hsi yu Liao[A] Shu-an　昔有廖叔安。

Hsia Ching　下徑。

Hsia Pei Ts'un　下北村。

Hsiang　鄉。

Hsiang-chin　鄉津。

hsiang-hsia　鄉下。

Hsiang she-chi chih shen　鄉社稷之神。

Hsiang-shen　鄉紳。

Hsiang-tu-li　鄉都里。

hsieh-tou　械鬥。

hsien　縣。

Hsien-ch'eng　縣丞。

Hsien Ch'eng T'ang　顯承堂。

Hsin-an Hsien　新安縣。

hsin-wei (year)　辛未。

Hsin Wei Tzu　新圍仔。

Hsing Jen Li　興仁里。

Hsiu-chih-lang　修職郎。

Hsüan-chou tz'u-shih　宣州刺史。

hsüeh-ku　學穀。

Hsün-chien-ssu　巡檢司。

Hsün-tao　訓導。

Hsün-ting　巡丁。

Hu-Kuang chün-shou　湖廣郡守。

Hu-Kuang ts'an-cheng ta-fu　湖廣參政大夫。

hua-p'ai　花牌。

Huang (lineage)　黃。

Hui Yang　惠陽。

Hung-ch'iao　紅橋。

Hung Hom　紅磡。

Hung Sheng　洪聖。

I-hsiang-sheng　邑庠生。

Ju-lin-lang　儒林郎。

k'ai-kuang　開光。

k'ai-teng　開燈。

k'ai-t'ou　開投。

Kak Chun Hui　隔圳墟。

Kak Chun Tsuen　隔圳村。

Kak Tin　隔田。

Kam Tin　錦田。

Kam Tsin　金錢。

Kat Hing Wai　吉慶圍。

Kong Ha　岡下。

Kowloon (City)　九龍（城）。

Kuan Fu　官富。

Kuan-tai shou-kuan　冠帶壽官。

Kuan Yin　觀音。

kung-chai　公債。

kung-jen　工人。

kung-ming　功名。

kung-ming-p'ai　功名牌。

Kuo-hsüeh-sheng　國學生。

Kweishan Hsien　歸善縣。

Kwangchow Prefecture　廣州府。

Lam Tsuen　林村。

li　里。

Li (surname)　李。

Li Pu　吏部。

Li Wan-jung　李萬榮。

liang　兩。

liang-t'ou-sheng　兩頭勝。

Liao (lineage)　廖。

Liao[A]　廖。

Liao-shih tsung-ch'in tsung-hui　廖氏宗親總會。

Lin (lineage)　林。

Lin-pu tseng-sheng　廩補增生。

Ling Ha　嶺下。

Lo Wu　羅湖。

Loi Tung　萊洞。

Long Keng　浪逕。

Loyang　洛陽。

Lu-tung-hsiang　路洞鄉。

Luen Wo Hui　聯和墟。

Lungnan　龍南。

Lung Ngan Yuen　龍眼園。

Lung Yeuk Tau　龍躍頭。

Man Kam To　文錦渡。

Meichuan　梅川。

Men K'ou Ts'un　門口村。

Ming Huan Tz'u　名宦祠。

Ming Te T'ang　明德堂。

Mui Lam　梅林。

mui-tsai　妹仔。

na-mo-lao　南巫佬。

Nam Tau　南頭。

New Territories　新界。

New Territories Administration　新界民政署。

Ninghua Hsien　寧化縣。

pai-ke-piao　白鴿標。

p'ai-lou　牌樓。

p'ai-ming　排名。

Pan-yu Hsien　番禺縣。

Pao-an Hsien　寶安縣。

Pat Heung　八鄉。

Pei Tou　北斗。

P'eng (lineage)　彭。

ping-hsü (year)　丙戌。

Ping Kong　丙崗。

Ping Shan　屏山。

Pu Shang Ts'un　莆上村。

Punti　本地。

Rural Committee　鄉事委員會。

Sai Kung　西貢。

San Tin　新田。

Sha Ling　沙嶺。

Sha Tau (Hui)　沙頭墟。

Sha Tau Kok (Hui)　沙頭角（墟）。

Sha Tin　沙田。

Sham Chun　深圳。

Sham Shui Po　深水埗。

Shang Pei Ts'un　上北村。

shang-shou　上壽。

Shap Pat Heung　十八鄉。

Shek Pei Tau　石陂頭。

Shek Wu Hui　石湖墟。

Q

shen　神。

shen-ch'i　紳耆。

shen-chu　神主。

shen-wei　神位。

sheng-yuan　生員。

Sheung Pou　上步（莆）。

Sheung Shui (Heung)　上水（鄉）。

Sheung U Tung　雙魚洞。

Shou-kuan　壽官。

shu-yüan　書院。

Shuang-yü-ling　雙魚嶺。

Shui Pui　水貝。

Siu Hang　小坑。

ssu-shu　私塾。

Ssu-tu-li　司都里。

Ssu-tu-t'u　司都圖。

sui　歲。

sui-kung-sheng　歲貢生。

Sun Kong　筍崗。

ta-chiao　打醮。

ta-hsiang-li　大鄉里。

ta-kung　打工。

Ta Kwu Ling　打鼓嶺。

Ta T'ing Ts'un　大廳村。

Ta Wang Temple　大王廟。

Ta Yüan Ts'un　大園村。

Tai Hang　太坑。

Tai Leng Shan　大嶺山。

Tai Pang　大鵬。

Tai Po District　大埔區。

Tai Po (Hui)　大埔（墟）。

Tai Po Tau　大埔頭。

Tai Po Tsat Yeuk　大埔七約。

Tai Om Shan　大菴山。

T'ai-shih-tsu　太始祖。

Tai Tau Leng　大頭嶺。

T'ang　堂。

Te-an Fu t'ung-p'an　德安府通判。

Teng (lineage)　鄧。

Teng-shih-lang　登仕郎。

Teng-shih-tso-lang　登仕佐郎。

Teo Chiu　潮州。

Tiaochou　釣州。

t'iao-tsu　祧祖。

Tien-li　典吏。

t'ien　天。

T'ien Hou Temple　天后廟。

Tin Kong Hui　天岡墟。

ting　丁。

Tingchow Prefecture　汀州府。

Tou　斗。

Ts'ai (lineage)　蔡。

Ts'an-i ta-fu　參議大夫。

tseng-li kung-sheng　增例貢生。

Tsim Sha Tsui　尖沙咀。

Tsing Shan　青山。

Tsiu Keng　蕉徑。

tso-fu　作福。

Tso-wei chen-kuo ta-chiang-chün　左衞鎮國大將軍。

Tsu　祖。

Tsu-chang　族長。

Ts'un　村。

Ts'un-chang　村長。

Ts'un-tai-piao　村代表。

Ts'un-wu wei-yüan-hui　村務委員會。

Tsung Pak Long　松柏朗。

Tsz-yi　諮議。

tu (cabinet)　櫝。

tu　都。

t'u　圖。

Tuen Mun　屯門。

Tung　洞。

Tung-chih　冬至。

Tung Ch'ing T'ang　東慶堂。

Tung-hsing-ch'iao　東興橋。

Tungkwan Hsien　東莞縣。

Tung Lo　東路。

Tung P'ing Kuk　東平局。

Tzu-wei-tui　自衞隊。

tz'u-t'ang-kung　祠堂公。

Village Council　村務委員會。

Village Council Hall　村公所。

Village Headman　村長。

Village Representative　村代表。

Village Watch　自衞隊。

Wa Mei Shan　畫眉山。

Wa Shan Tsuen　華山村。

Waichow Prefecture　惠州府。

Wan Shih T'ang　萬石堂。

Wang Hsün-fu Tz'u　王巡撫祠。

Wang Lai-jen　王來任。

Wang Mei Shan　橫眉山。

Wei Nei　圍內。

Wen (lineage)　文。

Wen-hsüeh-shih　文學士。

Wen Kang Shu Yüan　文岡書院。

Wen-lin-lang　文林郎。

Wen T'ien-hsiang　文天祥。

Wong Pui Ling　黃貝嶺。

Wu (emperor)　武帝。

Wu Hu　五胡。

Wu Kai Sha　烏雞沙。

Wu Pui　湖貝。

Wu-te ch'i-yü-lang　武德騎尉郎。

Wu-wei chün-kung　武威郡公。

Wu-wei t'ai-shou　武威太守。

Yang-chou t'ai-shou　楊州太守。

yin-chai　陰宅。

Yin Kong 燕崗。

Ying-shou-fu 營守府。

yu-hsing hsüeh-sheng 優行學生。

Yüan (lineage) 袁。

Yuen Long 元朗。

Yün Sheng T'ang 允升堂。

Yungting 永定。

Index

233